**Government Management Internships
and Executive Development**

Government Management Internships and Executive Development

Education for Change

Thomas P. Murphy
University of Maryland

Lexington Books
D.C. Heath and Company
Lexington, Massachusetts
Toronto   London

Library of Congress Cataloging in Publication Data

Murphy, Thomas P   1931-
   Government management internships and executive development.

   1. Interns (Civil service) – United States
2. Interns (Civil service) – United States – States.
I. Title.
JK718.M85   353.001'5   73-950
ISBN 0-669-86363-7

Published simultaneously in Canada.

Printed in the United States of America.

International Standard Book Number: 0-669-86363-7

Library of Congress Catalog Card Number: 73-950

For Marcella

Table of Contents

List of Figures

Figure

List of Tables

Preface

The current emphasis on relevance has drawn new attention to internships as an educational approach. Public administration programs as well as certain political science departments have long made use of the internship. Now other disciplines such as sociology and interdisciplinary urban programs are also using interns. The change is timely because leadership and the involvement in public affairs of persons whose value scales emphasize the "public welfare" over personal gain or parochial interest are among the most pressing of our contemporary needs.

American society has long been praised for its pluralism, yet it is currently under great stress from youth in general, blacks, Chicanos, and others who question not only the relevance but also the integrity of governments and leaders. If government is to reduce its negativistic establishment image, develop realistic citizen participation, and bridge the alleged credibility gap, people in government must establish new lines of communication with those groups feeling alienated, disenfranchised, or otherwise outside the mainstream.

Failure to accomplish these objectives will mean that governments will have increasing difficulty in securing acceptance and support of their programs. If government cannot draw upon an increasing supply of high quality young graduates having social consciousness and a grasp of the public's future needs, it will not be able to develop the desperately needed managers in the years ahead. Without such new-breed managers, a governmental management gap at the state and local level is a real possibility.

It is understandable, therefore, that greater attention is now being paid to making curricula more relevant. This should be especially true in the public administration programs which exist primarily to provide a supply of competent young managers and administrators with a background in, and empathy for, our governmental system. Internships long have been a part of public administration programs, generally serving as a capstone to the theoretical work in political science, economics, sociology, and administration that characterizes most public administration programs. The master's degree in Public Administration is generally viewed as a professional degree, that is, essentially a terminal degree providing a graduate student some specifics in, and an appreciation for, the management tools of analysis and evaluation that contribute to success in managing government programs where resources are always limited. Increasingly, urban studies programs are taking on some of the same appearances and adopting similar objectives.

Much current governmental attention is directed toward urban affairs. This is as true for one working at the federal level as it is for those at the state, city, and county levels. Most major urban counties are now performing urban functions formerly performed by cities. State governmental departments are heavily involved in programming federal funds passed through the states for the resolution of urban problems. All levels of government, therefore, are involved with urban affairs, but there are differences of emphasis and format. The federal and state governments tend to be program directors or brokers of urban services, whereas those at the city and county level are more likely to be providing direct services to the urban consumer. In many respects, however, all of these governmental units are now working to a greater extent than ever before through citizens groups and nonprofit groups operating at the local level with governmental money. Each of these levels of government provides good internship possibilities.

A variety of internship and fellowship programs has been developed at all levels of government to acquaint students with the realities of governmental service. If properly managed, internships can be extremely enriching experiences in which advanced students in public administration receive the opportunity to work directly for experienced administrators at the policy level, see at first hand the realities of governmental administration, and apply some of the theories and philosophies they have studied in the classroom.

This book treats some of the academic questions involved in internships, presents the view of a student as to the opportunities and pitfalls of an internship experience, and then reviews the historical development of city-manager internships, the new urban internships, the HUD Urban Fellowship Program, and internships at the state level in both executive and legislative branches. At the federal level the general management internship programs, Office of Education fellowships; Congressional fellowships, the White House fellowships, and Washington Semester programs are discussed. These represent the tip of the iceberg. There are many other specialized programs such as the Public Administration Fellowships for faculty members sponsored by the National Association of Schools of Public Affairs and Administration and the American Society for Public Administration with the cooperation of the U.S. Civil Service Commission.

The book concludes with chapters analyzing how the federal executive development programs attempt to broaden the horizons of specialists who have been promoted to positions requiring generalist and administrative talents, how behavioral science applies to current developments in local government organization and function, and how the Intergovernmental Personnel Act of 1970 proposes to strengthen the evolving federal system and make revenue sharing feasible.

The authors contributing to this book have had a deep and diverse involvement with internships and executive development at all levels of government. A few of them have even been involved in all aspects — as student interns, governmental intern supervisors, and university internship professors. Table P-1 shows that collectively they have had experience with twenty-one different city, state, federal, and public interest group internship programs. Several authors wrote their chapters while they were still students.

The other contributors are primarily professors who have worked in government or practitioners who have taught in evening programs. They represent the new style of teacher-practitioner who is capable of tackling urban and public administration problems from both inside and outside government. As such, they are providing leadership to the new breed of relevance-seeking students, and their message — along with that of the students — should be of interest to all who are concerned about the emerging patterns in education and public management. It is hoped that this book will fill an existing gap in the public and urban administration literature.

Internships are currently one of the most dynamic areas in education. Innovative educators are expanding the intern concept to cover a variety of "schools without walls" approaches. New associations are being organized to coordinate the development of these new concepts. In June 1972 the National Center for Public Service Internships was created with a board of directors representing virtually all of the diverse programs mentioned in this book. Robert Sexton of the Kentucky state government, who provided much of the leadership for the organizing phase, was selected as the first chairman of the group. It is headquartered at 1140 Connecticut Avenue NW, Washington, DC, 20036.

My colleagues F. Gerald Brown and Robert J. Saunders and City Manager James Kunde assisted in the formulation of this book. The Citizens Conference on State Legislatures, under the leadership of Larry Margolis, assisted in state data collection. Gail Burton, Thomas Edgerton, Peter Goodrich, Richard Heimovics, Larry Hughes, and Gordon Seyffert played vital research roles as graduate assistants. Barbara Gilmore Spear, Martha Gresham, Rosemary Minni, and Ann Taylor did an outstanding job of preparing the manuscript. My interns in the public administration program at the University of Missouri — Kansas City and the Department of Government and Politics at the University of Maryland contributed more than they realize. As usual, my wife, Marcella, and Kevin, Mike, Tom, Dolores, and Danny contributed by letting me work Saturdays to prepare the book.

Table P.1. Internship Backgrounds of Contributors

Contributor	Intern Experience	Governmental Intern Supervisor	Governmental Experience	University Intern Supervisor	Teaching at University Level
Asbell	No	No	Federal	No	Yes
Banovetz	Yes	Yes	City	Yes	Yes
Cookingham	Yes	Yes	City	No	Yes
Eddy	No	No	City	Yes	Yes
Fisher	Yes	No	City	No	Yes
Hedlund	Yes	No	Federal-City	Yes	Yes
Heimovics	Yes	No	Federal	No[a]	No
Hughes	Yes	No	City	No	No
Jadlos	Yes	Yes	Federal	No	No
Murphy	Yes	Yes	Federal-County	Yes	Yes
Paper	Yes	No	Federal	No	No
Rehfuss	Yes	Yes[b]	Federal	No	Yes
Sherwood	Yes	Yes[b]	City	Yes	Yes
Trachtenberg	Yes	Yes	Federal	Yes	Yes
Walker	Yes	Yes	Federal	No	No
Weaver	No	Yes	Federal	Yes	Yes

[a] As assistant to the director of masters program in Public Administration – assisted with interns.

[b] Experience in federal executive development centers at Charlottesville and Berkeley.

**Part I
Internship Dynamics**

1

An Academic Perspective on Internships

Thomas P. Murphy

The public management internship is an educational innovation that is assuming increasing significance in academic programs whose purpose is to train and educate public administrators. The use of the term "intern" is intended to connote the transition between learning and practice, much in the manner of the medical internship. Transition is really the key to the creation of internships; the primary intent is to bridge the gap between academic and professional worlds for the fledgling administrator. The success of the early internship programs has led to many and varied imitations, and any further generalization is probably subject to challenge. It can be safely said, however, that most of the new emphasis is coming as a consequence of our changing times.

The pressures behind this trend are therefore complex. As the spotlight of change is focused on local government, where urban pressures are centered, clientele groups in the cities are demanding more. Those governments are in turn pleading for state and federal help. These new urban challenges are driving out business-as-usual public management and thrusting activist public administrators into high level positions. Paralleling this shift, universities have been driven from their traditional intellectual isolationism into increased involvement in community problem-solving. Academia is now being badgered by governmental leaders to do much more, especially to assist governments in meeting their manpower needs. Concurrent with these changes, students are demanding participation and are becoming more impatient with their lack of involvement in real problem-solving.[1]

The internship has developed into an elaborate mosaic incorporating elements of city halls, court houses, state houses, federal buildings, and seminar rooms. Professors and government officials working together have developed internship mechanisms that meet many of the needs and demands of the diverse participants. For a student an internship provides a constructive approach to improving his community and also offers a special kind of learning experience. Government officials have found interns to be highly motivated and energetic, able to make important contributions despite the often short duration of the internship, and interested in moving permanently into public service employment. The universities have benefited from liberal injections of realism into formerly outdated lecture notes and also from the suggestion of new opportunities for research.

3

Interns frequently provide important linkages between previously isolated interests. Although most interns develop a total personal commitment to the agency, figure 1.1 illustrates the multiple responsibilities borne by the intern. This multiple bond is a key strength of internships, but it involves potential hazards. It means, for example, that there are some decisions and projects to which the intern may be denied access. However, apart from these exceptional circumstances, most interns experience considerable trust and openness due to their status as free agents.

Figure 1.1. Interrelationships in Internship Programs

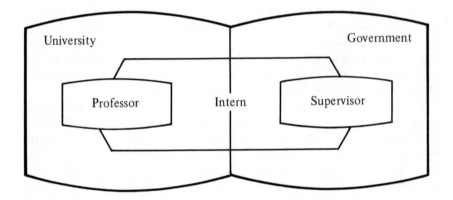

The Rationale of Internships

The popularity of internships, especially in graduate programs, is a manifestation of support for programs of professional education as opposed to those promoting study for the sake of liberal education. As public administration programs have developed, they have expanded their scope beyond staff functions such as budget, personnel, and management to incorporate a systemic approach to the governmental process.[2] This development is leading at the graduate level to the establishment of independent schools of administration, public affairs, or public administration. These independent entities have greater flexibility in pursuing grant funds, in identifying more directly with their governmental clientele, and in developing internship programs than do programs ensconced within arts and sciences colleges and graduate schools. Of course, there are exceptions depending upon the leadership of the department in question, as well as upon the governmental environment in which the school is located. Nevertheless, schools of public administration or larger schools including public administration as a major thrust are becoming established professional schools on a par with law schools, dental schools, medical schools, and schools of education.

One of the questions often raised with regard to public administration schools and the internship programs they frequently sponsor is whether or not administration is a skill which lends itself to teaching. Some argue, for example, that it is not possible to teach one to be an artist and that administrators as well are born with innate talents rather than developed by education. Yet it is clear that while virtually all artists study the classical works, they also have performed under the eye of accomplished artists early in their careers. Internships follow a similar pattern. When the graduate student is assigned to a senior manager in an appropriate governmental position, the new intern will not only learn a variety of techniques with which to implement administrative policies and to accomplish specified tasks, but he will also be given the opportunity to observe and evaluate the philosophy, administrative theories, personal skills, and attitudes toward public service exhibited by the senior man. Equally important to the intern is the professional appraisal he receives. Each separate experience provides specific training, of course, but the strength of internships lies in their power to develop within the individual a real "feel" for the reality of administration, all within a perspective that classroom lectures cannot convey.

Basic to the idea of the internship is the concept of the generalist administrator. Public administration literature provides such a wide range of definitions of the term generalist that each new context in which it is used provokes misunderstanding. Aside from this drawback, a sampling of characteristics often associated with the concept should be sufficient to indicate why there is a demand for students with knowledge of governmental theory, structure, and processes. Briefly, it is thought that a generalist who possesses these attributes is more capable of handling complex and ever-changing problems than a specialist with a conditioned "mind-set."

Michael Cohen has identified three major usages of the generalist term.[3] The first is that of the man engaged in advisory or policy-making work whose primary background consists of a liberal education, good judgment, and leadership abilities. He offers the British civil service as an example of a system that effectively employed essentially amateur administrators in policy and advisory positions. These generalist administrators were, of course, not limited to any one organization or policy area. A second usage identified by Cohen is that of an administrative specialist proficient in the implementation of policy. Such a man is hardly an amateur administrator, yet no one specific technical skill will meet his needs. Because he draws upon several, he is thereby categorized as a generalist. A third kind of generalist is so designated because of the priority his job places on administration at the expense of previous specialist duties. Persons in this generalist category may be management specialists who have acquired technical knowledge in a specific substantive area or who were at one time technically trained personnel who have now become managers as they have climbed the promotion ladders of their fields. However, few persons in generalist positions who have arrived there by moving up through technical programs in their organizations are true generalists. They often are not highly skilled in management, though success in their position would seemingly require that they be.

Commenting on the ambiguous content of the term "generalist," Cohen summarizes the situation as follows:

The elusive generalist may be an amateur or a professional. He may be someone devoted to policy matters or someone contributing to administrative support. He may be someone whose job strongly emphasizes administrative duties, or someone whose job has roughly equivalent amounts of administrative and substantive professional content, or even someone who is a professional first but has added some administrative skills later. . . . Two main ideas stand out. The first is the idea of mobility, variously expressed as flexibility of assignment, transferability between jobs or agencies, or self-propelled career progression across agency and department lines. The second is the idea of job content, which is usually thought of as high level, with administrative or executive activity, or policy-influencing activity.[4]

Robert Golembiewski develops these thoughts further in an article demonstrating that traditional organization theory works to reduce job rotation and reward specialization at the expense of generalist performance. He concludes that organizations with traditional structures "tend to eliminate the generalist, make him cynical, or alter his orientation. This amounts to a kind of devouring of its young by an organization that could use the generalist inclinations of its employees to advantage later in their careers."[5]

These theories are important to the study of internships because the accepted practice has been to place interns with supervisors who are thought to be closest to the generalist mold. Furthermore, as has been indicated, the objective of most graduate public administration programs is to develop generalist administrators. This in part accounts for the theory that public administration is not a discipline in itself, but rather feeds off the basic social science fields of political science, economics, sociology, psychology, and history as well as the quantitative and life sciences.

While early city managers tended to be persons with engineering backgrounds who may have later earned an MPA degree as a means of securing their generalist qualifications, even current city manager training programs now stress the humanities and organizational behavior skills. Thus, while public administration draws from the knowledge and research of specific disciplines, it is problem-oriented and deals with policy and administrative questions requiring broad knowledge. The academic disciplines also produce many graduate students who will be involved in public careers. These graduates, however, are likely to begin with more specialized work in the local, state, and federal governments, eventually rising perhaps to positions at a level requiring the skills of generalists.

In addition to their effort to introduce students to public service, provide feedback adding to the realism of the campus, improve the efficacy of public administration teaching, and enhance the education of students regarding the problems and purposes of government, internships also serve a number of other purposes. In the minds of the governmental managers, one of the primary goals is to provide a flow of new ideas into their working environments. This occurs to some extent during the internship but is best achieved if the interns later accept full-time jobs in the agency. In general, internships have both met this expectation and served as good recruiting channels for urban, state, and federal governments. Governmental administrators who have supervised interns generally agree that the experience has provided a learning stimulus for the sponsor as well as for the intern.

There is another advantage to management accruing from intern programs. Where universities have provided interns and new insights to government leaders and managers, the university has usually been used more extensively as a resource, leading to major contributions in some cases. Professional administrators have often "grown" as a result of contact with the "relevance conscious" interns, who acquire and transmit the intellectual interest of their professors. Because the intern is the essential element that brings the university and the agency together, almost without exception interns will state that they derive much more out of the experience than either the agency or the university.

In a well-managed program the assignments given to interns are carefully selected. Nevertheless, daily intern duties often alternate between fire-fighting tasks and long-range projects. Both give the intern an opportunity to observe the agency in action, while at the same time the agency can appraise the intern and evaluate the academic program of which he is a product. The ready availability of an intern's time and talents may also give the agency an opportunity to complete important projects that have been postponed due to more urgent demands. Such assignments, it is necessary to point out, should be clearly differentiated from assignments given to interns because nobody else wants to do them. These latter assignments are usually neither educational nor satisfying to the intern.

From the standpoint of the interns themselves, the introduction to the governmental work environment prior to graduation provides an important springboard into a career with the host government or some other public service agency. Not only does the student develop an "in" with the governmental unit that will aid him should he apply for permanent employment with the agency; additionally, receiving the experience while in a special capacity as intern generally enables the student to get a more profound overview of the governmental unit than would be possible if he were hired directly and permanently into any individual department. Thus he will be in a better position to select the best area in which to begin his career following graduation. Finally, where internships grant stipends they also serve as a form of scholarship or fellowship which may prove essential to the completion of a student's education.

Academically, internship programs help schools with a professional orientation achieve their objective of mixing theory and practice by providing some of their students with experience in government and a more sophisticated perspective from which to evaluate the words of professors. Few professors have themselves had the unique opportunity to observe government first hand so that they have difficulty teaching how government operates. Interns learn that being a member of an organization provides special insights not available even to the professor-researcher.

Writing of internships as opportunities for research, R.J. Snow concludes that this relationship "may allow access to data otherwise unavailable. When the researcher earns confidences and is accepted in his research environment, he may probe for access to guarded data sources, tune in on "scuttlebutt" and gossip, and ask questions which he could not ask as an interviewer on a brief visit."[6] The learning experience may be even more propitious if the intern is not using the insight for research; very likely his co-workers will feel even more open with him if they do not fear being "studied."

Since the selection process tends to insure that interns are among the better students and an internship provides rapid infusions of new knowledge, the level of classroom discussions is inevitably raised. Finally, the existence of interns and the relationships that develop because of them among administrators and academicians help to break down suspicions so that research opportunities become available both to students and faculty which would not have been possible without the relationship fostered by the interns.

Types of Internships

Internships can be categorized according to their length, their sequence in the academic career, whether they have voluntary or mandatory status within the academic program, the level of government at which they occur, or whether they are located in executive, legislative, or political organizations. Most internships run concurrently with academic semesters. They are either part-time or full-time and are taken in summers or during the last year of a two-year master's degree program. A few programs schedule internships in the summer prior to the commencement of graduate studies. But in a number of instances, especially where the internships are taken far from the campus, the internship is reserved until the end of the program and extends for a full academic year. The length of internship programs may thus vary from three months to a year. Of the two, full-year durations are preferred since many of the participating governments insist on the longer internships, feeling that significant benefit is not derived unless the intern has time to fully develop personal contributions. There are merits to both sides of this question.

Most internships are found at the federal level, but they are also becoming more numerous at the city, county, and state levels. In most programs the internship is voluntary rather than mandatory. Master's degree programs concentrating on producing city managers are an exception to this principle for obvious reasons.[7] By contrast, many other programs make the internship optional because a substantial portion of students are part-time. Many already have had several years of governmental employment to provide them with a reservoir of experience against which to measure the classroom theory.

Although public administration internships have been primarily with executive agencies of government, there have been several significant legislative internship programs as well. Political internships also exist, but are in some respects a special case. Internships with city, county, and state committees of political parties have been rare, especially where the university has a separate political science department which engages in these programs. Again, key elements favoring the use of interns are their youth, energy, and lack of organizational allegiances. In the case of political internships, the absence of political allegiance could be a detriment, but often political leaders do not insist on this as it often develops as an intern works on the elected official's staff.

The same caliber of feedback an intern can provide about an organization can also be provided to elected governing boards, commissions, councils, and legislators. The intern may become an effective liaison person, delivering messages and impressions that otherwise might be left unsaid and so left to grow into major problems. In this role the intern may make a contribution to the agency's responsiveness to citizens as well as to elected officials.

In examining the special characteristics of political internships, Bernard Hennessy indicates that three elements are essential to any definition of internships: "a real work situation; the opportunity for the intern to participate on the same basis as other workers; and the opportunity for the systematic and continuous examination of the experience in relation to generalizations of political science."[8] These criteria apply as well to administrative or management internships, although the experience will also be evaluated in terms of the general theories of organizational behavior, management style, personal development, and organizational effectiveness — questions having less appeal to political scientists.

Selling the Program

Governments generally are pleased to participate in internship programs. Many agencies with professional administrators seek out universities which will develop such programs. In other cases, a certain amount of salesmanship is essential, but consists more of satisfying the doubts of managers as to how the program would be administrered than it does of selling the validity of such an approach. Most administrators are flattered to be approached by the university and told that they have been selected as managers capable of assisting in the education of graduate students. Besides, appointments of interns are generally reported in local mass media and this publicity helps to enhance the image of the professional administrator as one who is both in touch with students and directing an open operation that has the support of the university.

A further selling point of an internship program is the motivation of the intern and the exposure of the organization to his enthusiasm. Eager young interns, while lacking experience, will generally make up the difference in energy and intelligence. A highly motivated intern will often volunteer extra hours to the program if his lack of experience is preventing him from performing effectively during regular office hours. As a result, interns will generally produce more than they cost relative to full-time employees.

Another potential benefit is the opportunity for top management to receive an objective evaluation of its organization. While the intern may develop an intense loyalty to the agency, it is a loyalty unclouded by personal defensiveness about job security. The pervading concern of an intern is in learning effective management behavior, hopefully by generating successful ideas and observing effective administrators. Other benefits of the program may not develop until after the intern has completed his assignment with the agency. Then he is likely to receive a job offer.

Even administrators who have been skeptical of universities find it hard to resist a well-sold program. For one thing, if they have been very outspoken about their feelings, it has often been because of the apathy observed in universities that have not attempted to make themselves active in urban problem-solving. Having made such charges, it is difficult for an administrator to resist the overtures of a competent faculty member asserting that he and his students want to become actively involved, but need an open door to the governmental unit to succeed.

At other times it is preferable to avoid a "hard sell." The chief reason for selecting a modest explanation of the advantages and disadvantages of a program rests in the knowledge that a chief administrator who remains personally unconvinced probably would set expectations that an intern would find impossible to meet. If realistic expectations cannot be established in early conversations, then the likelihood of a beneficial intern experience developing in such an agency is not bright. One of the key factors in the success of an internship program is the assigning of an intern to an administrator with sufficient breadth of experience and risk acceptance that the intern will receive good exposure and training. An administrator who cannot appreciate the potential of an internship program is probably not qualified to be an intern supervisor and to "talk him into it" would tend to be self-defeating for both intern and program.

Another potential barrier in the establishment of a program can be the question of whether or not the intern should be paid. There have been many extremely successful intern programs where the interns were not granted stipends. However, this is extremely rare for a full-time internship. Where the internship is part-time, there are many factors that enter into the selection of the assignments the intern receives. Generally speaking, if the program provides that the intern will not be paid, there is a strong likelihood the intern will not receive appropriate assignments. There are good reasons, therefore, for insisting that interns be allotted a salary by the governmental agency. In addition to providing the intern with the financial assistance he may need to complete his education, paying for the services received is likely to cause the agency to take greater interest in how the intern is utilized. Payment also serves to reduce participation by administrators who do not have the intention of using the intern effectively, but who would accept an internship because it didn't cost them anything. The amount paid to the intern, while generally less than that paid a permanent employee with similar background, represents a commitment of resources on the part of the agency that hopefully will lead to an atmosphere in which the intern can maximize his experience through active participation.

The terms of pay sometimes represent a problem in that the faculty member responsible for the program will negotiate salaries with the hiring jurisdictions. Often he may not be able to secure the same rates with all of the agencies, leading to some inequities for the students. In other situations a particularly good intern may perform so well that the organization will raise the salary above the amount agreed upon. The monetary difference between jurisdictions is generally not significant, though, and since financial return is only one aspect of the total internship experience, this is not necessarily a serious problem. Nevertheless, a better alternative might be for the governmental units hiring interns to make payment to the public administration program, which would then divide payments evenly among the students. In really favorable situations, it might be possible to convince the governments to pay a stipend larger than that which the students would ordinarily receive in order to provide some additional funds for guest lecturers and field trips.

Selecting Interns

One of the primary considerations in selecting interns is the student's academic record. It is important to note, however, that while grades are clearly important they may not be the most critical indicators of performance potential. That is, the intern's academic record ought to be above average, but the internship need not be looked upon as the equivalent of an honors program. There is probably too much of a tendency to emphasize past academic performance because it offers the only hard data available for measuring one prospective intern against another. Accordingly some effort ought to be made to examine the other characteristics of an applicant that might contribute to the internship experience. If the intern has shown himself to be successful in dealing with people, he will unquestionably fare better than the nonpersonable intern. Conversely, if the intern should alienate others, future interns may thereby be deprived of their opportunity and the university will lose the enriching feedback effects that result from internships.

Motivation and maturity represent two considerations which also outweigh the academic record. An intern who is highly motivated to enter a career of public service will consider the internship an opportunity for important career planning and decision-making. It should be a time during which the intern can experiment with the administrative process and take exploratory risks under the guidance and challenge of an experienced administrator. The internship becomes a process during which the intern's qualities are spotlighted and tested in a manner that provides him with an opportunity to adapt to achieve policy and program goals. Meaningful experimentation and personal growth depend to a large extent on the intern's attitude. Applicants who see the internship only as an income supplement are not as likely as others to benefit from the program or to deliver the kinds of input the agency expects.

Maturity is another vital element in intern selection. An applicant who is short on maturity may cause problems within his sponsoring agency by violating confidences, causing dissension among regular employees, or proving unreliable when given deadlines to meet. All of this will have the effect of reducing the potentialities of the program inasmuch as interns will be more likely to be assigned to support departments rather than as aides to city managers, mayors, or chief budget officers. In building an internship program, it is of great importance to weigh heavily the maturity of potential interns. Students who have had military, Peace Corps, or similar experience often enhance the image of the internship program.

Maturity is a factor in limiting some programs to students in their final semester. Not only will these students have assimilated another year of academic work before attempting the internship, but also those who lack motivation will often have dropped from the degree program by that point. This precludes the embarrassment of having students resign in the midst of an internship. If all criteria – academic record, emotional maturity, previous experience, high motivation, and age – are properly applied, this can usually be avoided. It may therefore be unwise to make it an absolute requirement that all students complete a year of academic work before being granted a field assignment.

Special attention is needed in the selection and placement of female interns and those who are members of other minority groups. Some internship environments contain additional roadblocks, real or perceived, that may have an effect on the success of the internship program. In the present administrative environment it is generally not difficult to place black, chicano, or American Indian interns because of legal incentives or the desire of managers to advertise their broad-mindedness to superiors and colleagues. However, placing a woman intern may still be quite difficult. This is not only because the incentives for employing women are not as tangible as those for employing other minorities, but also because some male managers still have doubts that a woman is as suitable a prospect for career employment. For the intern advisor, each situation must be handled individually with special attention to be paid to the maturity and emotional stability of the particular intern as well as to the attitudes and management style of the supervisor with whom the intern will work.

The selection process varies from program to program. One approach is to appoint one professor to be responsible for the internship course and the selection of interns from student applicants. Other programs use a faculty committee to conduct interviews of applicants and make formal selections. However, academic committees are likely to encounter problems concerning the development of appropriate criteria for the selection of interns. Such committees have had a tendency to rely heavily on the selection criteria used for awarding the more conventional fellowships and assistantships, whereas an intern selection must be based on more than the level of academic attainment. Don Herzberg and Jesse Unruh comment on this problem as follows:

It is these requirements – a greater degree of extrovertism, an enhanced ability to write clearly, succinctly, and under pressure, a commitment to politics, and an appreciation of the role of the politician – that are rarely reflected in the present criteria governing the selection of academic fellows.[9]

One of the most important ingredients to the success of the internship program is the appointment of the right faculty member to head the program. To be effective, the faculty advisor must have the respect both of his colleagues and of the personnel in the agencies with which he deals. Herzberg and Unruh comment that, "ideally, he should be both a scholar and a man who may have had some experience as a governmental or political advisor himself."[10] The faculty advisor must also be able to exhibit a high degree of sensitivity toward the interns and their adjustments to the people for whom they work.

Even in programs where a faculty committee is responsible for selections, a single faculty member should manage the internship program. This type of arrangement assures consistent dealings and contacts with the agencies and with the interns. The arrangement also encourages consistency in grading and course requirements.

The Placement of Interns

The key factor in the placement of an intern is the supervisor to whom he is assigned. He needs a supervisor who knows how to use him correctly and whose own stage of personal and professional development is such that he has a valid contribution to make to the experience of the intern. The supervisor must also realize that the academic advisor who places the intern cannot guarantee that the interns who serve will be good prospects to become permanent employees. Nonetheless, most professional administrators are broad enough in their outlook and mobile enough themselves that they appreciate – even when an intern moves to another agency, another city, or to private industry — that the experience is not wasted. Such a person is likely to become a future colleague and resource or even be appointed a member of a governing body or citizens committee. In such a case, the former supervisor or one of his successors is likely to have an ally who understands the perspective of public managers and the pressures they face.

In addition to the personal considerations mentioned, it is generally best to attempt to secure assignments in those offices having access to top-level decisions and offering close personal relationship. The front office in particular receives communications from throughout the organization and passes instructions and decisions on to lower offices. One of the most vital insights the intern can develop is an understanding of how the whole organization fits together as a working system. This type of observation is most easily made from the top. It is for this reason that an office such as the budget office is generally a good place to assign an intern. Not only does it offer an overview, but frequently such an office is also charged with a management analysis responsibility permitting the intern to focus special attention on reviewing the organizational structure and its relationships. For the intern the opportunity to participate in the struggles and decision-making of high-level management is a considerable growth experience.

Aside from the personal and organizational location criteria, a third criterion may justify placing an intern in an office that is not only not at the top but not even in an overview position. This office might be characterized as one having a "high degree of action." Valuable experience can be obtained in a new program where precedents are lacking, where most of the participants are learning themselves, and where assignments are less procedurally structured. The intern is often permitted to participate on a free-wheeling basis in all of the activities of such an office. This has been, for example, the experience of many interns assigned to Model Cities offices. In one case an intern had a similar experience in, of all places, a public works department. A city earnings tax referendum had been approved to finance the establishment of a city-wide trash pickup system and the intern was given the job of designing the pickup system. Although not a glamorous assignment, this challenge included a broad variety of administrative problems and involved the securing of support from other departments to such a degree that it provided a top-to-bottom perspective of the total organization. Surprisingly, it also added significantly to the perspectives of the interns serving in staff positions. Comparing and contrasting their unique assignments became one of the focuses of the internship seminar.

The timing of assignments is also crucial to the successful placement of interns. There are many budget offices that do not have or do not exercise a management analysis responsibility. These may be poor places for an intern to be located at the wrong part of the budget cycle. In the absence of management analysis responsibilities and a year-round budgeting approach, things can be quite routine in the off-season. Whereas the intern might learn much about procedures and regulations, he would learn relatively little about process. There are other times not especially conducive to learning. For example, in the period just prior to an election, many agencies consciously reduce their risk-taking activities and delay making final decisions or starting new projects. This means that only routine activities are maintained. Innovation is avoided. In a situation where there are insufficient assignments for the regular staff, the intern may be used as little more than a file clerk.

The rotation of intern assignments is another significant placement question. In many internship programs, the participants serve a specified time in each of several agencies so that each intern might receive a well-rounded experience. As has been indicated, this same effect is best developed by assigning the intern to an office where he will have a continuing overview of the total organization. Nevertheless, such positions are not always available, particularly if the internships are not unpaid undergraduate students. The main drawback in rotating an intern even once during an internship program lasting less than a year is that the impermanence of the assignment will generally not motivate the supervisor to give an intern the best possible exposure. On the other hand, rotating an intern within elements of the same branch of a total organization can be a useful approach where major relearning is not necessary for each assignment and where the same supervisor continues to be in reasonably close contact with the intern.

Some observations may be made about selection of governments and their organizational units as appropriate places for internships. The established practice has been for the academician to place the intern in a professionally oriented government where values of professional public management are held in high esteem. Such governments tend to be places where political rivalries are insignificant, where the government is nonpartisan in nature, and where a "clean room" environment exists. Assignments to such governments can be good for the intern provided all the other criteria for the assignment — personal characteristics of the supervisor, existence of overview, availability of action, and willingness to use the intern — are present.

However, sometimes internships in less "pure" organizations may be equally beneficial. For four years interns were assigned to the highly professionalized government of Kansas City, Missouri, one of the largest cities in the nation to employ the city manager form of government. During the same period interns were also placed with Jackson County, Missouri, which over the years has been a bastion of spoils government intent upon avoiding most of its governmental responsibilities.[11] A reform county government took office in 1967 and, being underfinanced, could afford only a few professional administrators. In trying to raise the quality of its performance, the new administration was willing to use interns on assignments not normally entrusted to inexperienced staff members. Thus in their postinternship evaluations the the interns provided indications that those who served with Jackson County were more likely to receive challenging top-level assignments. Those assigned to the more stable Kansas City government were likely to have more narrow assignments, to be less in demand, and to deal with only a phase of a total problem.

Jackson County, it can now be seen, had no choice. There was no one else to do the job, and professional administrators had to delegate projects to the interns that a larger professional staff would have normally undertaken directly. The interns were provided with fantastic opportunity to learn and grow in a situation where risk-taking was encouraged. The net result was beneficial for the county even though some mistakes were made. The city government, on the other hand, could not have afforded to give the interns such wide-ranging assignments, nor would it have been able to allow the mistakes. Timing, therefore, can be very important to the program, and with a key administrator available at the right time and under the right circumstances, the intern can be entrusted to virtually any kind of government regardless of its prior reputation.

Another situation suggesting good opportunity for personal initiative is one in a metropolitan or regional agency. A regional council of governments or planning commission, for example, can provide a significant challenge for innovative and aggressive governmental interchange in a metropolitan area. It will also afford a view of at least a slice of the functional organization within several governmental units.

Different placement arrangements provide different opportunity benefits. In small organizations internship arrangements are most often negotiated by the professor with the cooperation of the top administrative official, such as the city or county manager. In large cities the manager may designate one of his chief deputies or the personnel officer to be responsible for the interns. Sometimes no central coordinating point is established and individual department heads make their own arrangements. Each of these patterns has both advantages and disadvantages to the intern program. The university, too, may practice administrative pluralism, and besides being all the more confusing to the participants, this method can act in such a way as to jeopardize the internship program. If several schools or departments of the university have internship programs, and if these are not coordinated, they will appear to be competitive in the eyes of the governmental administrators whose cooperation is solicited by various professors. Given that situation, none of the intern programs is likely to achieve an optimum environment. In fact, where there are a number of departments from competing universities attempting to place interns with larger governments – Washington, New York, and Los Angeles for example – the governmental departments and agencies are often large enough and sufficiently sophisticated that they are able to take over a large part of the responsibility for integrating the programs.

Formal Educational Aspects

Virtually all graduate internship programs provide academic credit for the participants. Part-time internships generally provide three credit hours during each of two semesters while full-time internships are offered for six credit hours in one semester. The academic requirements usually include preparation of a major graduate research paper or in some cases a thesis. Often interns are also required to write an analytical report or memorandum summarizing their internship and making suggestions to improve the program.

The research subjects may relate to the internship assignment, an administrative problem, a political-administrative relations problem, an intergovernmental relations problem, the installation of a new system, analysis of a key event, a case history of a significant decision, or some other application of administrative theory to a practical problem. The area of research may even be in a field requiring the advice and guidance of a professor other than the one heading the internship program; university procedures should be flexible enough to permit this. The interns, of course, meet at frequent intervals with the faculty both to review progress on the research projects and to evaluate personal internship experience.

The research aspect of the internship is receiving increasing attention in the literature because of the growing dissatisfaction with the adequacy of social science research methods.[12] The internship offers the opportunity for a participant-observer approach to research as a supplement to other methods. As Webb, Campbell, Schwartz, and Sechrest wrote:

Some 90 percent of social science research is based upon interviews and questionnaires. We lament this overdependence upon a single fallible method. Interviews and questionnaires intrude as a foreign element into the social setting they would describe, they create as well as measure attitudes, they elicit atypical roles and responses . . . . *But the principal objection is that they are used alone.*[13]

Many intern programs have dropped the requirement for a research paper on the basis that the sponsoring governments object to the practice of interns devoting substantial portions of office time to work on their research projects. But often this is an excuse based on fears held by many supervisors that outsiders will make detailed observations of their operations, leading to unfavorable publicity concerning perceived errors in procedures, criteria, and values which only an "insider" could fully interpret. That such fears are not uncommon or, in fact, unfounded only serves to point up the significance of the maturity factor and the need to instruct interns in the need to protect confidences received as an intern. Interns who quickly establish loyalty to the supervisor have fewer problems with such distrustful reactions and reservations.

In addition to research assignments, most programs include a periodic internship seminar at which interns present for discussion the kinds of problems they are having, their evaluations of the governmental unit they serve, and observations they have made about the governmental system and its relation to what they have learned from their academic work. The internship seminar meetings should always focus on some particular aspect of public administration, such as administrative or organizational theory. This concurrent approach assures that field practice can be directly related to academic theory. Additional seminars are held in most programs during which invited guests speak on a selected subject and then answer questions directed by the interns. Faculty members from the public administration program are invited to participate in most such sessions. Very often, the governmental supervisors of the interns are also present for these seminars. In those programs where an extended internship is undertaken, the common practice is to bring the interns back periodically for extended seminars that because of the travel costs involved, usually consist of two or three days of intensive reporting and interaction.

One of the most valuable educational experiences available to the intern is the opportunity to observe the behavior of his supervisor, his co-workers, the top management of the governmental unit, the supervisor's subordinates, subordinates of other organizational units, and the response of the entire governmental unit and its various components to interest groups in the community and its governing board. The internship seminar presents an opportunity to develop such observations. Some key questions that may lead to significant educational discussion are the following:

1. How are policy issues articulated?
2. What types and uses of power exist in the jurisdiction?
3. Who are the key actors and what are their roles?
4. What are the major differences between the political and professional, the line and the staff, and the official and citizen groups?
5. Who are the real leaders? How do they express their leadership? What significance does structure, personal behavior, or official role play in leadership?
6. How do the public administration professionals manage their resources, including employees and volunteers?
7. What kinds of data are available, how does information flow, and how does the public administrator influence the flow?
8. What managerial bottlenecks exist and how do the administrators deal with them?
9. What different management styles are being employed by different managers?
10. What clientele groups exist and who is dealing with them?
11. What role does the press play and why?
12. What seem to be the primary value assumptions of the managers and the other participants in decision-making?
13. How much decision-making is taking place in private?
14. What constitutes professional behavior?
15. What kinds of career patterns exist and which ones appeal to you?

16. What structural characteristics contribute to, or detract from, administrative effectiveness?

The observations of the interns are expressed in seminar sessions and generally relate to process concerns. This tends to balance the research projects which usually de-emphasize process comments in favor of the substantive content of subject areas such as finance, budget, labor relations or EDP systems. It is through the seminar that the interns develop the learning potential of the internship.

In his monograph on political internships, Bernard Hennessy stresses the importance of advanced planning so that the intern will be properly prepared for the experience. Relating the preparation and training of the internship in a pragmatic way that squares with the experience of a variety of seasoned intern directors, Hennessy concludes:

Most obviously, the prospective intern should be familiar with some of the existing knowledge in the area of his field experience to come. The more he knows about the literature the better — though knowledge of the literature in the uncritical mind may carry with it some conceptual and perceptual blinders (interns, like non-interns, often find in the field what their reading has told them they would find in the field).

It is not to be thought that relevant course work and reading should necessarily *precede* the internship. The internship might be more valuable, in fact, if it were experienced *concurrently* with relevant course work and reading. We have never investigated comparative educational structuring for internships, and therefore we are ill-prepared to make generalizations. But if I were asked to speculate, I would suggest that general courses and readings in American politics should precede internships, and relevant specialized courses should be taken concurrently with the internships.[14]

Whichever way training is handled, the intern professor will play an important role in facilitating educational processes. Because of his experience, the professor may serve to help an intern maximize his learning capacity. At the same time, the professor has a responsibility for carrying on a continuing relationship with the governmental sponsors to insure that they also derive benefits from the program. By maintaining direct relationships with both the intern and the sponsor, the professor is in a unique position to detect when an internship is not meeting its promise, and can take the appropriate corrective action. At such times the credibility of the faculty member with the governmental agency becomes very important. If the relationship is good, the necessary changes probably will be successfully made or at least an appropriate reassignment might be arranged without causing hard feelings. Even so, it is generally best to let an intern work out his own on-the-job relationship with his supervisor. This avoids creating the expectation that the professor will intervene every time a decision goes against an intern. When there are situations the intern cannot handle himself and in which the professor must become involved, he should then move rapidly to prevent damage to the internship program or to remove any potentially harmful pressures from the intern.

Other kinds of interactions are valuable in the intern program. The academic supervisor also monitors the agency supervisor's evaluation of the performance of the intern, and in most cases this is a factor in the student's grade, either directly or indirectly. Independent evaluation presents the professor with an excellent opportunity to secure feedback concerning each intern as well as to go into any matters of a management nature with the superior. Supervisors sometimes even use such sessions to discuss personal career development with the professor. Often they will also inquire as to whether there are any part-time teaching positions at the university that they might be able to fill, as the kinds of supervisors who consistently use interns effectively are likely to have a desire to teach. This motivation fits well into such a program, but the requests to teach will far exceed the available openings.

Conclusion

As an educational device for universities, internships differ from fellowships in several important respects. First, they are less prestigious in the academic world and, as a consequence, are less attractive to "scholarly" students to the point of being disdained by some academicians. Second, internships remove the student from campus for substantial periods of time, minimizing his exposure to the intellectual fringe benefits of full-time involvement in the academic community. Third, internships often tend to prolong the student's formal schooling, thereby delaying the award of a degree and increasing the costs involved in obtaining such a degree. Finally, there are numerous logistical problems associated with internships, particularly for schools located in rural environments, well removed from easy access to any significant number of governmental agencies.

But in many other respects, the internship is, or can be, a more effective recruiting device for universities than the fellowship. In addition to the support money involved, it provides the intern with personal job experiences that increase the relevance of classroom instruction and offer direct contact with professionals already in the field. Most importantly, by opening professional doors the internship makes a local government career a more viable option for the individual student.

Too, internships frequently have some unique educational advantages. Interns receive a taste of the real life of administration. They have an opportunity to see how things are done and to experience the problems, pressures, challenges, and drama that are a part of any meaningful administrative position. Further, the intern discovers that administrative work is not solely concerned with major policy decisions. He learns instead that the system used in refuse collection can be a prime determinant of voter disfavor or alienation, or that voters are more concerned with dog leash laws than with air pollution ordinances. In short, interns will begin to relate to the "client," and to the kinds of ways people respond to government in a democratic society.

The internship is a peculiarly good educational tool because it provides relevant educational experience in organizational activity. James Banovetz quotes one of the interns in his program at Northern Illinois University as saying:

The typical academic program awards individual excellence; the scholarly task is solitary and independent. Yet the skills most needed in an organizational setting relate to working with and through people. The organization man who works with and through people is called "a good administrator." The student who operates in this fashion is usually called a "cheater."

Thus the student gains an understanding of a particular operational pattern of working with people that he doesn't get in a typical academic setting.

The internship is a window to reality for the intern. But those who oppose the existence of internships as being a form of indentured servitude or as constituting simple work-study programs that should not be dignified by the provision of academic credit will have a basis for those charges if the professor guiding the internship program is not sufficiently sophisticated in his understanding of how governments operate or his ability to provide the enriching side experiences that crown the internship.

Yet the internship has distinct advantages both as a recruitment and as an educational device. It is a useful weapon in the campaign to professionalize governmental manpower. As such, it deserves greater utilization than it currently receives. Unfortunately this chapter must conclude, however, that much improvement remains to be injected into current programs. Hennessy discusses this point as follows:

It seems quite apparent that the best preparation, assignment, and supervision of interns can only be done by teachers who have themselves had extensive experience as participant-observers. Here indeed may be the major contemporary bottleneck to greater use of political internships — that the academic world has, as yet, neither the personnel nor the will to provide optimum supervision of participant-observation.[15]

In pointing to this specific problem, Hennessy has provided part of the solution. As intern programs continue to prosper, future students will have the advantage of having more professors who themselves have been interns. Also, as later chapters indicate, the increasing tendency for professionals to migrate from university to government to university will also increase the number of knowledgeable intern professors. This factor and the momentum of success should provide a better reservoir of intern professors for the future.

Notes

1. Robert F. Wilcox, "The New Public Administration: Have Things Really

Changed That Much?" *Public Management*, March 1971, pp. 4-7.

2. John C. Honey, "A Report: Higher Education for Public Service," *Public Administration Review*, November 1967, pp. 294-320, with commentaries by James M. Banovetz, Frederick C. Mosher, J. Kenneth Mulligan, Herman G. Pope, Henry Reining, Jr., Harvey Sherman, Paul P. Van Riper, and Rufus E. Miles, Jr., pp. 321-356. See also Sigmund G. Ginsburg and Armand F. Schumacher, "Graduate Training in Public Administration: What's Wrong, What's Right?" *Public Management*, June 1969.

3. Michael Cohen, "The Generalist and Organizational Mobility," *Public Administration Review*, September-October 1970, pp, 544-52.

4. Ibid., pp. 545-46.

5. Robert T. Golembiewski, "Specialist or Generalist?: Structure as a Crucial Factor" *Public Administration Review*, June 1965, p. 137. See also James W. Fesler, "Specialist and Generalist," *Public Administration Review*, August 1958 and Robert V. Presthus, "Decline of the Generalist Myth," *Public Administration Review*, December 1964.

6. R.J. Snow, "Participant Observer Analysis," in Donald M. Freeman (ed.), *An Introduction to the Science of Politics*, New York: The Free Press, 1971.

7. See L.P. Cookingham, Chairman, Committee on Professional Training of the International City Managers' Association, *City Management – A Growing Profession*, Chicago: The International City Managers' Association, 1957 and Robert L. Brunton and William E. Besuden, *Internship Training for City Management*, Chicago: The International City Managers' Association, June 1960.

8. Bernard C. Hennessy, *Political Internships: Theory, Practice, Evaluation* (University Park: Pennsylvania State University Press, 1970), p. 9.

9. Donald G. Herzberg and Jesse M. Unruh, *Essays on the State Legislative Process* (New York: Holt, Rinehart, Winston, 1970), p. 92.

10. Ibid.

11. Thomas P. Murphy, *Metropolitics and the Urban County* (Washington: Washington National Press and the National Association of Counties, 1970), pp. 126-80.

12. See especially Stephen K. Bailey, *Congress Makes A Law*, New York: Columbia University Press, 1950; Peter M. Blau, *The Dynamics of Bureaucracy*, Chicago: University of Chicago Press, 1963; Severyn T. Bruyn, *The Human Perspective in Sociology: The Methodology of Participant Observation*, Englewood Cliffs, New Jersey: Prentice-Hall, 1966; Charles L. Clapp, The Congressman: *His Work as He Sees It*, Washington: Brookings Institution, 1963; Harry Cohen, *The Demonics of Bureaucracy*, Ames Iowa: Iowa State University Press, 1965; Eugene Eidenberg and Roy D. Morey, *An Act of Congress*, New York: Norton, 1969; Alan Fiellen, "The Functions of Informal Groups in Legislative Institutions," in R. Peabody and N. Polsby (eds.), *New Perspectives on the House of Representatives*, Chicago: Rand-McNally, 1963, pp. 59-78; Herbert Gans, *The Urban Villagers*, Glencoe: Free Press, 1962; Donald R. Matthews, *U.S.*

Senators and Their World, Chapel Hill: University of North Carolina Press, 1960; and James A. Robinson, "Participant Observation, Political Internships, and Research," in James A. Robinson (ed.), *Political Science Annual: An International Review,* vol. 2, 1969.

13. Eugene J. Webb, Donald T. Campbell, Richard D. Schwartz, and Lee Sechrest, *Unobtrusive Measures: Non-Reactive Research in the Social Sciences* (Chicago: Rand-McNally, 1966), p. 1.

14. Hennessy, *Political Internships,* pp. 114-15.

15. Ibid., p. 117.

16. Summaries of a variety of interesting internship programs at the federal, regional, state, and local levels are contained in *Who Administers?*, a report for the Ford Foundation by Frank Logue, October 1, 1972. Logue is director of the National Urban Fellows program based at Yale University, New Haven, Connecticut.

2

An Intern's Perspective

RICHARD D. HEIMOVICS

Once on the new job, a first concern of the public administration intern is to "get something accomplished." And why not? The student spends a significant part of his life in training to become a professional administrator. Furthermore, emphasis in most university classrooms is directed at doing and actions; performance is evaluated on evidence of task accomplishment. Accordingly, the temptation is to view the internship in terms of learning how to "get the job done" or learning how to "do something" about a specific problem in public management. The internship conceived in this context is described in an International City Management Association (ICMA) guidebook for internships.[1] The guidebook, *Internship Training for City Management*, suggests as the individual goals of the internship:

The educational goal is achieved if the intern gains a perspective of administration. A well-planned program gives the intern an opportunity to observe, analyze, participate in the development of general theories and concepts of governmental administration. It also gives him an opportunity to apply those theories and concepts to specific situations during a period closely connected to his academic study. A broad-gauged internship helps develop his sensitivity to a management environment in which he applies his academic training to practical situations.[2]

The ICMA concern about learning how to get the job done is stated again when referring to the value of the internship learning experience:

1. It provides an opportunity to apply university training to actual situations.
2. It is an organized means to familiarize the student with applied administrative practice.
3. It provides the most effective means of teaching an over-all approach to management.
4. It provides the student with practical experience in organized fashion.
5. It provides the intangible benefits of contact between the intern and the experienced administrator.[3]

These are important considerations. But are they the reality of the experience?

This chapter grew out of the author's nine-month internship with the city of Kansas City while a graduate student in public administration.

The situation of most interns might be stated as "look, but don't touch." He is the new member of the management team, untried and untested. Usually employed for a short time, he is given little responsibility or authority. Thus it is difficult for the intern to understand the real feelings of the responsibilities of management: the "sweat" of pressured decision-making or the "heat" when the manager knows his decision may not have been the best one. The intern comes to the task anticipating action, hoping to create change and influence policy. He is skilled at conceptualization, steeped in the latest tools of systems analysis and decision-making and anxious "to do the job." But he finds he has only the limited right of recommendation or suggestion. His only opportunity for influence usually rides on the skill with which he prepares a project or the persuasion with which he attempts to sell it. In fact, he finds himself using only the same skills he became so adept at in the classroom. It is but old wine in new bottles with seemingly little potential for new learning.

Creating the bridge from the classroom to the administrative world is not a simple task. Nor is making the internship experience unique and meaningful an easy thing. The internship is at most a maturation process, clearly not described adequately in either academic or administrative worlds. But if it is to be an experience in administration different than that of the university classroom while at the same action-oriented, where is the middle ground?

It may not exist; or better stated, perhaps we need another perspective from which to discuss internships. Although the intern can seek maximum exposure to problems and processes and can test his decision-making skills against those of the senior managers, he nonetheless is still often without influence. He can carefully prepare his work project with diligence, but the experience is really not much different than authorship of a term paper.

If the student himself is to create a bridge, his first recognition must be that the success of the internship is largely his own responsibility. Secondly, it is helpful if the intern can place the experience in an individually satisfying perspective. For example, it may be helpful to accept an orientation that maintains the goal of the internship is not learning how to accomplish a task, but how to form attitudes toward the meaning of the experience. Even though learning how to apply a growing amount of academic knowledge to the accomplishment of problems in public management is at the heart of the profession, there may be more realistic ways to think about the intern experience. Instead of placing emphasis upon "accomplishing something" perhaps the orientation might be one of how the intern relates the personal experience of his learning to what it is he is *becoming*. Accordingly, the issues for the internship would be: What changes has my learning brought about in me? What does this experience mean in terms of helping me build bridges from learning to practice? What is it about my experience that is meaningful, and how does that relate to my career objectives? These questions mirror a personal conviction that the student intern is entering an important juncture of life when he can ask: "Who I am to *be,* and how?"

Unfortunately the tendency in most internships is to proceed with specific learning tasks for the student. The production of services and the attainment of departmental objectives are said to be concerns of most public agencies and should continue to be. But under this reasoning the student too often inquires: "How much do I know?" Perhaps the intern needs to avoid the daily task of *doing* or learning to *do* in favor of considering what it is he is *becoming.* Otherwise, the potential consequence is the often unresolved tension surrounding such statements as: "They will not let me do enough," or "I walk around with nothing to do," or "I do not have enough time to accomplish everything they want me to do. The trouble is none of it is important."

As an example of the task orientation, consider the typical first assignment undertaken by almost every new intern in a public agency. He is asked to carefully review the agency's budget and operation manual in order to derive some insight into the structure and operation of the agency. But necessary as it may seem, the intern is normally out of the mainstream of operations. His major duties are those of short duration: staff research, a project report. Truthfully, it may be helpful to be introduced to the department by way of the manual. But what if the first task for the intern could be to assess very carefully what it is *he* hopes to accomplish during the internship, what he wants to learn about himself, and how he wants to grow individually? Possibly what the intern needs is a "procedures manual" for his own internship experience – one he creates for himself, listing his own needs and expectations.

Consider, too, the commonly shared wisdom about internships held by most organizations. If the intern cannot influence policy or determine action, perhaps he should at least be placed in a position providing as broad a view of an agency's operation as is possible. In the language of the ICMA guidebook, "The internship reinforces his 'generalistic approach' to the problems of administration."[4] However, there are other considerations. Kenneth Boulding provides an insight:

I suspect, indeed, that the major task of formal education is likely to become that of learning the language of specialists so that communication among men may take place. This is perhaps only another way of saying that the major task of formal education in the future is to teach people how to learn, not to stuff their minds with particular content. The learning of content will have to go on during the whole life, and the period of formal education will be much too short to permit the transmission of the total knowledge stock. The principle sounds innocent but could involve a profound revolution in the whole system of education.[5]

The tasks of addressing the issue of *becoming* or the reorienting of learning are not easy ones. We have had so little practice. We may illustrate from the behavioral sciences as concerns role behavior. All of us have a large repertory of possible roles and styles of behavior we may bring into play in any given situation. But when there is uncertainty about one's perceived role, as is often the case in the internship, there is usually greater ambiguity of choice in the roles we perform. The intern entering this new experience will certainly be faced with the decision of what role he should play; he has a degree of choice in this new environment. He can be the passive listener, because it is expected of him; or he can be the aggressive learner, a behavior pattern which may have worked well in the past; or he can be the friendly social fellow, which has worked under other conditions. In any case, the intern needs to be aware that the problems he faces in entering the new agency stem from a set of underlying emotional and attitudinal issues relative to the question, "what and who am I to *be* in this setting?"

Carl Rogers provides an observation from his work in psychotherapy which may be helpful. Rogers suggests that the more open people are to the realities of their own behavior, the less apt they are to rush in and fix or do things. A person acting under this precondition might state: "I am much more content simply to be myself and to let another person be 'himself'." But Rogers suggests:

What is life for if we are not going to do things to people? What is life for if we are not going to mold them to our purposes? What is life for if we are not going to teach them the things that *we* think they should learn? What is life for if we are not going to make them think and feel as we do? How can anyone hold such an inactive point of view as the one I am expressing? I am sure that attitudes such as these must be a part of the reaction of many of you.

Yet the paradoxical aspect of my experience is that the more I am simply willing to be myself in all this complexity of life and the more I am willing to understand and accept the realities in myself and in the other person, the more change seems to be stirred up. It is a very paradoxical thing — that to the degree that each one of us is willing to be himself, then he finds not only himself changing, but he finds that other people to whom he relates are also changing.[6]

Rogers' view suggests other ways to think about the internship. One unique aspect of the internship period is that it is a time when the ability to pass examinations is not the best criterion for juding professional promise. It can be the time when knowledge does not have to mean the accumulation of brick and brick of content and information. Rather it can be a time when the intern comes face-to-face with questions often left unasked in the classroom and rarely addressed on the professional job:

1. Where and how do I want to grow as a professional?
2. What are my strengths and weaknesses as a potential administrator? Do I know what they are?
3. What is it about my experience that is really meaningful to me and how does that relate to my career objectives?
4. What is my agenda for learning for the next period in my life?
5. Am I now able to become responsible for my own learning?

Thinking about internship in a different framework does not suggest that learning about accomplishing tasks in the administration of public agencies is not important. What should concern us is the question of order and emphasis. In any case, the opportunity for learning is heightened if the intern gives careful consideration to many other issues than learning how to do a job.

Another way to view the internship is to consider the intern's own entry style into an organization. The style is largely a function of the role he wishes to play. The behavior can be viewed in three steps which interact and overlap: (1) initial contact with the agency; (2) defining the relationship; and (3) formal and psychological contracts.[7]

Initial contact with the agency sets the stage for a most important aspect of the internship. Gaining entry to an organization for the purposes of experience, research, and personal development of an intern is highly contingent upon the help of one or more internal people who are willing to initially expose the processes of the agency to the intern. Often these people have only the vaguest ideas of what internships are, but they can easily identify with the role of a student. An early spirit of inquiry by the intern is an essential characteristic of this first stage of a potentially successful intern-agency relationship.

The intern might consider an exploratory meeting as one of his first efforts. The purposes would be to determine more precisely what is expected. Now is the time for the intern to ask questions designed to: (1) sharpen and highlight his and the agency's interest in the internship concept and (2) test how open and frank the agency representatives are willing to be. If there is a sense of hedging or confusion about the internship, caution about the intern or his motives and/or confusion about his potential role, the intern should proceed cautiously. A successful internship is a function of clearly defined relationships. Too often internships have not been fruitful because the intern either moved too fast or blindly.

After this early testing of the relationship, the intern is best guided by a sense of openness and honesty, partly to determine how willing the agency is to be open and honest and partly to make it clear from the start to the agency how the intern views his role. During this process the stage is set to define the formal and psychological contracts that ultimately determine the parameters of the interaction between the intern and the agency.

There are two aspects of the contract: one is the formal decision such as what hours the intern is to devote and when — what specific tasks will be performed; the other aspect concerns the actual "psychological contract" — what the intern expects to gain from the relationship and what the agency expects to gain from the efforts of the intern. It is important for both the intern and the agency to explore both aspects of the contract, not just the formal ones. The intern who has established a healthy relationship can constantly renegotiate the psychological contract as a function of the degree of trust between him and the agency.

During the first part of the internship, opinions about task, role, and objectives for the intern may be unclear; this most likely will be the case. Confusion may exist if the agency's past experience with interns is minimal. The three steps suggested for entry into the internship are merely guideposts for finding one's way through this critical period.

In order to understand more of the entry problem, it may be helpful to think about the frame of mind of most agencies. For some, the student is talent at a cheap price. I recall reviewing job-training programs for high school dropouts while serving in an internship with the Model Cities program. Without exception, these job-training programs paid more than the graduate school internship. But this was my first recognition of the fact that most people in government services (particularly in local government) are not there for money. In fact, it helped to point out that most people in government service with whom the intern works are overworked and underpaid, motivated primarily by pride and faith in what they are doing.

Yet not all agencies seek interns because they are cheap labor. Organizations are always looking for new blood and a fresh view of problems. Furthermore, an internship program provides an agency with an opportunity to evaluate potential employees more extensively than can be accomplished through an interviewing procedure. As a variation on this theme the agency will often not know what to ask of the intern, largely because the intern's capabilities are not yet known or the agency does not know how to use his talent. This dilemma is heightened by the relatively short period of most internships. Increasing the potential frustration for the intern is the "look, but don't touch" nature of most internships. As mentioned earlier, the obligation for the successful experience is largely the student's. This reasoning would suggest that if "looking" is the name of the game, there must be ways to make the most of it.

Here again, it might be helpful not to think about the internship in the context of task accomplishment but rather, in this case, how skillful an observer the intern can be. A good place to begin is with attendance at numerous meetings. There are many to choose from. Perhaps the most obvious one is the weekly staff meeting. I recall a staff meeting at which I was purposely looking for signs of openness and cooperation – just as the books on organizational behavior suggest. When I found little, there were other things to look for. I discovered that those attending staff meetings are usually asked to report on problems and developments. Some administrators make concise statements when asked, leaving time to busily outline what they wish they were doing in place of attending the weekly staff meeting. I discovered as well that individuals who make lengthy progress reports are those whose projects are not going well. Everyone, including the boss, knows when good jobs happen without hearing about them at staff meetings. Attendance is not always obligatory; however, everyone expects to see the intern there. He should be. These meetings are a microcosm of the organization. The careful observer will soon learn the identity of the malcontents, the unhappy, and the ones who talk but do not perform. Every staff meeting has an agenda. This usually consists of a listing by an administrative assistant of the problems he believes to exist. At best, the successful administrator will use the staff meetings to carefully gauge the progress of his employees. He will facilitate face-to-face interaction for people on his staff who otherwise refuse to see each other. In a healthy organization, I discovered that the staff and administrator work together to build and process the agenda.

Similar problems surround problem-oriented meetings. Organizations that cannot solve a particular problem are inclined to call a meeting to bring together the best minds both within and without the organization. These meetings, I discovered, reflect the fact that a department is either unable or unwilling to solve problems through the usual channels. Normally a subcommittee will be appointed, requiring an additional meeting at which a report is made. (A problem-oriented meeting is almost a guarantee of a subsequent meeting.) Once again, I found it helpful to attend most of these latter meetings to learn best how to use them in the future.

Some of the most frustrating, but nonetheless entertaining meetings, are those that bring the organization's big minds together. Especially educational are meetings that attract highly paid consultants to unravel a complex organizational problem. The fun and fireworks occur when these consultants come to test their theories of administrative success. The intern can observe that often those in the agency who have the hardest time getting things done crowd the consultant after his presentation, asking lengthy esoteric questions about policy analysis, musing over input-output problems and testing the latest jargon. Their behavior illustrates the difficulty of making an adequate transition from classroom theory to day-by-day administrative actions – a problem that is not exclusive to internships.

There are still other meetings worth attending; some of the most valuable I recall were: (1) those involving "grass roots" politics, such as neighborhood planning meetings or Model Cities community meetings; (2) policy-making sessions, including those for political figures; and (3) the budget hearings of the agency. The budget hearings demonstrate how the budgetary review process often places much policy-making power in the hands of persons who are not directly responsible for accomplishment, and whose actions cannot be effectively policed. I recall that this insight came to me one afternoon while observing a city council deliberate eight minutes on a $8.7 million public works budget and fifty minutes on $47,000 for staffing a community service division. The occasion concerns one of the most bizarre features of our government – local, state, or federal. Cardinal choices have to be made by a handful of men who cannot have a first-hand knowledge of what those choices depend upon or what the results may be. Too often these policy and program choices are those which determine in the crudest sense whether the government is to be effective. The point is that by sitting through the lengthy budget hearings, I saw dramatized before me an insight that no textbook could have made so clear. All I had to do was watch.

There are other ways for the intern to keep his experience reality-conscious. One is the difficult process of learning a little about administrative risk-taking. The behavioral scientists tell us that people are willing to take imaginative risks with their skills when the atmosphere of an organization is supportive – that is, when it is free of threat. The intern alone is completely free (perhaps for the only time in his administrative career) to take full risks with his administrative and analytic skills. This is because administrative risk-taking includes awareness of the consequences of bad judgment, and the harshest consequences of bad judgment are rather limited for the intern. Thus, even if the organization is reluctant to give the intern little responsibility or authority, my experience was that I profited most by testing the limits of my administrative judgment whenever possible.

There is much to read in any office. I found helpful data in the job description manual. It is a good place to check pay levels; one needs to know ranges for future employment. Whatever the case, I soon learned that the good administrator often uses job descriptions to create new jobs for the good people he wants to hire who may not otherwise meet the prescribed experience requirements established by the merit system. In other words, there is a merit system game that few people talk about, but everyone plays.

There is much to learn about the merit system and personnel departments. My discovery was that the trouble with many personnel experts is they use the same techniques borrowed from manufacturing and production or cherished since the 1920s. Personnel files are often thumbed through much like inventories, and the replacement charts reflect a likeness to preventative maintenance charts in engineering operations. In any case, I discovered the reality that the philosophical underpinnings of the "merit system" are not absolutes.

And I did read the operations manual. It finally was not because I wanted to find out how work was to proceed, but rather why it was not proceeding according to the operation manual (as my boss suggested). First, I found the manuals overly general and not always useful. I would guess that the "how-to" manuals often restrain and discourage individual creativity, or they are read the first day on the job (along with the budget) and then placed on a shelf alongside the dictionary. I recall speculating that three kinds of people usually read operations manuals carefully: People who work at avoiding hard work, those who have written them, and those who must operate in a structured environment. The avoiders memorize the manual so they can say, "It's not in our jurisdiction," or simply "It can't be done." Those who write manuals often refer to them when they need leverage, or when they are unable to create a healthy environment where individuals want to do their jobs properly. Those who need a structured environment in which to work use the manual to frustrate creative and adventuresome minds. By careful observation I found out much about how people use, misuse, and do not use procedures. By careful observation, I became aware of many other realities of the administrative world.

The operations manual, or its counterpart the organization manual, provides a statement about the formal structure and operation of the agency. Perhaps the most valuable learning experience for me was to attempt to look for and understand the differences between the formal statement of operation and the actual operation. Someday as an administrator, I know I will have to make some sense of my own about the ambiguity between the two.

These brief descriptions of perceptions of the internship experience may have little to do with others' experience. It is not implied that they should. The point is only that the internship can be viewed as a host of valuable organizational experiences. Therefore, my concern was to attempt to make some sense of my own perceptions of the experience and to test those perceptions during the short time structure of the internship period, both within and without of the organizational context. The normative statement that the internship ought to address the question, "What is it that I, the intern, am being during this experience and what is it I am becoming in the process?" is suggested as a means of organizing perceptions into a meaningful frame of reference. This is not to suggest that this frame of reference is the most relevant or helpful for a specific intern. Rather it is presented as one intern's way of ordering his experience. In any case, my internship had much to do with what it is I have become and am now becoming. I know I carefully sharpened my organization observing skills — and I grew personally. I did not shake any mountains, but it was a good experience.

Notes

1. Robert L. Brunton and William E. Besuden, *Internship Training for City Management,* The International City Managers' Association, (ICMA), 1960.

2. Ibid. p. 2.

3. Ibid. p. 9.

4. Ibid. p. 2.

5. Kenneth Boulding, "The Specialist with a Universal Mind," *Management Science* 14,12 (Aug. 1968):653.

6. Carl R. Rogers, *On Becoming a Person* (Boston: Houghton Mifflin Co., 1961, pp. 21-22.

7. These stages were adapted from a discussion of entry behavior into organization by Edgar H. Shein, *Process Consultation* (Boston: Addison-Wesley, 1969), pp. 79-88.

3

Potential Pitfalls of Internships

THOMAS P. MURPHY

While an internship can be the highlight of preparation for a public service career, pitfalls exist which may detract from the experience. Interns invariably enter an agency with high spirits and energy, seasoned with mild trepidation; most leave the agency self-assured and eager to show what they can do in a permanent position. However, others may either become discouraged or disoriented by bureaucratic systems or else leave with no significant observations about themselves or the organization in which they served. Either way the result is a reflection of the degree of success the intern experienced in confronting the hazards that develop during an internship.

The most commonly observed pitfalls threatening the intern may be categorized as organizational, political, and personal. In addition to the hazards that may be avoided by tactful interns, other situations may arise in which even the most wily intern will have no control. Such would be the case where the internship professor would fail to perform his part of the job effectively or be prevented from doing so by his colleagues who may not understand the program or who may be motivated by professional jealousy. Any of these hazards may cause an intern to have an unsuccessful internship. However, the eager intern who makes an honest effort can succeed in avoiding the worst consequences of all these pitfalls.

The potential educational impact of an internship is indicated by the experience of one intern who took an internship early in his MPA program. He reported that much of the course work that followed his experience was anticlimactic. Yet equally important to an individual's professional training is the self-evaluation generated by a failure. Consider the experience of an intern whose personal style generated organizational hostilities against both his supervisor and himself, eventually forcing the intern from the agency. Under the direction of a skilled advisor this episode could provide valuable introspection for the young intern. Still other interns become "grey" interns — they meander around an organization for months and emerge just as they had entered! Under these circumstances the interns who "fail" might even be envied for their lesson. Fortunately, these nonproductive experiences are not frequent in well-run internship programs.

35

Participant Interrelationships

The proper mix of intern, agency supervisor, and academic advisor is essential to a productive internship. The importance of these three roles and their interaction in the development of a productive internship is indicated in table 3-1, which shows the responsibility the participants have for various aspects of the internship experience. While the roles played and the decisions made on various aspects of the relationship contain the elements of a healthy internship, they may also have a negative impact.

Table 3.1. Responsibility for Aspects of the Internship Experience

	Intern	Supervisor	Professor
Intern selection	A	D	A, D
Determining intern office assignment	A	D	A, D
Administrative knowledge	A	I	I
Task experience	P	D, I, R	I, R
Legitimacy in the organization	P	D	R
Inclusion in decisions	A, P	D, I	I, R
Administrative-political insight	A, P	I, R	I, R
Evaluation of the internship	R, P	D	D
Evaluation of the intern	P	D	D

A = Initiator, proposer, acceptor
D = Decision-maker
P = Influenced by his performance

I = Instructor, interpreter
R = Reviewer of decision, performance, or environment

Attribution of the agitator and initiator role primarily to the intern, and only secondarily to the professor is due to the primary decision-making role assumed by the supervisor with respect to what the intern does on the job. Were it not necessary for the supervisor to manage the programs of many interns, individual attention could conceivably be focused upon each intern to the extent that the agitator/initiator role would become superfluous. As in the classroom environment, a profitable internship experience results to a large extent not from the ability of the professor to effectively teach, but rests upon the ability of the student to discern personal interests within the framework of that teaching and, in a very real sense, to educate himself. The professor, teaching many, cannot be held responsible for the achievements, or lack thereof, for each individual student. Thus, in an internship, much of the responsibility for success rests with the intern. His ability to establish effective personal relationships for the transfer of knowledge and to perform on the job demonstrates his credentials and allows him to propose additional responsibilities or research opportunities.

But the success of these intern initiatives is also dependent on the sensitivity, competence, and organizational positions of the agency supervisor and the professor directing the program, and upon their past experience with interns. As table 3-1 shows, decisions as to who will be an intern, with which government, and under what conditions are the province of the professor. However, many key decisions on such factors as legitimization within the agency, inclusion of the intern in decision-making, and selection of task experiences are made by the supervisor. Further, each supervisor must agree to the intern's assignment and participate in evaluating him. The competence of the professor becomes most critical in maintaining the relationship between the schools and interns on the one hand, and the agencies and the supervisors on the other. If the professor is to be effective in his role of reviewing the supervisor's handling of decisions affecting the intern, he must have considerable rapport with the supervisor and the agency and be sufficiently accessible to play his role at critical decision points as well.

One of these initial decision points is the selection of projects to be assigned to the interns during their initial training. These projects are the means through which the intern undergoes his initiation into the agency and the administrative process. They may influence the intern's view of government as a career. The decisions on projects also represent either the conscious or unconscious decision as to whether an intern is to be a temporary participant in the agency's administrative and decision-making processes or whether the intern is to be instead just another pair of hands. There are various indicators that an intern may observe in determining the overall attitude towards his internship. For example, is he invited to sit in on policy discussions? Even routine decisions such as the physical location of work areas may provide clues to this attitude. If the intern's desk or office is near that of the top administrator, the potential for participation is generally greater. However, an intern may be within hearing of the top man and still be effectively isolated, again emphasizing the importance of developing the personal relationship between supervisor and intern.

Of equal ranking with the initial project assignment in setting a future course for the intern is his understanding of the administrative and political processes which form the environment of the agency. Such insight is most easily gained when the intern is accorded legitimacy by agency top management. In healthy organizations this legitimacy often proves adequate to "open doors" throughout the agency. In "closed" organizations this legitimacy may follow the intern only as far as the manager's door; elsewhere the intern will be expected to "win his wings." This foreknowledge will in itself be valuable to a newly appointed intern, for not uncommonly interns face a defensive attitude when they approach subdivisions of the organization that may consider then to be "front office spies." Interns even occasionally find themselves the victims of the bureaucratic runaround of which the agency's clients and the taxpayers so vehemently complain. While such experiences constitute excellent learning, they underscore the necessity of providing the intern with legitimacy sufficient to his needs.

In addition to providing simple access to information, the degree of legitimacy the intern receives in the organization influences the level of understanding to be reached between intern and agency. The formal processes by which the agency operates are generally written in an administrative code, if not in a charter or statute. But the administrative understanding sought by the intern includes as well a cognizance of the informal process areas. Learning is achieved through observing and participating in discussions of management styles, professional goals and allegiances, organizational rivalries, interdepartmental relationships, and extra-organizational factors impinging upon the decisions that become policy and action through the formal process. As with other aspects of a successful internship experience, learning is promoted only to the extent that mutual confidence is cultivated between the intern and the agency.

Nonetheless, there are various administrative environments in which an "open" relationship is difficult to develop in a limited time. For example, the formal organization of an agency may be an inhibiting factor. At one extreme are those departments in which each division is a separate fiefdom so that organizational effectiveness becomes a victim of inadequate coordination of policy and decision-making. This type of organization provides a variety of pitfalls as the barriers inherent in the formal organization are compounded by organization alliances which characterize the local informal process. While an intern may in time find his way through such a maze, a semester or even a year might provide considerable knowledge about the organization but little feeling of accomplishment.

This means that the internship must be a collaborative effort on the part of the three principal performers as well as by the agency and university as organizations. Table 3-1 indicates that the performers have different degrees of influence at different stages of the internship. Even the most able professor with considerable credibility in an agency cannot affect or change role factors for an intern who has failed to gain the confidence of the supervisor. And yet, the interaction of the intern and the administrator is crucial and represents an informal learning experience that the student may reflect upon as his career develops. The administrator must be willing to take the time and develop the confidence of the intern so that an open cooperative interaction may develop between them. The professor must use all his skills to insure that this occurs.

Open collaboration of the three principal participants is essential to a viable internship experience. While these participants may all be highly motivated and able people, their perspectives and approaches will differ. As a consequence, their efforts may not be synchronized so as to maximize the learning aspects of the internship. When such personal attitudes are not a problem, there are still other potential pitfalls of an organizational and political nature that even a high level of collaboration may be be able to overcome. These deterrents to productive interaction will now be examined.

Organizational Pitfalls

In addition to the hazards peculiar to individual organizations, there are a few problems that manifest themselves in organizations generally. One of the most dangerous to interns and internship programs alike is the absence of real commitment on the part of governmental organizations agreeing to accept the internship program. Some agencies or supervisors within those agencies may be motivated primarily because of the status such programs often provide. Internships have become an indicator of the willingness of an agency to be innovative. Furthermore, the internship is often looked upon as an effective device to recruit inexpensive but talented staff support. These attitudes result in a sublimation of the learning goals of the internship in favor of agency needs that could be achieved through the existing framework of agency operations.

Organizational attitudes toward internship programs become most apparent in times of organizational stress. These are periods of agency- or government-wide tension and/or change in which an intern can benefit immensely if allowed to participate. Among these periods are:

1. Changes in governmental form
2. Redirection following an election
3. The realignment of top management
4. Decision-making periods in budget preparation
5. Program evaluation by higher authorities
6. Challenges by external forces
7. Innovations or changes in major policies

However, in organizations where commitment to the intern program is not high, the intern may find himself isolated from top management, seen but not admitted to the councils of analysis and decision.

This reaction can occasionally be costly to the organization as well as to the intern. While lacking experience and sophistication, a reasonably perceptive intern can contribute to agency functioning by questioning some of the assumptions that insiders may be taking for granted or protecting for selfish reasons.

A second major intern problem is the dead-end assignment to useful but shallow projects. Interns may receive assignments involving a policy or action recommendation, yet at the same time be so remote from "the action" that virtually any recommendation would suffice. Interns assigned to routine or wheel-spinning projects may be highly lauded for their efforts but are really missing out. They cannot gain the experience that is the goal of the program if they are continually closeted with low-priority projects and not permitted to observe or participate in the more significant decisions.

One variation of the dead-end assignment is the assignment that never quite gets off the ground. Intern projects sometimes fall victim to agency politics or hostile circumstances generated from the outside environment. In this special case it is not the intent of the agency to detour the intern into low priority or irrelevant assignments. Nevertheless, the result is much the same; the intern fails to receive assignments that permit the risk-taking responsibilities so necessary to proper professional development.

One example of this difficulty is provided by the experience of two interns assigned to a research project in an agency personnel division. The stated task — that of designing a computerized position control register — was potentially of great importance to the agency, insofar as the new system would have provided important budget and personnel information to the chief administrator and department heads.

Unfortunately, internal staff problems took the interns by surprise. Although the intern supervisor regarded professional management systems development as having high priority, his enthusiasm was not shared by either his superiors or the budget and personnel offices — the two key staff offices whose cooperation would be required to optimize professional management capabilities. Other problems emerged from the inexperience of the interns in handling sophisticated problems in data processing because of their ignorance of the organizational "culture." In the first place, neither intern had any real knowledge of EDP. Such knowledge was a basic qualification for determining the capabilities of the present system and the nature of future data and reporting requirements. As a consequence of their inexperience, it took nearly a month to reach the point where an inventory of present data storage could be undertaken.

At this point the second barrier was encountered. The EDP Department was completely entangled in the development of a new tax assessing and billing system, a computerized budgeting system, and court and law enforcement records system. Under these circumstances harassed EDP people could not afford to allocate scarce time and personnel resources to a position control register project which would delay establishment of their existing priorities. But to the further detriment of the project, the EDP personnel felt obligated to simulate the true cooperation they could not afford to give, rather than admit to the interns that they could not sacrifice their department's projects.

In this particular case the project was stimulating to both interns and professional personnel, but because of hidden organizational realities the interns were incapable of fathoming, this potentially useful project was doomed to an agonizingly slow death. Little valuable cooperation was provided either by the line personnel who were grossly overworked or by the department heads who were somewhat suspicious of the motivations of top management.

Looking back on their experience, the interns admitted that possibly they could have done more to develop the system had they not used the organizational roadblocks they encountered as a shield to cover their lack of experience. Even with the intervention of top management in this case, it is doubtful that such an ill-prepared project could have succeeded in the organizational environment that existed.

While this particular case illustrates the hazards of a fragmented organization, other examples of dead-end projects may be encountered in highly centralized, highly professionalized bureaucracies. In such agencies it is frequently difficult for interns to maintain positive and open relationships with key decision-makers. Because policies and procedures in these agencies are highly centralized and highly structured, interns are seldom included in either routine or major decisions even though they may be housed with members of the top management support staff. On the contrary, projects assigned them are often related to ideas that have surfaced intermittently within the agency over a period of several months or years. Often the justification for such assignments lies in the assumption that a "fresh" examination will encourage new solutions to long-standing problems. Naturally this approach usually proves fallacious as interns run into the same organizational barriers that have prevented solutions in the past. In addition, interns are placed at greater disadvantages than are regular staff personnel by their part-time status within the organization and the resulting credibility problems.

The mention of intern credibility raises a third and final major organizational pitfall, which is that the intern may be jeopardized by being absent when he is needed. It is particularly ironic that the major advantage of the internship to students is its work-study opportunity. There is some feeling that this very division of labor between academic and professional pursuits denies full commitment to either. The intern can neither devote himself to academic excellence nor place himself fully in the service of his organization. Whereas he may reap the benefits from both opportunities, he must also endure the traumas generated from his division of loyalties.

Within the organization this problem translates into a lack of dependability. The intern fortunate enough to be assigned to a timely and critical organization problem may find himself as the weaker link in a chain where all the other linkages are fastened through a 40-hour time commitment. Phone calls or memoranda directed to the intern may frequently arrive at a time of day or during the part of the week when the intern is not available. Likewise, meetings and confrontations will often occur at times when his academic commitments force him to be absent. At the very least these disruptions may impinge upon his ability to fully grasp the development of problems on which he is working, but more importantly he may incur the wrath of professional colleagues who must depend upon his ability to produce results upon short notice at critical junctures.

Even though this problem is primarily related to the structure of the internship program, it is the intern himself who suffers the consequence of ill-fitted priorities. The structure of the program will force him to miss formal and informal gatherings of key administrators; but it is the intern and not the program who will suffer from the loss of important sources of information and agency attitudes important to his understanding of the total governmental process. As a consequence of structural inconveniences the intern must bear the brunt of staff criticism and disinterest. Under such conditions even the most enthusiastic interns quickly lose interest as they discover that few persons take their work seriously. Of all the intern hazards, this is perhaps the most unkind.

Political Hazards

While organizational hazards can block effective intern participation, political battles may also intervene in unpredictable ways leading to situations dangerous to both intern and internship programs. Most governmental agencies exist in a political climate which by its nature may be potentially threatening to the inexperienced intern. In addition, agencies that become engulfed in changing political climates may offer additional dangers to the unsuspecting intern. For example, an agency in which top management is elected rather than appointed through civil service or other merit systems may be unstable in its dedication to internship program goals.

The formal and informal factors in such a situation are of equal significance. Many jurisdictions formerly led by part-time elected officials have found that the growing complexities and demands of administering public bodies are beyond the time and energy resources of such elected officials. Thus, in many cases, cities, towns, and counties have circumvented outmoded constitutions and statutes to appoint administrative officers. Such officers are empowered not by charter, but by the compact arranged between the appointed officers and the responsible elected officials. Prime examples are cities and counties where elected officials are responsible for the management of public business, yet have delegated those powers to city or county administrators. In such cases the administrator has some of the trappings of a city manager in a council-manager city, but his powers are only as extensive as he is able to negotiate from the political leadership.

Under such conditions the wise intern will seek to assess the political/professional balance of power before venturing forth with politically dubious projects. Understandably, internships in such agencies provide unique opportunities as well as personal and professional challenges. Intern assignments in such organizations may produce in the end a more satisfying professional experience than the comparatively safe research assignments in traditional council-manager cities.

A case in point is provided by the example of an intern who was instructed to initiate legal research into the politically explosive issue of tax assessments in a medium-sized local government. The intern supervisor in this case was an administrator who was personally committed to changing the assessment process in hopes of increasing revenues and correcting historical inequities in the tax system. From an administrative point of view the administrator's concern was most noble, because the government's budget was under great strain and services were being reduced under the combined stress of accelerating inflation-generated costs and declining-revenue increases from a near-static property tax base.

Unfortunately, the political powers were solidly opposed to such a study. Public opposition to any increases in real estate taxation was mounting, and the elected assessor who was from a different political group had declared his opposition to any reassessment studies. Objective observers believed that the project was hopeless until at least after the next election. In most governmental situations such as this, political sensitivities would have dictated that no action be taken; however, the intern report was completed according to plan and a copy was provided to the intern supervisor. Learning that he had finished a staff study concerning assessment practices, political leaders called the intern into a meeting to discuss his findings. Soon this unfortunate intern found himself and his report quickly engulfed by considerable political heat generated both by the meeting and by the newspaper report of the political deliberations. A showdown was avoided when the administrator took a different job. The moral of this episode may be that in a government where the political leadership is active in management matters, the potential for a dangerous crossing of jurisdictional lines between professionals and politicians may be enough to sabotage a workable internship program. Nevertheless, this is the reality of many governmental situations and interns need to learn that too.

Another intern in a similarly structured organization found himself appointed as trouble shooter for a social welfare agency during one of its periods of crisis. The intern was given primary responsibility for expediting repairs, maintenance and supply requirements for one of the agency's embattled divisions. Unfortunately, this service area was of current concern to the most garrulous member of the governing board. While the intern was pleading with the budget, purchasing, and public works departments, the board member was holding regular staff meetings with various professional groups within the agency, often with media representatives present. These meetings usually resulted in a rehash of a laundry list of real and not-so-real needs, with charges that the administration (the intern) was not responding to the governing board. This was a case of political intervention in an area normally considered to be solely administrative. Yet the intern was in a political-administrative situation that could be resolved only by the dissipation of interest over time, progress in meeting the real needs, or the emergence of new issues in other departments to divert the political attention. There is always a possibility of conflict of political and administrative values in public agencies. However, the government in which the final management word can come from a political leader presents a much greater likelihood for political intervention.

Yet another variation of this occurs in a government where political and administrative spheres are sharply defined by charter or statute. Here an intern may work for the administration or for the political leadership, but very rarely for both simultaneously. In such a government it is possible for an intern to work for a public program yet never have contact with the elected political decision-makers. His experience is thus missing a vital element of the world of public service. On the other hand, an intern serving a political internship will fully experience the strengths and weaknesses of the administrative organization through the eyes of the political leaders. Elected officials must depend on the administration for answers to questions directed to them by the citizenry, yet the administrators often fail to provide meaningful replies. The approach of the intern is significant in that an aggressive and perceptive intern can experience elements of both the political and administrative viewpoint.

Those who argue against placing interns in organizations where political influence is strong are unduly pessimistic. Political experiences are often extremely valuable and productive for the mature intern, but only under circumstances where the safety of the program is reasonably protected against permanent damage. Admittedly, the determination of what is and what is not a politically threatening situation can never be suitably defined in advance. In the business of political internship program management, hindsight is of little value to the advisor whose efforts on the part of many interns have been destroyed by the involvement of political considerations in a single explosive situation. Even in circumstances where university sanctions might exist, it is sometimes best to let the chips fall where they may. For even if intervention might prove initially productive, the long-term political results might prove to be even more formidable than the short-run circumstances to be resolved.

By and large, the most valuable service of the intern professor may be that of acting in the role of "decompression chamber" for those interns who find themselves submerged in the political wars. An experienced professor wise to the ways of the "real" world may prove invaluable in helping the intern to sift through his experience for lessons he may carry forth to his professional future. In this regard the intern professor may be seen as filling a void where the host agency cannot provide the staff professionalism necessary to enrich the internship program. In such cases the professor may find himself to be in high demand for his services inasmuch as the very nonprofessionalism of the agency, which permits challenging assignments for his interns, will demand superior commitment on his part in order to compensate for the difference between challenge and direction.

The Personal Pitfalls

Turning to personal pitfalls, one "fatal" mistake an intern can make is to fail to observe the statements or signals his administrative supervisor may set forth during the course of the internship. In particular, failure to adhere to an administrative confidence may prove disastrous to the personal relationship the intern and the supervisor attempt to build. Insensitivity to organizational realities is most generally the cause of indiscretion, rather than a deliberate effort to be thought important by peer groups or to embarass the administrative supervisor. Nevertheless, the effect can be the same. Innocent indiscretions on the part of the intern may prove to damage irreparably the fabric of personal understanding that has been developed in prior program years.

Another important oversight is the incapability on the part of the intern to recognize professional feedback. The provider of such feedback does not always hold up a flag to indicate his intent, and the intern must always be alert to the comments that may indicate the need for a redirection of efforts or a reappraisal of attitudes. Interns may fail because of poor judgment, indiscretion, and even for conflict of interest, but failure due to intellectual incompetence is rarely observed. By the time an intern has passed the not inconsequential hurdles of selection and placement, it may usually be assumed that he possesses the basic qualitites of intellect and bearing necessary to pursue his success. Yet his pursuit of success must be as considerate as it is cautious; he must not construe a period of arms-length dealings as being agency rejection, but must calmly attempt to prove his merit to those whose trust he must respect. In many respects the intern must initially persevere on the basis of faith rather than confidence. He can never be secure in his acceptance, but must always strive under the assumption that his diligence and loyalty will be rewarded. Not all interns pass this period of initiation, and future improvements of internship programs may rest upon the installation of more reliable selection procedures as well as the perfection of more sophisticated means of "briefing" the intern as to the nature of his alien world.

These potential obstacles are illustrated by a case study included in a report by the American Political Science Association on their State and Local Internship Program. One of the interns was highly committed to a particular social action program to the extent that his awareness of the agency position was partially blinded. His high resolve and motivation in behalf of his personalized cause endangered the effectiveness of the agency in meeting many of its goals and nearly eroded the confidence of the elected governing body in the program. This was a case of an intern's personal philosophy becoming an emotional hang-up to the extent that both the internship and the agency were threatened.

As the intern learns about the organization and the political environment of public management, he also learns about himself — if he is able to analyze his own roles and reactions as well as those of others. The personal hazards that can weaken or destroy an internship program develop from individual "styles" and personalities. The intern learns that the supervisor's style is a mix of personality, learned skills, and organizational realities.

The style of the supervising administrator may be an asset or pitfall for the intern. Some managers are open and communicative about their organization. Others are administrative loners, their real motives and plans are seldom expressed. Still others are limited in their openness by administrative and political alliances. Many have become experienced in internship relationships and maximize the opportunities to use and teach the intern. But until a management style incorporates this art, a valuable resource is often wasted on irrelevant tasks.

A second category of mistakes frequently made by interns concerns overconfidence. If the intern assumes a "Mr. Big From the Front Office" role, he can expect closed doors and little support from his supervisor and co-workers. Overconfidence is frequently confused with aggressiveness and arrogance. In one case, an intern who was officed adjacent to a city manager was handed several substantial assignments of the type that are of obvious importance to all office personnel. The intern unwisely reacted to his assignment through feelings of egocentric pride. When two regular staff members asked his collaboration on a brush-fire assignment, he responded by pointing out how much more important were the projects on which he was already working. To his great misfortune, both individuals represented divisions generating key information. By his approach the intern not only squelched an important opportunity to make contacts for himself, but also created credibility problems for three other interns in the agency.

The intern must be aware that the same elements which make for such a rich opportunity also represent hazards. Because the intern is encouraged to take risks to a greater extent than others in the agency, he potentially represents a threat to them. In a highly competitive agency where communication is low and bureaucratic paranoia is high, the intern might even be perceived as a spy for top management or as a competitor for one's job. This problem is especially crucial if the intern is not sensitive to these potential reactions.

A final pitfall stems from the intern's performance and the agency's expectation of what he will produce. This again depends in large part on the professor and how carefully he has structured the relationship. If questions arise, he will be the only university person knowing what the governmental body really promised to provide the program. The professor's close relationship with the intern is indispensable to maximize the learning experience. However, even this asset could become a major source of disappointment if the intern should rely on the professor for intervention in administrative decision-making in the organization. While the professor may lay the groundwork for an intern, and provide guidance and interpretation during the internship, intervention in behalf of the intern could well end the chances of productive experiences for that intern as well as for others to follow him. An inexperienced professor could become emotionally involved in such a situation and do irreparable damage to the internship program.

Conclusion

The hazards affecting an internship negatively are as many and various as the agencies in which interns work, experiment, and learn. They must be anticipated as inevitable but unknown quantities. When organizational, political, or personal pitfalls emerge, as they almost always do when an internship is providing the experience intended, major growth opportunities also emerge. In this manner each internship develops into an individualized learning and growth experience.

Organizational and political pitfalls are often much easier to recognize and negotiate. This is largely because it is easier to evaluate and judge an agency or a city council than to examine one's personal behavior and interaction in the agency. When it comes to analyzing personal pitfalls that develop between the intern and supervisor or the intern and the agency, the challenge of interpreting feedback about personal behavior is commonly avoided by interns. It is easier to blame the agency, the supervisor, or the director of the program. This is not to say that these participants are always blameless. It is, however, vital that the intern be sensitive to his impact on the agency as well as to both obvious and subtle feedback. These informal mechanisms will provide him with tools with which to avoid pitfalls or minimize their impact.

An internship is an experimental learning experience involving three interrelated elements. If pitfalls are to be avoided:

1. The governmental supervisor *must* be knowledgeable about the problems facing the agency and the intricacies of the formal and informal activities of his organization. He also must be willing to develop a relationship with the intern that permits a free and open interchange of observations and ideas and must not look upon the intern as an additional position not charged to his staffing table.

2. The intern must become immersed in the organization as quickly and productively as possible and with attitudes likely to encourage a collaborative relationship with his supervisor. He must also respond openly to his professor and objectively try to evaluate his performance as an intern.

3. The professor directing the internship must assure that interns are placed in live agencies, with perceptive supervisors, and are not used as if they were in a work-study program. He must also be available to interns and supervisors for guidance, instruction, and intervention.

The absence or malfunction of any one of these participants reduces the effectiveness of the internship for the intern and the agency.

Finally, it might be noted that "pitfalls" may be a question of attitude and definition. Clearly, one intern's pitfall is another's opportunity. If these political, organizational, and personal pitfalls did not exist, the intern surely would not learn as much. In fact, if there were no pitfalls in governmental organizations, innovative people would probably not be interested in working in government and there would be little need for internship programs or internship professors.

**Part 2
Urban and State Internships
and Fellowships**

4

Early City Management Internships

L. P. COOKINGHAM

The attitude of the average citizen seems to be that anyone with normal intelligence is qualified to fill a local public job. This attitude appears to be prevalent even in communities where the voters have long supported good municipal government. This "home-town boy" feeling is probably an outgrowth of the spoils system when those who helped the winner were entitled to the jobs regardless of qualifications.

When the functions of local government were minor compared with those of the later years of the twentieth century this was not too unrealistic. However, as local government assumed greater responsibilities and expanded its functions, the need for trained personnel increased. But how to get this type of city employee within the city limits became a problem which increased with the complexity of government. A greater problem was the controversy that arose when "outsiders" were brought in to take a job at city hall. The opposing political group was sure to make capital out of every "imported expert" hired by the city.

In one medium-sized city, when the position of finance director became vacant, recommendations for filling the position came from many local sources, suggesting persons with talents ranging from an insurance salesman to a bank cashier. The president of the largest bank in the city strongly recommended one of his tellers for the position. His qualifications were a "pleasing personality, honesty, a neat dresser and well liked by his associates and the bank's customers." It was later discovered that the bank was really trying to "promote" the teller to a responsible city position as he had not been filling his job to the bank's satisfaction. But the president was sincere in his belief that the position of director of finance in that city did not require specific training and experience. He failed to understand the scope of the job which required training in many phases of finance, including municipal accounting, assessing, purchasing, budgeting, tax billing, bond management and many other elements of municipal finance unknown to an untrained and inexperienced person in this particular field.

The position was filled by the importation of an experienced finance director from another city who could take over the job without months or even years of training at public expense and perhaps much mismanagement.

Because of unfavorable public reaction and the political hazards involved in bringing in "outsiders", many city officials took the easy route by placing incompetents in positions that required higher degrees of skill and much more experience than anyone in the local community might have.

In the years following World War I, universities began to train students in political science and public administration and step by step key positions in local government became more of a profession than a job. However it was not until after the Great Depression of the late 1920s and early 1930s that the professional came to be recognized as necessary if local government was to function effectively. More and more functions were assumed by local government. New processes and equipment requiring skilled hands and trained minds to operate and manage became commonplace in the more progressive cities of America. How to get these trained people into the city service without creating unfavorable public reaction was a problem for every administrator, especially those who were sensitive to public criticism.

Late in the 1930s a few schools offered to send their graduate students to cities where an opportunity for gaining experience in a good environment existed. In some cases the students received stipends from their universities to finance a year of practical experience and came to acceptable cities without cost to the city. In other cases the students worked without any compensation, considering the cost of the year's experience as much a part of the expense of their training as their on-campus costs.

The opportunity to accept graduate students for a year's training at little or no cost to the local government provided the means to bring in outsiders without local opposition. Alert public officials were quick to realize this advantage, and it was not long before cities began to compete for students for this period of training, hoping that those with exceptional ability would remain in the service after becoming "residents" of the city in which they received their training.

My first experience with graduate students in public administration came in the late 1930s when a midwestern university offered to send two students to the city I served for a year of practical experience at the local level. The city was to pay a nominal monthly salary and the students were to be given a stipend from a grant which was available to the university for this purpose.

The students reported for duty at the conclusion of their college work. The city's responsibility was to give the students an opportunity to get the "feel" of municipal employment and to learn as much as possible about the functions of local government. In this way they could obtain experience that would qualify them to continue in their chosen field of activity.

As the city had not previously offered experience to men who had more academic training in government than anyone else in city hall, an informal "cut and try" program was initiated. The students were first required to read the City Charter and the Administrative Code. Several hours were devoted to discussing the past political and economic history of the city and the characteristics of its people. They were then assigned to the several staff and operating departments for a minimum of one week in order that they could become briefly familiar with the duties and functions of each. This was done with the idea of later reassigning them to the city manager's office as aides to him.

The contributions these young men made to the administrative program soon became evident and they were readily accepted by the council, department heads and employees, principally because their services were so valuable, their enthusiasm so great, and their recent education in current subjects relating to municipal government so helpful. In addition, the public knew the city was making only a small financial contribution to the students who were contributing so much so that there was little adverse public reaction to the experiment.

Because these young men were working at rather modest salaries in order to gain experience necessary for them to advance in the profession, the title "intern" was applied to them. Their place in the city government was not unlike the newly graduated medical student who required actual experience before becoming a full-fledged M.D. able to function independently. Unfortunately the first two interns chose the federal government for their careers and the local government lost the service of two capable administrators.

After the change from political to professional administration in Kansas City with the defeat of the Pendergast machine in 1940, a number of young men with degrees in business or public administration applied for positions in the city government hoping to get the experience they required following completion of their academic training. Some offered to work without any compensation and others for subsistence pay in order to get the experience needed to assume greater responsibilities in Kansas City or in other cities seeking professionally trained and experienced people to fill positions in local government.

As soon as the professionalization of the city government was established and the unusual volume of work caused by the change subsided, consideration was given to establishing a more formal training program in which persons with graduate degrees in political science or public administration would be given the opportunity to gain practical experience in local government administration.

In June 1945 a new department designated as the Department of Research and Information was established, principally as a device for shifting some of the work load from the city manager's office and to do research work in social and economic fields which heretofore had not been possible. This department was headed by a highly competent person with long and valuable experience in these disciplines. In April 1950 the preparation and execution of the annual budget was assigned to this department and the word "budget" was substituted for the word "information" in the title of the department, and a budget and systems specialist was selected to head the department. The staff consisted of people with training and experience in local government and with some management skills. The department continued the social and economic research and in addition to the budget responsibilities began to make studies in method and systems in an effort to improve administrative efficiency. Following the placing of the added responsibilities in the department, all of the interns were assigned to that department and received their assignments from the director who was a skilled administrator and had a rating and compensation equal to that of assistant city manager. In fact the city manager leaned heavily on the Research and Budget Department for the study and thinking he had so little time to do. The association of the interns with the director of research and budget was as important to their training as direct contact with the city manager would have been.

The training program for those young graduates already in the service and those to follow was developed around the work of this newly formed department. It was evident that a graduate student fresh out of college could be of little immediate assistance to the city manager in a city as large as Kansas City, therefore it was decided that a greater opportunity to gain practical knowledge at the top management level could be provided for the interns in the Department of Research and Budget. Here they were given tasks to be performed under the direction of an older staff member, usually an administrative analyst with several years experience in the city government.

Applicants for intern training were carefully screened either by personal interviews by the staff or by review of their academic records, extra curricular activities and appraisals by their professors. An attempt was made to determine their dedication to the public service which must be intense if one is to succeed in the field of local government administration. Married students were asked to bring their wives with them on interviews as it seemed important for them to know what the public service job entailed, including frequent moves, adverse as well as favorable publicity, the political hazards of the job, and something of the role of the wife of the public official.

In the screening process candidates were sought who understood the principles of democracy in local government, who were dedicated to public service, who had a sense of humor, who subscribed to the ethics of the profession, and who were educable. Their grooming was also observed as well as their personalities and their physical stature. During their period of training their temperaments, leadership ability, compatability, analytical ability, productivity, objectivity, aggressiveness, and other characteristics essential characteristics for leadership were carefully observed.

Not all of these characteristics could be discovered in every intern during his one year of training. However, close observation by supervisory personnel led to an awareness of the more important traits.

Ratings in these and other characteristics were maintained on each intern and those showing the greatest promise of advancement in the service and with the qualities necessary for assuming leadership roles in city government were offered opportunities to remain with the city in order to gain broader experience and thus be prepared for greater responsibilities.

The interns were assigned to one or more departments for a specified period and then shifted to other departments so they might understand the functions of each department and learn how each related to the overall municipal program.

As the annual budget process began about six months after the interns arrived, their immediate supervisors had ample opportunity to observe their progress and then assign them to work in connection with budget preparation. Interns were permitted to attend the formal and informal budget hearings with the department heads and the City Council to observe how the department heads supported their requests, how the manager justified the adjustments that he had made in the original budget requests, how the elected officials reacted to budget cuts, increases, program changes, tax and revenue increases or decreases, and other policy and strategy devices used by the manager in guiding his budget through the council.

The training program also proposed an occasional meeting with the city manager in order to "pick his brain," listen to his philosophy of public service, and discuss recent actions of the City Council. Often such council actions might not be understood by these young men who therefore may not have agreed with the council policy. The interchange gave them the opportunity to understand the political and organizational dynamics underlying the decision.

Another element of the training program was attendance at the precouncil and formal sessions of the City Council. Usually one or two of the interns attended the precouncil meetings, where they observed how the council reacted to recommendations of the administration, how the political mind functions, why some worthy suggestions were rejected, and many other problems of the relationship of the elected officials and the appointed executive.

The interns were given assignments of varying types, principally in the area of research. These studies might be requested by the city manager, by the head of a staff or operating department or by the director of research and budget. In some cases the idea for the project would originate in the mind of the intern who would seek approval for the work.

Some of the assignments given to the interns were:

1. A comprehensive study of the modern concept of city planning and the preparation of a report for the city manager. (Incidentally this study made possible an increase of 500 percent in the budget for planning.)
2. Custodial costs at city hall and other public buildings.
3. Advantages, disadvantages, costs, and possible results of fluoridation of the water supply.
4. An analysis of the disposal of garbage through a hog feeding program which had been successfully operated for a number of years.
5. A study of the economics and public reaction to the integration of the general hospitals.
6. A study of the city hospitals' operation of the ambulance service.
7. A study of the revenue to be derived and the organization necessary to administer a payroll tax.

The interns also assisted in the analysis of departmental budget requests, reviewed monthly revenue and expenditure reports, reviewed all requests for new or replacement personnel, studied methods and procedures to provide for efficiency and economy, worked with administrative analysts in setting up new activities authorized by the council, and performed many other management tasks normally done by the city manager or his assistant in smaller jurisdictions. Actually the entire staff of the Research and Budget Department was considered a vital part of the city manager's office, doing the administrative planning and much of the thinking and writing for that office.

Occasionally an intern would work for several days or even weeks on a research project, make his report to the director of the R & B Department who in turn would prepare for the manager a formal report and recommendation to be submitted to the City Council. The council might reject the recommendation, often with only minutes of consideration or the manager might decide to delay the presentation until a later and more opportune time. The intern who had worked so long and diligently on the project would evidence concern over such rejection or delay. In at least one instance the intern developed ulcers due to his concern over failure to get action on a project he knew was worthy and in the best interest of the service. In my long and interesting career, I never developed an ulcer or other evidence of frustration, as early in my career I learned to "laugh-off" my defeats and let the less experienced and temperamental associates suffer the pains of defeat while learning to accept them.

Usually after such an occasion the manager would meet with the R & B staff to discuss the council rejection or his decision to delay submission of the report. The object of such meetings was to teach the lesson that the manager cannot expect to get every recommendation accepted, must forget the rejections, then try something else but never to be personally offended by such council action. They were taught that some very worthy projects die that way, also that those same projects may be revived by the council or resubmitted by the manager at a more opportune time.

They were also told the reason for the manager's decision to delay submission of a recommendation, if that procedure was followed. This was a lesson in timing which is so very important for an administrator, dealing with an elected legislative body, to understand. Timing and patience were two of the lessons learned in situations such as described here.

During the early stages of their training period the interns were carefully observed by the department heads, the administrative analysts for whom they worked, and by the manager and his assistants. Those interns who showed exceptional ability were encouraged to remain with the city after their internship ended, while those with less apparent competence, or those who decided against local government careers, left after completing their year of experience.

The training program briefly described herein was outlined to the City Council at one of its informal sessions in June 1942 and after the presentation, the council encourated the continuance of the program. The council thereafter approved budgets providing for the admission of as many graduate students and others who showed signs of developing into capable administrators as could be utilized. In some years as many as eight graduate students were admitted to the program. As the effectiveness of the internships became known the city received applications from three to four times as many students as could be adequately trained.

The interns were generally accepted by the department heads, most of whom had many years of experience in this or other local governments. In the indoctrination period the interns were instructed in ways in which they were to work with department heads and their staffs. We realized that they would have ideas for improving service and, because of their recent academic training, might feel many changes should be made in methods and procedures. They were instructed to report their suggestions to their own department head rather than be critical of an operation or appear to be giving instructions to a staff or operating department head. All such suggestions were to be made to the department head by the R & B administrative analyst assigned to the particular department, by the head of the Research and Budget Department, or, if the suggestion was of great enough importance, by the city manager himself.

When it was felt an intern had developed proper rapport with a department head, he was given more freedom to discuss changes and improvements directly with him, but this was not permitted until the department head had indicated to the manager or R & B Department head that he was interested in having the intern make suggestions to him. On many occasions, when it came time to transfer an intern from one department to another, the department head would ask that the intern remain for a longer period. If acceptable to R & B and to the intern a longer stay was permitted. In some cases interns spent their entire internship in one of the major departments. This was an acceptable practice as we were always anxious to find an intern who might develop an interest in continuing his experience at the department level rather than spreading his short stay over many departments hoping to obtain a city manager position at the conclusion of his internship.

The objective of the training program was to train for positions in local government, and we were as anxious to turn out future finance directors, public works directors, hospital administrators, and capable people for other positions below the top level as we were to train only for city manager positions.

The young interns brought to the city government the latest teaching in the field of local government which tended to keep the city government up to date. They brought new vision and unlimited energy and enthusiasm to an aging staff that "rubbed off" on them and their subordinates. This also tended to keep the staff "on its toes." I am certain that one of the reasons for the extra long tenure of the administration from 1940 to 1959 was due in large part to the new ideas, the vigor, and the enthusiasm brought to the city government by the interns.

One important asset discovered in the work of the interns was that they served as listening posts and provided a means of communication with second and third level management and rank and file employees which helped uncover weaknesses in top level management. They also brought to R & B suggestions for improvement or changes that might not have otherwise been discovered. We did not use these men as "spies" nor did we violate any confidence. We carefully screened the information they received and took such remedial action as we thought necessary. We cautioned them to always keep their eyes and ears open but to talk as little as necessary to obtain helpful information. Naturally much of the information they obtained was known to us, but occasionally some important information, helpful to the leadership, was obtained.

Because these bright, energetic young men were so conspicuous by their presence, sometimes long after the work day ended, the council members called them the "Whiz Kids."

In later years as the council personnel changed, I was never certain of its acceptance of these young people until at one of the informal budget meetings when the manager and council were discussing the final phases of the budget in a closed-door session. In order to balance the estimated expenditures with available revenue and after every item had been dropped that seemed feasible to eliminate, it was still necessary to remove another sixty-thousand dollars from a fifty-million dollar budget. I suggested that the R & B budget be reduced by that amount which would have meant the elimination of a number of interns and administrative analysts.

Much to my surprise and gratitude, one of the most "machine" minded members of the council, who had never shown too much enthusiasm over professionals in government, spoke out against the cut. He said "there surely is some other way to reduce expenditures." "These men" he said, "are the smartest people in city hall and I get more help from them than I get from any other group and I would hate to see even one of them displaced." The rest of the council agreed and from that time on I had no hesitancy in continuing the intern program in Kansas City.

Occasionally when an intern showed exceptional ability or completed an important research project he would be permitted to present his findings in person at an informal or special meeting of the City Council. This afforded him the opportunity to gain experience in making an appearance before the legislative body. This also gave the council the opportunity to observe the competence of these young men, and to give them a chance to view the vast difference between the average city employee and the highly trained individual who was dedicating his life to a career in local governnment.

As the trainees and the higher level employees were leaving the service to accept city manager positions in other cities, naturally there were stories in the news media regarding their employment with the city and the new responsibilities they were to assume in another city. To some it seemed the city was constantly losing its most competent employees, but there were always others in training to fill the gaps left by the departing employee. In one week four interns or former interns "graduated" to city manager positions.

On one occasion when the assistant to the city manager was reported as leaving to accept the city manager position in a fairly large city, an industrial executive with whom I was visiting asked why, if these men were such capable administrators, local industry did not recognize their capabilities and employ them instead of letting them go to another city.

I indicated two reasons. First, I said I did not believe that private business had yet learned that people trained in local government were equal to those filling management positions in private enterprise. Second, I said those men who were leaving to more responsible positions were truly dedicated people. They had trained for the public service, and I doubted if they would change their careers at this point for double the salary offered by local government.

Because of the large number of city managers who were developed in the Kansas City program and the nationwide recognition it received, many mayors or city councils began their search for a city manager by contacting Kansas City to determine the availability of a prospective candidate. On one occasion a mayor from a distant state called to inquire about the possibility of getting a manager for his city. He was from a city of under 10,000 population. He was told that we had no one at that time who we considered a finished product and well enough qualified to go out on his own. The mayor then asked who we considered the furthest advanced in his training as both he and the council desired a man from the Kansas City program. We mentioned the name of the fellow we thought showed the greatest potential within the group and the mayor then invited that person to come to his city for an interview. The members of the council were so well satisfied with him they appointed him forthwith without even letting him return to discuss the position with his associates. This "unfinished product" remained with that city for a number of years and now is in his third city, much larger than the first he served, and with much greater responsibilities.

This incident points up clearly the importance of a good academic background and a few months of practice, even though limited in scope, gives the student the "feel" of city government and enough confidence to tackle the city manager job in a smaller city where he can continue to gain experience for the greater responsibility he will be called on to assume as he advances to larger cities.

The interns who remained in the R & B Department one or two years usually became city managers of smaller cities – with populations from 5,000 to 10,000 – where they stayed two, three, or four years before going on to larger cities. Those who remained with the Kansas City program as long as six to eight years obtained their first city manager positions in larger cities. In fact, most of the interns planned their careers that way. Some wanted the small city experience, while others desired a greater amount of experience, hoping to get their first assignment in a larger city, thus avoiding using the smaller city as a "stepping stone" to the larger city.

It is normal for the graduate student upon entering the service as an intern to immediately serve as assistant to the city manager where he can work closely with the top man in the organization. This is possible in the smaller city but in the larger cities, the manager's assistants must be highly trained, capable of decision-making and of executing administrative policies with little or no direct supervision from the manager. The assistants to the manager were usually drawn from the more capable R & B Department administrative analysts who had spent five or more years with the city. In some instances the director of R & B was moved to the city manager's office and one of the analysts was promoted to the position of director of R & B.

Some of the larger cities that obtained managers directly from the training program in Kansas City are Phoenix and Tucson, Arizona; Tacoma, Washington; and Fort Worth, Texas. One of these men stayed in his first city until he reached retirement age, another left after five years to enter private business and two others went on to what are considered the two top local management jobs in the country.

In Saginaw, Kansas City, and Fort Worth where the intern program was conducted, a total of approximately eighty interns were given the opportunity to gain experience in city government. Of this group forty-seven became city managers and the majority of the others continued in the public service or in a related field.

The greatest number of the interns came from the University of Kansas. Second in order of number came from the Fels Institute at the University of Pennsylvania; third from the University of Denver; then in declining order from Colorado, Michigan, Minnesota, Syracuse, Missouri, Connecticut, Northwestern, Harvard, Oklahoma and the balance from a varied list of colleges and universities, and some were selected from employees within the service who showed extraordinary capabilities.

The program with which the writer was associated extended over a period of thirty-five years. During this period the functions and complexity of local government increased many fold. It was interesting to observe how well the academic training kept pace with the changes in functions and responsibilities of local government. Each new group of interns brought new ideas, new concepts and new vigor to the city government. Each year the professionals in responsible positions looked forward to the opportunity to help these young people get started in their chosen field and to the new ideas they would bring with them.

I can say, without any reservation, that the greatest satisfaction I had from my many years of service as a city manager was the opportunity given me by a number of city councils to conduct this program of offering experience to young people who had been trained for careers in city government.

These people brought much more to the city than was evidenced by the salaries they received. The experience they obtained and the opportunities that came to them after gaining actual experience in the art of municipal administration were of immeasurable benefit, both to them and to the cities where they later served, as well as to the city providing the training opportunity.

The training program could not be considered perfect in all respects. There were pitfalls that concerned both the sponsor and the intern. These pitfalls were so interrelated that it would be difficult to allocate them to either the sponsor or the intern. Some of the pitfalls were:

Lack of opportunity for the intern to maintain close relationship with the city manager.

Too frequent reassignment from one department or activity to another.

Awakening of the intern to the fact that he lacked the power and authority he had anticipated.

Modest compensation necessary to maintain harmony with permanent employees.

Too frequent assignments unrelated to his thesis subject.

Frustrations due to lack of understanding of importance of political implications and timing.

Open and indiscrete criticism in outer circles of long established practices or programs which yet were to be changed to meet changing conditions.

Problems of adjusting to practical application of theory.

Occasional friction with department heads or their subordinates.

This listing of pitfalls certainly is not all inclusive. I am sure there were many more, the reader can determine whether they are pitfalls of the sponsoring agency or the intern.

When the students concluded their internship, we gave them what we thought was sound advice in a few simple words. We told them to believe the city they served was the best city in the world and to try to make it better; be loyal to their councils; honest, patient, and sincere with their citizens; work hard and do the best job they could possibly do, never wavering from what they believed to be right and in the best interest of the city they served.

We also told them they might lose their job by doing what their conscience told them was right, but they would soon get another job and that one would be better than the one they lost. This would not be the case, they were told, if they were guilty of misconduct or actions they knew were wrong.

When the "graduates" got their first city manager job, we wrote them a letter we tried to have on their desk their first day on the job. The letter contained the following guideposts which my experience had taught me were helpful in fulfilling the obligations to the council, to the public, and to administration.

These are the guideposts we proposed:

Relations with the City Council

1. Never forget that the council, to the best of its ability, expresses the will of the people. There will be times when you will not understand why the council takes certain actions, but you will find that the council is generally right and that the members express public opinion as they see it and as they learn it from their constituents.

2. Formal acts of the council become public policy, and you as city manager must always do your best to translate these policies into action. You should do this in a manner to best realize the intent of the council. In some cases you may not agree with the policy, but it is your duty as city manager to carry out the policy to the best of your ability unless it is illegal or fraudulent.

3. Lead those whom you contact – members of the council, subordinate employees, and citizens – into the proper channel by tactful suggestion rather than by too persuasive argument. Make them feel that they have had a major part in making the decisions and in establishing the policies which you deem to be in the best interest of the individual and the government.

4. Give credit where credit belongs and always give the council members all the credit you can. They have to be re-elected.

5. Work hard to gain and keep the full confidence of the council and the respect of your department heads and your job will be easier. The confidence of the council is of utmost importance in doing a successful job.

6. Keep your eyes and ears open and your mouth shut during council meetings. This is one of the most important principles in the field of council-manager relations. I have known more managers who have talked themselves out of jobs than into jobs. The members of the council are elected by the people and know something about the business of municipal government. When they want information from the manager, they will ask for it, and it is well to have the information when requested.

Relations with the Public

1. Remember that the average fellow with whom you talk, whether he is a member of the council, one of the city's staff, or a citizen, does not know as much about the job of municipal administration as you know now or will know in the years ahead; so don't get too far beyond him, for he will not be able to follow you.

2. Be as humble as the humblest with whom you deal, and subdue by your patience those who are inclined to be too arrogant. You must give as much time as is necessary to the person who is slow in understanding, and you must be patient with those who may be impatient with you.

3. Treat everyone in the city, friend or foe, as if your success depended on the manner in which you handled his problem. I have often told my employees to consider everyone with whom they talk to be a member of the city council, and, by doing this, they will give their best to all.

4. Never forget that you are a servant of the people, and instill that philosophy in each of your employees. If you find one who cannot understand this philosophy, remove him, for he will be no good to you or

to the city. If you ever get the idea that you are ruler, you, also will be no good to the city or to the form of government.

5. Don't let the "cranks" worry you too much, for if you do they will outlive you.

6. Be sure to develop good press relations; give all the time necessary to help the press, radio, and other media to keep the public informed, because any of these media can ruin your program with very little effort.

7. Always take the chip off the complainant's shoulder before you let him go. This will be a hard task in some cases, but use every resource at your command to make friends out of potential enemies.

8. Always think of the city in which you work as your city. Participate in civic movements for its betterment and, above all, live in your city.

Guides in Administration

1. You have to "give and take" all along the way, but when you must give ground to the "left," be sure that, when you return toward the center, you go the "right" as far as possible. In "giving," never do anything which may be illegal or contrary to the basic principles of the plan of government with which you are working.

2. Don't let any problems frighten you, for there is a logical solution to each one you have to face. If they seem too tough for today, let them go until tomorrow whenever possible, for then they will seem simpler. The problems concerning you today may be completely forgotten in a week or two.

3. Get acquainted with your employees as rapidly as possible, and take time to let them show you what they have in their departments and how they do their work. (If you do not approve, go slowly in making drastic changes — the results will be much better and the improvements more lasting.)

4. Don't pursue your program at a faster pace than the council, the employees, and public can follow. You will always see plenty of things to do and have plenty of changes to make, but be sure that everyone understands why you are doing this and how it will benefit the city or its government before you proceed.

5. Always remember that you will never get in trouble or be embarrassed by doing what is right. You may lose your job for standing up for what you think is right, but you'll always get another and better job. Besides, you will be able to sleep soundly every night.

6. Keep your personal contacts with other city managers. The greatest compliment you can pay them is to ask how they handle a certain problem.

7. Keep a framed copy of "The City Manager's Code of Ethics" in your office. Read it once in a while. Always abide by it.

Public attitude toward the "outsider" has changed in the past quarter century and cities now are competing for skilled personnel and are willing to pay the price required to get them. The intern program has been widely accepted by cities throughout the country and many more people with graduate degrees in local government or public administration could be placed in intern programs than there are graduates to fill them. The intern program provides the "polish" required to produce a finished product and the cities that utilize interns are making outstanding contributions to good local government, and the students through these programs are afforded the best means of starting on a long and interesting career of public service.

5 Emerging City Internship Patterns

FREDERICK E. FISHER

A few years ago a small number of selected cities were committed to training urban generalists (city managers, mostly) by providing six-to-twelve month internship experiences, usually at the end of a graduate academic program in public or governmental administration. As Perry Cookingham has pointed out in chapter 4, there was a pipeline from a few committed graduate schools to an equally small number of enlightened committees through which dedicated students traveled to gain exposure to the "real world of public administration." It was a unique and valuable tutoring system, seasoning the bright young generalists in the practical world of urban management, preparing them for early entry into the profession. Men like Perry Cookingham, Woodbury Brackett, and Robert Morris became identified as mentors to be trusted and called upon frequently to provide the personal capstone touch to a budding career. They took particular pride in their mission and readily sacrificed privacy and gave long hours of patient counseling to assure their young proteges a good start.

The early years of city manager internships were a bold and noble experiment in the preparation of professional management talent for our nation's cities. In a sense, it developed an elite corp of professionals woven together by bonds of loyalty to schools and mentors, reinforced by Christmas newsletters, annual get togethers at ICMA conferences, and a good word at the right time from the academics when their "boys" were under consideration for a new job. It was a system that worked — and worked well — in the unharried world of decades past. It provided a high level of confidence among elected officials seeking new talent in the market place, reasonably met the needs of a slowly expanding profession, and, no doubt, developed consternation among competing job seekers from lesser known schools when they were up against this cartel of academics and practitioners.

While remnants of the old cloth of city management internism are still with us, the weave has been weakened by the retirement of the directors of a few key schools and the growth of new schools offering urban masters degrees. There are other factors, of course, and we will want to consider them as we look at some of the emerging city internship patterns.

The mobile nature of the modern professional, a growing need for large numbers of urban generalists in a variety of organizational settings, and increasing opportunities for exposure to the municipal working world at an

65

earlier age have all taken the edge off the earlier approach to city management internships. This is not to say that the intern's world that Perry Cookingham has shared with us in the previous chapter is dead. Far from it. Many dedicated urban administrators of recent vintage are still performing the role of mentor with rare distinction. But their slice of the pie continues to shrink in the face of expanding competition. Some of the emerging trends in municipal intern-ships — the Urban Corps, the Southern Regional Education Board's Resource Development Project, a metropolitan, a state-wide, and an individual city program, as well as the National Urban Fellows program will be reviewed.

The Urban Corps

The Urban Corps National Development Office has announced that Urban Corps in 1970 encompassed over seventy cities and a minimum of fifteen thousand students. This is pretty impressive for a program that is no more than five years old. Urban Corp is a unique program, dependent in large measure on funds from a program that was not designed with Urban Corps in mind. The College Work Study Program, from which Urban Corps has drawn life, was established under Title IV-C of the 1965 Higher Education Act to provide needy students with the opportunity for summer and part-time employment. In the beginning, the bulk of CWSP funds were kept on campus, providing students jobs within the academic setting. Dr. Timothy Costello, now deputy city administrator of New York City, is credited with the development of the Urban Corps concept. In an appearance before a group of students and faculty at the City College of New York in 1965, Dr. Costello stated that "our young people and our cities can no longer afford to be strangers." He proposed an Urban Corps to provide the framework for this interaction, offering college students the opportunity to participate directly in the government of the city as full time summer interns or part-time workers during the academic year.

New York City Mayor John Lindsay saw great hope in the Urban Corps concept, and when he brought Dr. Costello into his administration in early 1966 the concept was implemented. In just three years, the New York Urban Corps had built an annual student work force in excess of three thousand representing 120 colleges and universities. Urban Corps was an immediate success in New York City. The Ford Foundation responded by providing funds to establish the Urban Corps National Development Office. Its mission is to advise and assist cities throughout the nation to emulate New York's pioneering effort. The National Development Office, operating under a grant from the Ford Founda-tion, has been successful in spreading the word as dozens of Urban Corps have been established throughout the country.

The development of the Urban Corps concept, while pushed by the National Development Office, would not have achieved such immediate success with-out: (1) access to College Work Study Program funds available to colleges and universities through the U.S. Department of Health, Education and Welfare; and (2) the cooperation of the educational institutions receiving the funds. Cities have always been interested in employing students but rarely have they had the funds available to hire large numbers. The CWSP provides 80 percent financing under its guidelines, thus allowing municipalities to hire five students for the price of one.

While 80 percent of the College Work Study Program funds are still spent on campus, the 20 percent available to off-campus public agencies is, nevertheless, substantial. Fiscal year 1970-71's appropriation was 154 million dollars. The previous year's appropriation was considerably less and yet nearly 25 million dollars went unused.

Perhaps a word about how the CWSP works would be appropriate at this time. Students (graduate or undergraduate) to be eligible for funds under the College Work Study Program must be: (1) enrolled fulltime; (2) in good academic standing; (3) United States citizens, or have filed the intent; and (4) demonstrate, to their school's satisfaction, that they need the income to continue their education.

On the final criteria, it should be pointed out that CWSP is not a poverty program. Eligibility determination is a discretionary matter with school administrators and often they adopt a liberal interpretation.

The administrative machinery is not complicated in spite of the fact that it is a federal program. A simple contract between the hiring agency and the school is all that is necessary. And there is great flexibility in organization and implementation. Urban Corps can be structured to meet the needs and desires of a given geographic area. In fact, the development of a formal Urban Corps is not necessary for cities to participate in CWSP funding. (The term Urban Corps can be a bit misleading since there are no hard and fast rules dictating their development and operation.) A small town may be hiring only one student using CWSP monies while large cities employ several hundred or even thousands. When the numbers get above a few, it makes sense to provide structure and direction, thus Urban Corps has been established in close to 100 cities. Let us take a closer look at the Urban Corps concept as it has developed in Atlanta, Dayton, Grand Rapids, and Boulder.

Atlanta, Georgia

The Atlanta Urban Corps was started in the summer of 1969. Over 1000 college students (graduate and undergraduate) applied for the 225 internships available. Sam Williams, originator of the Atlanta program, and a staff of fifteen provided guidance to the program in its initial months of operation. Attention was given to the academic growth of each intern and his awareness to urban problems. The staff worked with interns and supervisors to resolve problems and to make sure maximum service was being obtained.

Leon W. Lindsay's report in the *Christian Science Monitor* provides insight into the involvement of college youth that summer in Atlanta.

These interns – from 45 colleges and universities, 18 of them in Georgia – worked in 16 divisions of the city government, several Fulton County Departments, and 38 private agencies.

They served in 53 job categories, including management assistant, labor relations worker, urban planning assistant, surveyor, draftsman, dietary assistant, social worker assistant, camp counselor, mental health researcher, teaching assistant and vocational teaching assistant.

One intern, working with a church related agency in a ghetto neighborhood, organized a buying club for poor families. Another worked under the direction of the local head of the National Welfare Rights Organization, helping to organize chapters and get people out to meetings. Six interns ran a day camp for retarded children for a month, then moved on to other projects for the rest of their 10 weeks.

A group of interns performed a land use study for the Fulton County Planning Department. Another group worked on plans for setting up neighborhood mental health centers for the Fulton County Health Department.

In the Community Services Division of the Mayor's office, interns studied waste disposal problems, a bugaboo for most large cities. One of their proposals, which is likely to be activated, is to establish a division charged with the specific job of removing junk cars.[1]

The Atlanta Urban Corps is a significant departure from the traditional city intern program that involves a few graduate students in the top administrator's office. Beyond involving large numbers of students, it broadens the concept of public service by encompassing private agencies often not viewed as part of the public response to community problems. This is an important dimension of the Urban Corps program, or any municipally generated effort involving students.

The Atlanta program also demonstrates the cooperative funding concept that is gaining favor in other areas of the public domain. While the city of Atlanta put up $52,000 to launch the 1969 summer effort, the bulk came from other sources: $78,000 from HEW's College Work Study Program; $40,000 from the Southern Regional Education Board; and $35,000 from private business sources.

Dayton, Ohio

Dayton started its Urban Corps program in 1968 with approximately sixty students working for the City's Bureau of Recreation. The program rapidly spread to other departments of the city, particularly those concerned with providing social services. Dayton's Urban Corps, with the strong backing of City Manager Graham Watt, stressed the employment of minority students. The 1969 program was able to establish a ratio of 53 percent black students to 47 percent white in the second year of operation. This is another significant factor in the Urban Corps approach – a move long overdue. Cities have traditionally employed blacks and chicanos in menial jobs. Now minority students are getting a vocational shot at the full range of municipal activities. Hopefully, many will decide to seek careers in the local public service.

A post evaluation of the 1969 program in Dayton showed the immediate supervisors to be enthusiastic about the employment of students in their departments. Nearly 92 percent indicated they would rehire the interns who worked for them that summer. This finding should provide encouragement to those mayors and chief administrators who have difficulty convincing their line agency chiefs that hiring students is good business.

Grand Rapids, Michigan

The Grand Rapids 1970 Urban Corps program involved ninety-two students from twelve different colleges and universities. Their work assignments covered twenty different city departments and a range of unique experiences. The program was under the direction of a three-man coordinating committee. In addition to the daily problems of keeping Urban Corps running smoothly, they analyzed the program at its completion, projected potential job slots for a modified program during the academic year, and held a series of summer seminars for the working interns.

Intern assignments included the following:

1. Assisting the art museum staff with a new artmobile program
2. Compiling data for analysis of the city's motor equipment system
3. Administering a college recruitment program for minorities
4. Surveying and compiling data on Model Cities
5. Assisting in the city museum's archaeological laboratory
6. Counseling and supervising neighborhood youth corps students
7. Developing an educational program for young visitors to the Children's zoo
8. Coordinating planning efforts for the city's youth employment program which provided summer jobs for 200 youngsters 14-16 years of age

More than 36 thousand hours of youthful vigor was Grand Rapids' gain as a result of Urban Corps in the summer of 1970. It cost a total of $106,365.00, with the city paying only $25,894.00. The rest came from College Work Study Program funds. Better bargains are tough to find in this world of spiraling prices.

Boulder, Colorado

Urban Corps has proved valuable to the city officials in Boulder, Colorado, a university community beset by youthful transients. Urban Corps workers have done much to close the gap between the city "establishment" and dissident youths in search of new lifestyles. Jim Grayer, a twenty-five year-old psychology major, heading up the Boulder student task force assigned to work on the potential problems of an influx of transients during the summer of 1970, made this observation: "Urban Corps is benefitting the community by getting young people involved in the community, in the mechanics of city government; by bringing new, fresh ideas to the municipal government scene; by stimulating new thought to change. It's benefitting me in the knowledge I'm gaining of people."[2]

Ted Tedesco, one of the nation's most innovative city managers, is concerned that the work experience students have in Boulder will be beneficial to their career goals. A look at a few job assignments indicates the program is being successful from this point of view. A young woman majoring in library science works in the children's section of the Boulder Library. A student specializing in criminology and juvenile delinquency works in the Youth Service Bureau counseling adolescents with potential problems and learning disabilities. A psychology major, who speaks Spanish, works with tenants living in housing leased by the city under a federal rental housing program. Her language facility aids her work with the Mexican-Americans in Boulder and her experience with the housing program will be valuable when she returns to southern Colorado after graduation. A first-year architecture student works in the city planner's office helping to develop a financial plan for a new civic center. And so it goes, linking valuable student talent to specific job tasks within the community to the benefit of all. That's really the purpose of Urban Corps — an exciting program born in the bowels of Manhattan and spreading across the land with contagious enthusiasm.

SREB's Resource Development Project

Although Urban Corps, with the blessing of the Ford Foundation, has been attracting much of the national press coverage in the past two or three years, there are many fine regional, metropolitan, and city programs that merit attention. The Southern Regional Educational Board's (SREB) Resource Development Project is one of them. Initiated in 1967, the project involves a series of internship programs in the fifteen Southern states. In the first three years of operation it placed more than 850 college students from over 150 colleges and universities in 250 local, state, and regional agencies.

William Ramsay, project director for SREB, says that "each internship, regardless of sponsoring agency or local assignment, conforms generally to the basic SREB internship design. This design calls for the intern to concern himself with a development task identified by a host agency; to relate to a project committee (consisting of a host agency representative, a university faculty counselor and a technical advisor); to be responsible for independent initiative while on the project; to participate in educational seminars with other interns; and to prepare a final report for the host agency."[3] By involving nearby university and college faculty members, the program fosters cooperation between local public agencies and the academic community.

A recent SREB publication entitled *Manpower for Public Service, 1970* lists the following program objectives:

1. To provide immediate student manpower to economic and social development agencies

2. To give students seeking to participate in the solution of social and economic problems constructive service opportunities

3. To encourage young people to consider careers and citizen leadership roles in development programs and to provide a pool of trained personnel for recruitment by sponsoring agencies

4. To give students in social sciences and related studies a more relevant education and training in the complexities of resource development

5. To provide an avenue of communication between institutions of higher education and programs of development; to make the resources of universities and colleges more accessible to the community; and to relate curriculum, teaching and research to society's needs[4]

"Financial support for the program," according to SREB, "is provided primarily from federal grants supplemented by a variety of cost sharing arrangements with local, state and regional agencies."[5] Federal support for the SREB internship program comes from such diverse agencies as the Coastal Plains Regional Commission, Economic Development Administration, Office of Economic Opportunity, Tennessee Valley Authority and the U.S. Department of Labor.

"The internship experience," according to SREB's Bill Ramsay, "adds a new dimension to the student's education background and gives him a chance to contribute constructively to activities aimed at meeting some of the needs of our society. It also introduces him to career opportunities in the field and shows him the vital role civic leadership can play in resource development."[6]

The resource development area is becoming increasingly important to cities and graduating students with practical experience in these areas will be sought with increasing vigor in city halls across the country. SREB interns have sought career employment in the following areas upon graduation — community development, education, housing, community health, legal services, manpower, personnel, planning, urban finance, and social welfare.

The record of accomplishments by SREB interns has been impressive and the program's popularity has taxed the board's ability to match requests with students. A look at some of the projects completed by these summer interns clearly demonstrates why interest runs so high.

1. One intern's recommendations on improving the appearance and design of ten Georgia towns has resulted in citizen action in at least three communities.

2. In Olive Hill, Kentucky, another intern counseled high school dropouts (girls) on such things as grooming, nutrition, money management, and job interview skills. Her summer's work was so successful that the local Neighborhood Youth Corps employed a staff person full-time to continue the services when the intern returned to school.

3. Another intern identified a way that one small town could reduce sanitation department costs by $14,000 yearly while improving services.

4. Nonmedical students, working in the health field, helped establish a mental health education program, formed a community health council, and identified serious water contamination problems in another community.

A Metropolitan Program

An Urban Careers Program has been administered by American University and the District of Columbia Personnel Office for the past two years in the Washington metropolitan area.[7] The program, funded under Title I of the Higher Education Act of 1965 in 1968-69, was designed to encourage undergraduate students to pursue administrative, professional, and technical careers in the local public service. In two years, over 300 students were recruited for summer internship experiences in local government in the Washington metropolitan area. The intern program was open to all academic disciplines, and students in political science, sociology, psychology, physics, history, education, engineering, economics, and public administration participated. Special attention was given to the placement of the student to assure challenging work assignments for the student and potential contribution to the agency providing the work experience.

Since the students were all working in a closely defined geographic area, the university was able to add a new dimension to the experience that is not always possible in similar programs — a series of seminars for the interns. A slightly different format was used each year of the program. The first year, two well known local officials made half-hour presentations in a particular problem area. These were followed by a question and answer period, after which the student group broke down into small workshop sessions for informal in-depth discussions. These sessions were guided by practitioners and educators from the area, A variety of topics were covered, including public safety, planning and physical development, public management, housing, community development, recreation, and employment. In 1969 the formal presentations were dropped and students met in small discussion groups with a local government official, a professor, and a citizen interested in community affairs.

American University's Urban Careers Program for the Washington metropolitan area had some interesting spinoffs. First, several of the summer interns were hired by the agencies where they had served their internships. Secondly, the program prompted some changes in the curriculum of American's School of

Government and Public Administration. Two new courses were added. One, a semester internship places students in local government agencies for two days a week and brings them together once each week for a seminar focusing on the political system of the Washington metropolitan area. The students' practical experiences provide for lively seminars and enhanced learning.

The other new course, prompted by the Urban Careers Program, is called the Urban Affairs Semester. Students meet with a variety of key policy-making or influencing officials from the Washington area two or three times a week to discuss a variety of issues. American University's unique location provides access to congressmen, officials of national associations concerned with urban affairs and administrators from federal programs geared to the urban scene. All of this makes for pretty exciting learning.

A survey of the 1968-69 internship program showed the following average responses for the two years: 84 percent said their work experience related to their academic major; 93 percent thought it a constructive and worthwhile experience; 86 percent increased their interest in urban careers as a result of the internship; 96 percent thought the Urban Careers program an effective way to stimulate interest in local public service among students; and, of course, the clincher, 98 percent were willing to recommend the program to their friends. The supervisors' evaluation of the program was just as enthusiastic with 92 percent indicating they would recommend their interns for employment within their own departments.

A Statewide Intern Program

One of the most exciting men to ever serve the public was responsible for creating an effective state-wide internship in community service for New Jersey. Paul Ylvisaker, former Commissioner of Community Affairs in that state, said at opening ceremonies for the first intern program in 1967, "Nothing our Department will do for New Jersey's communities — and we intend to do a lot — can compare in importance to what we are beginning today: which is to recruit the brightest young minds and the most enterprising young spirits we find into careers which will shape the future of our State's community affairs . . . and while formal education is a necessity, the solutions we are looking for and the talents we want engaged can't spring full-blown out of the classroom. The classroom has to be convened on the frontier; the mind that matters will have to go where the action is."

The New Jersey Interns in Community Service program started with 83 interns the first year. By 1969 it had expanded to 171, and in 1970 189 college and graduate students were selected from more than 1300 applicants. The 1970 crop was assigned to jobs in thirty-seven municipalities, seven counties, a number of state government agencies, fifteen community action (antipoverty) agencies, nine Model Cities agencies, fifteen local legal service organizations, and several public-oriented organizations in the private sector. The eleven-week intern program begins with a preliminary orientation session to brief the students on some of the problems they can expect and what resources are available to aid in solving them.

The heart of the program, as with all internship efforts, is the actual work experience in the public service. The students are assigned to an advisor-supervisor, designated by the hiring agency and approved by the Community Affairs Department. These supervisors provide any necessary on-the-job training and evaluate their progress and contributions on a regular basis and at the end of the program. Both student and supervisor submit required periodic reports on assignments and performances. Weekly seminars are held for interns, supervisors, and Community Affairs representatives featuring nationally and regionally known guest speakers from a range of related fields. To many interns, the seminar series has been the intellectual highlight of the program, allowing them an opportunity to probe issues critical to our society.

The 1967 Intern program, the first of a continuous effort, was subject to intensive evaluation by a University of Pennsylvania study team and dubbed "truly outstanding." In a detailed report, the team said:

1. More than 98% of the interns participating in the evaluation rated the program as "good" or "better."
2. 76% of the interns said their interest in public service was strengthened as a result of the internship experience, which "suggests that the program is likely to achieve its long range goal of attracting a significant number of highly qualified personnel to local and state government work."
3. Almost 75% of those supervising the interns on the job rated the students' service as either "highly satisfactory" or "exceptionally good."[8]

Some of the student intern reactions during the evaluation are interesting:

1. *Interns in Community Service* could have been just a summer job but this time the title implied substance . . . . It has demanded of you a decisiveness and a creativity you had not experienced before in summer work.
2. This has not been an easy summer, but then, an easy summer was not what I had in mind when I applied for the internship.
3. It hasn't been all great: you've been at sea more than once and you've done the wrong thing and stepped on the wrong toes more than once; you've gotten irritated with hangups and frustrated with your own and other's lack of expertise. But you've also learned more about your own state than you ever thought you wanted to know, and you've gotten excited about it.[9]

As with American University's Urban Careers program, the New Jersey Interns in Community Service produced some immediate results. Of the eighty interns in the first year's program, twelve were asked to stay on an additional three weeks, until school started. At least two were hired immediately and several others were offered employment at the end of their formal schooling. The usual amount of skepticism prevailed at the beginning of the program but as one suburban mayor stated, "our officials, after working with . . . [interns] this summer, have become enthusiastic believers in what can be done by and for these outstanding students. A wide variety of projects were accelerated to the policy making or decision stage due to the fact finding and analytical talents and coordinating efforts of [interns]. In addition to these tangible municipal management gains can be added the less tangible but very real intellectual stimulus received by our contact with an idealistic, questioning, young man committed to the objectives and values of effective local government."[10]

Individual City Programs

There are a number of significant internship programs that are run on a city basis without the benefit of outside funds or which were originated without such funds. The International City Management Association polled its members in early 1970 and found that 297 cities had plans to employ one or more interns for the summer. It was the first time for the survey and, undoubtedly, it reflected a modest count of the intern efforts nationwide. A number of cities declined listing their intern positions for applicants nationally because of their continuing relationship with a neighboring college or university.

One of the most impressive large city internship programs is in Phoenix, Arizona. The program, running continuously since 1950, employs three students yearly who have completed graduate training in public administration or related fields to serve one-year internships. These interns receive experience in the whole spectrum of municipal government. In addition to doing municipal research and analytical work, interns participate in the preparation of operating and capital budgets. They work with a variety of committees, attend staff meetings called by the city manager, and have opportunities to go to local and regional conferences where they rub shoulders with veteran public managers from all levels of government.

The Phoenix internship program has an illustrious alumni group. Sixteen are city managers and another fifteen hold responsible administrative positions in city government. Seven work for other levels of government, one is associate editor of the *American City* magazine, two have joined consulting firms, two are with state municipal leagues, and another is associate director of the American Public Works Association. Nine former Phoenix interns work for the city of Phoenix, holding a variety of top administrative positions. The program has been far from parochial in its search for talent — no less than twenty-five different graduate schools have been represented in the Phoenix program.

There are, of course, many fine internship programs, modest in scale, which cover a wide range of cities across the nation. Bob Morris, Village Manager, Glencoe, Illinois, has tutored nearly 100 young men and women in the fine art of municipal management from his small suburban city hall on the outskirts of Chicago. Woodbury Brackett, just retired from forty years of managing cities in northern New England, has students in his office for longer than lots of them would like to remember. Although never in what is now considered a large city, "Woody" Brackett attracted some fine budding talent. Two of his interns ended up vice-presidents of the International City Management Association, while another was honored with the presidency of that professional organization.

Often these individual city programs were modest in size and in the dollar investment made, while the return in talent and dedication was king-sized and enduring. It makes one ponder the chances for similar success with some of the high-powered fellowship programs that are now breaking. One such program is the National Urban Fellows program.

The National Urban Fellows

The National Urban Fellows program was launched in the summer of 1969 by the National League of Cities, U.S. Conference of Mayors, and Yale University with the financial blessing of the Ford Foundation. Twenty-four persons, mostly from ethnic minorities with demonstrated potential for positions of urban leadership, were placed with carefully picked and widely respected mentors. The program was initiated by a six-weeks intensive academic experience at Yale University. It relied heavily upon the seminar and brought in key urban practitioners, academics, and specialists from all over the country to work with the Fellows in small groups, relating conceptual material on the city to gutty urban issues. After completing the intensive Urban Studies program at Yale, they began their ten-month assignments as special assistants to city managers, mayors, school superintendents, and other urban executives. They supplemented their ten month on-the-job experience with graduate courses at universities in the communities where they were assigned. In addition, they attended three special one-week seminars devoted to current urban issues.

While no particular professional or technical background was required, the first round of Urban Fellows had solid experience in government service, law, the ministry, business, and community development. Compensation at their preentry salary levels with adjustments for cost of living and moving expenses made the involvement of older persons with family commitments possible.

The thirty-six 1970 fellows were selected from 265 candidates and also represent a wide range of ethnic and occupational backgrounds. A gathering of the 1970 Urban Fellows clan will resemble a mini-United Nations with at least one Aluet, American Indian, black, Eskimo, Japanese-American, Mexican-American, Puerto Rican, and white. The National Urban Fellows program, although small in numbers, will compensate in a modest way for the lack of ethnic minorities who have had opportunities to penetrate the top echelons of urban management. These fellows should make a valuable contribution in the near future to the dilemma that grips our nation's cities.

Where Do We Go From Here?

These emerging patterns of urban internships indicate a growing acceptance and a spread of service learning as a lead-in to careers in the public service. Certainly the base of operation and concern has broadened from a rather parochial administrative intern-to-the-city-manager approach to a wide array of intern offerings open to all academic disciplines and majors.

Bernard Hennessy, one time affiliate of the National Center for Education in Politics, made the observation that "internships are remarkable effective learning experiences. Some fail, of course, but only a few can be judged to be complete failures, and the almost universal testimony of interns, teachers and politicians is that internships work." Hennessy went on to say that "internships work not so much as devices for gaining knowledge of a factual kind, as for gaining knowledge in the sense of 'feel' and understanding. Internships work because they personalize data. They work because they give to political life and events a reality that makes them part of the intern's own being. That is, they not only give to facts some of the warmth and color of the human condition, but they merge, to some extent, the self with the otherwise foreign and non-self stuff of the world."[11]

Notes

1. Leon W. Lindsay, "Urban Corps Fights for Survival," *Christian Science Monitor,* August 26, 1969, p. 5.

2. *Boulder Daily Camera,* May 6, 1970, p. 8.

3. Personal correspondance between the author and William Ramsay, director of the Southern Regional Education Board, July 14, 1970.

4. Resources Development Project, *Manpower for Public Service, 1970,* Atlanta, Georgia, 1970, pp. 3-4.

5. Ibid., p. 4.

6. Ramsay, personal correspondance, July 14, 1970.

7. Bernard H. Ross, "The University and the City," *Nation's Cities,* July 1970, pp. 12-13, 23.

8. Thomas J. Davy, *Evaluation of New Jersey's Interns in Community Service Program,* Report of the Fels Institute of Local and State Government (Philadelphia, Pennsylvania: University of Pennsylvania, 1967)

9. Ibid., p. 11.

10. Ibid., p. 12.

11. Bernard C. Hennessy, *Political Internships: Theory, Practice and Evaluation* (University Park, Pennsylvania: The Pennsylvania State University, 1970), p. 103.

6

The HUD Urban Fellowship Program — A Partial Response to the Urban Manpower Crisis

JAMES BANOVETZ

The United States today faces a strange situation. It is, without doubt, history's most advanced nation technologically, capable of sending men to distant celestial bodies or literally destroying life on its own celestial body. Yet it is also a nation fundamentally incapable of resolving its domestic problems, or eradicating hunger and poverty, of guaranteeing its young an adequate education, of controlling its own ecology, or of instilling within its citizens a sense of respect, appreciation, and Judeo-Christian love for one another.

Many blame this sorry state of affairs upon the nation's international entanglements which divert national resources away from pressing problems at home. This, however, is a simplistic argument advanced by those who seek easy answers to complex problems. If the Congress were to announce tomorrow that it was transferring $50 billion from the Department of Defense budget to rebuilding the cities and reconstituting human living conditions, the nation's internal problems would not only persist, they would scarcely be affected.

Money alone is not the basic problem; neither is technological capability. The United States could, if money and technology were all that was needed, move expeditiously toward the resolution of its difficulties, despite extant international commitments and involvements. Political capacity and manpower capability — these are the missing ingredients that must be supplied if existing problems are to be ameliorated.

The nation lacks, first, the political capability to make the hard decisions needed to resolve its urban and other public problems: the nation can't make needed political decisions. For example, it can't bring itself to yielding up its second cars, expensive vacations, rock festivals, cosmetics, drugs, and other accouterments of affluent life to fight poverty; it can't decide whether persons on welfare should be treated as unfortunate widows or cheating chiselers; it can't reconcile its desire to sustain local government autonomy and importance with its suspicion of local government's fiscal integrity; it can't clean up the environment, not because of an absence of technology, but because it can't decide how to use existing technology. As long as the nation remains incapable of making difficult choices, of paying the kinds of prices that must be paid, its social and economic problems will not be solved.

Equally significant, and the topic of this chapter, is the inadequacy of the educated manpower pool available to administer an expanded level of governmental programming on domestic concerns. The nation has experienced,

79

to its dismay but unfortunately not to its enlightenment, the veracity of this fact. The initial impact of the federal government's 701 planning program, for example, was to create a new class of wealthy citizens — private planning consultants — since governments had no manpower pool available to undertake expanded planning activites. As might have been expected, furthermore, the work of the private consultants was mediocre at the start and remains highly suspect today.

The War on Poverty should have been even more enlightening. It represented an effort to increase the nation's social welfare programming on a crash, literally overnight basis. What it did, in fact, was to spread the nation's limited pool of social welfare professionals more thinly than before, but at much higher salaries. Social problems, meanwhile, have seemingly persisted unabated.

This chapter, as already indicated, will discuss this manpower crisis. Specifically, it will present two propositions: (1) that there is a strong and growing disparity between the demand for and supply of administrative, technical, and professional people trained for careers in the public service, and (2) that young people select careers upon the basis of the options to which they are exposed at critical moments during their development years, and that a proper exposure to public service options can markedly balance demand and supply. Having made these points, I will contrast the use of fellowships and internships as devices for expanding the career options made available to students. In so doing, I will also review the principal administrative complications inherent in the operation of a national fellowship program.

The Need Factor

Every public administrator today can cite chapter and verse of his favorite statistics on government's professional manpower problems. Senator Edmund Muskie aptly summarized the situation when he termed such problems the "Achilles Heel of Creative Federalism:" Typical statistics include the following:

1. Over 500 new jobs will develop in city planning alone every year for the next ten years.
2. During the same period, one third of all city managers now in office will become eligible for retirement.
3. A 1968 ICMA survey showed an average of eight vacancies in managerial and technical positions in 309 middle-sized cities, or 6.5 percent of all such positions in those cities.
4. A 1968 study in Illinois showed that the state would need 136,000 additional administrative, professional and technical personnel between 1965 and 1975. Only a tiny fraction of that number were being educated by Illinois colleges and universities.
5. The Chicago office of the U.S. Civil Service Commission reported in 1968

that the federal government alone would need 500 administrative people in June 1969, yet Illinois colleges and universities were destined to graduate less than 10 percent of that number with appropriate educational preparation for those jobs.

To cite more statistics would be redundant. Every analysis has reached the same conclusion: governmental agencies, particularly at the state and local level, face a manpower crisis. There are not enough trained professionals to fill current administrative positions; the gap between supply and demand will increase in the future. The nation's educational system is simply failing to interest a sufficient portion of its students in public affairs and to provide training designed specifically for a public affairs career.

There are now indications that the federal government's manpower shortage is easing. This would be a good sign if there were convincing evidence that unsuccessful candidates for federal jobs subsequently seek positions at the state and local level, but no such evidence exists. Meanwhile, the manpower crisis at the state and local level continues and worsens.

This is not to suggest that professional, administrative, and technical jobs in state and local government will go unfilled; it does suggest that they will not be — and in too many cases are not now being — filled by persons with the level of background preparation routinely expected by private employers for comparable positions.

The Career Motivation Factor

The career motivational factor is largely a matter of psychological identification. Young people choose careers in a haphazard manner in which the most important considerations are their capabilities and the kinds of opportunities to which they are exposed. Youngsters start out planning to be policemen, firemen, truck drivers, or airplane pilots because they are enhanced by uniforms; these occupations capture their imaginations, and their preschool books expose them frequently to these jobs. As youngsters grow older, they are influenced by their neighbors, teachers, and experiences: they are likely to consider as viable options only those careers to which they have some personal exposure.

A student will typically not consider a career with which he is totally unfamiliar. For example, a student who has never known an architect has only a vague notion of what an architect does, and if never encouraged to consider architecture by a teacher, career counselor, or friend, is most unlikely to pursue an architectural career. Careers in governmental administration are no different in appeal or visibility.

Most young people destined for college make their initial occupational choice during their college years. While most students enter college with some notions about career alternatives, most change major fields during their college days as they respond to the influence of the academic environment. If that environment does not make certain choices visible and viable, students are not likely to pursue them. A college without an archaeology department will produce few, if any, archeologists; a school without a public administration program or emphasis will produce few public administrators — particularly from among its best students.

Students, in other words, will not opt for a vocational choice to which they have not been exposed. Four kinds of exposure have been proven effective in encouraging students to pursue careers in government.

The first is an academic introduction to the career, either through coursework or through the personal encouragement of members of the academic staff. Related to this is a second encouragement common to most professional fields: fellowships, assistantships, internships, and other forms of financial aid for persons interested in studying in that field. Money attracts: it attracts good students just as, in the business world, it attracts good employees.

The third kind of exposure is recruitment by professionals in the field. The city manager educational program at the University of Kansas, for example, has maintained a national recruitment base largely through the efforts of their alumni who encourage young people to go into city management and then encourage them to study at Kansas.

Finally, personal work experience is an effective, and perhaps the most effective, recruiting device. Nothing makes a career choice so viable as a meaningful, challenging involvement in that profession for some period of time. Such involvement defines the option more clearly, points out career advancement possibilities, creates professional attachments, and stimulates the student's creative energies in that field. Most of all, it offers the student a sense of mission, purpose, and accomplishment — the sense that is so frequently and painfully missing from the lives of young adults in today's society.

Best of all, of course, are combinations of the above motivational inducements. Each of them has been effective; when used in tandem, they provide mutual reinforcement for each other. Yet, none of these inducements have yet been applied to government careers on a very widespread scale in the United States. Courses in public administration are still relatively rare in college curricula; half the states have no graduate level academic programs in public administration in either their public or private universities; support money for graduate study is even scarcer; and internships, while increasing in number, are still very limited in comparison with the dimensions of the manpower shortage.

Yet, there is no reason to believe that a motivational program designed to make government career options more viable for more students cannot increase recruitment by the requisite amount. To evaluate this proposition, and to examine the problems inherent in developing better options as government career recruitment devices, this chapter will examine the Urban Fellowship program operated by the U.S. Department of Housing and Urban Development.

From the statistics presented to Congress, the HUD program seems impressive. Although funded at a level of only $500 thousand per year, it has had a very high rate of success in sending persons into the urban public service, which is its avowed purpose.

The HUD Urban Fellowship Program

The Record

As of February, 1970, 113 persons had completed their study under HUD sponsorship. Of these, all but 14 had completed or were expected to complete the degree work for which they were supported. Of these,

37 were employed by government
9 were in related teaching or private profit positions
28 were not yet in the job market
6 were in nonurban employment or the military service
28 were dropped from the program or are unknown as to their whereabouts.

Thus, about 90 percent of employable fellows upon whom information is available have selected occupations in urban-related fields. Only half of the total fellows, however, are actually engaged in urban government positions (30 of 60 now employed).

There is also some evidence that the program has increased the number of persons engaged in graduate study. The University of Illinois reported that the program helped increace its enrollments in urban planning from 14 to 25. The University of Chicago combined HUD fellowships with other awards to increase its urban study enrollments from 22 to 32 students. Yale University upped its urban studies enrollments from 30 to 45. In each instance, the HUD fellowships directly supported only two or three students yet, the universities seemed to consider the fellowships crucial because of the kinds of fellows they enabled to attend graduate school. This is the kind of data presented to Congress in support of the program. It is valid data supporting a program that is sorely needed at a vastly higher level of financial support. These figures do not, however, tell the whole story. They do not indicate, for example, that they were compiled during a period of generally rising enrollments nor do they indicate why the particular institutions cited could not have supported these "better quality" students from their own comparatively ample student-support resources.

In any analysis of the HUD program, it must be clearly stated at the start that the program's principal failing — and the cause of the obfuscation in the above figures — is the miniscule level of support provided by the Congress. Nationally, the $500 thousand supported only 99 fellowships in fiscal year 1969 and 107 in fiscal year 1970. This is less than the proverbial drop in the bucket when compared with needs. HUD's Fellowship Advisory Board has estimated that the program would have to be doubled in size even to begin to have a consequential impact on the nation's needs.

Administrative Problems: Applicant Review

Even if the program were to double in size, however, there would remain a number of administrative problems affecting the program's ultimate goal achievement. A review of these problems is interesting, partly because it provides some insight into the difficulties that are inevitably encountered in the recruitment of students for a particular field, partly because it describes the difficulties inherent in rendering decisions about the allocation of financial support, and partly, too, because it summarizes problems of managing such a program at the national level.

First, there are several problems directly related to the selection of fellowship recipients. One is a product of the contemporary era: how should the quality of an applicant be reconciled with such distributive factors as race, sex, age, schools, fields of previous collegiate study, congressional sponsors, and geographic areas of residence? Essentially, the question is this: should those fellows be selected who have the best academic record or should this consideration be modified so that blacks, Spanish-speaking peoples, native Americans, and other minority groups will have improved opportunities? This consideration is rendered even more difficult in light of the established tendency for persons from such minority groups to compile relatively poorer academic records because of the inferiority of their elementary and secondary educational experiences. The other distributive characteristics pose equally difficult questions, yet questions which are very important to those individual applicants affected by them.

A second fellowship selection problem, also related to quality, is the question of a student's potential for a career in the urban public service. The purpose of fellowship programs is to increase the number of students in the urban public service career. An outstanding student in urban economics, for instance, is likely to continue his studies toward the Ph.D., yet there are very few positions in the urban public service for Ph.D.s in economics. Few such persons are employed by urban governments except as consultants; there are few local governments needing a full-time research economist on their staff. Evaluations of urban service career potential are particularly difficult to make because there is no hard data which can be used in making such judgments. HUD's Fellowship Advisory Board did consider, for example, using an applicant's past work record for this purpose, giving some preference to those who had worked in the Peace Corps, VISTA, or with various community action agencies. Such a practice, however, tends to favor applicants from affluent families — students who have to support their college education without financial support from home can rarely afford to pass up better paying jobs in favor of the low-pay, high social service positions — so it was discarded.

Related is the question of preference in awards between new applicants for graduate study and those applicants seeking support for their second or third year of study. On the one hand, Congress established the program with the intent of encouraging as many *more* students as possible to pursue careers in the urban public service. This consideration would argue for giving awards only to new applicants for graduate study; students already in graduate school have already made a commitment and are likely to enter the urban public service even without such support while applicants for graduate study may still be weighing several commitments. On the other hand, Congress also wants the program to get a good track record, to graduate as many persons as possible for the urban public service. This consideration would suggest giving as many awards as possible to students already in graduate school since they have proven their ability to do graduate study and they already have a commitment to urban-related work.

A most difficult question related to quality concerns support for students who plan to pursue doctoral study, or who are likely to do so. Urban governmental agencies have few positions requiring an earned doctorate, and so are rarely in a position to pay persons with such training a salary commensurate with other employment opportunities. Urban government consulting firms employ many holders of the doctorate, but the Advisory Board quickly and unequivocally ruled against supporting persons destined for careers in private consulting. Yet holders of the doctorate, through research and instructional activities, can make a major contribution to the improvement of urban life. This fact not withstanding, however, the Advisory Board has recommended that the purpose of the fellowship program — the education of persons for professional positions in urban government employment — should be kept paramount by restricting fellowships to persons pursuing professionally oriented masters degrees in qualified programs.

Finally, the question of quality must also be measured against the question of financial need. Fellowship support provided varies, under the HUD program, from student to student depending upon such variables as the number of dependents and the cost of tuition at the school of study. If preference is given to applicants without dependents and applicants planning to attend lower-tuition schools, then the cost per fellowship can be reduced and more fellowships can be awarded. If such preference is not given, fewer fellowships can be given and the congressional intent to maximize the number of new students attracted to the urban public service is frustrated.

Administrative Problems: Program Selection

One way to avoid these problems is to award fellowships to particular schools and then let the schools select the recipients. This, however, merely substitutes the problem of school selection for the problem of recipient selection. The school selection problem is two-fold: (1) what kinds of programs ought to be selected for fellowship support, and (2) what concern, if any, should be given to geographical distribution of awards?

In fiscal year 1969, HUD awarded ninety-nine fellowships to students for study in fifty-seven departments in forty-six schools. In fiscal year 1970, 107 fellowships were awarded for study in only forty-six departments in forty schools. The change was caused, principally, by a change in procedures. For fiscal year 1969, schools were asked to nominate fellows. For fiscal year 1970, applicants applied directly to HUD and then were free to select their own school. The result, of course, was that most applicants chose to attend the "name" schools and the distribution of awards was circumscribed.

Herein lies the crux of the problem: should the fellowships be put into the best schools, where presumably the students will receive the best education, or should they be given to lesser-known universities seeking to develop or expand programs designed to train people for the urban public service? The latter option obviously has much to commend it: the manpower shortages of the urban public service will ultimately be solved only when more universities have developed programs to produce more graduates for such careers. The grant of fellowships to nonprestige universities would constitute a major boost to the development of new programs or the strengthening of small and weak programs. Consequently, such grants could constitute a major investment in the expansion of graduate education for public service careers in the United States.

As it is, with students selecting the school they wish to attend, most of the awards are currently made to high prestige institutions. In fiscal year 1970, for example, seven schools – Harvard, M.I.T., Yale, Chicago, University of California at Berkley, Columbia, North Carolina – received 48 of the 107 awards granted. At the other end of the scale, only 10 nonprestige universities received fellowships.

A related problem is that of geographic distribution. In fiscal year 1970, schools located in only seven states – those in the Mid-Atlantic and New England area – received 59 of the 107 awards. In other words, schools in seven states received over half of the total awards granted.

This pattern of distribution poses questions since most state and local government agencies follow the practice of recruiting professional help from local colleges and universities. With the exception of the planning and city management fields, the national manpower market in local government is extremely limited; few governments recruit on a national basis and few job candidates look beyond their immediate region for positions. Until this situation changes, or until there is an adequate geographic distribution of educational programs designed to prepare people for professional careers in government, state and local manpower problems will remain chronic and critical. The present distribution of academic programs is certainly not adequate: fully half the states have no university graduate programs in public administration operated within their boundaries, and the situation is similar in the field of planning. Consequently, there is a severe need for the development of an increased number of academic programs in these fields. This, in turn, generates certain pressures for the inclusion of geographic considerations in the allocation of fellowship awards.

Regardless of whether fellowship applications are submitted by individuals or schools, two additional, chronic problems remain. One of these is the question of qualified programs: which fields of study should be supported by the award of fellowship grants? Certain kinds of programs are obviously to be included: graduate programs in urban and regional planning, municipal administration, and urban studies clearly qualify. Similarly, traditional degree programs in geology, business administration, or elementary education do not qualify. Much more difficult to handle, however, are those fields that have not traditionally been urban-oriented but have had urban components added to them. How many urban-oriented modifications must be implemented in a law school program, for instance, to justify fellowships for the study of urban law? The field of social work has posed similar problems as, to a lesser extent, have programs in fields such as geography, health, civil engineering (with an urban transportation focus, for example) or real estate and land economics. Each of the fields mentioned has been supported with some fellowship grants, but the Advisory Board has become increasingly wary of supporting programs that have not been substantially redesigned with the professional needs of the urban public service in mind.

Finally, there is the continuing question of financial need. Although need per se is not legally a consideration the Advisory Board may take into account, nevertheless every fellowship given unnecessarily, either because other sources of financial aid are available or because the student would have pursued the degree program anyway, frustrates the program's purpose of attracting additional persons into professional careers in the urban public service. Financial need considerations thus continue to present themselves, phrased in such contexts as: "Should applicants already entitled to Veterans Administration benefits be granted fellowships?" "Should awardees be permitted external employment while receiving fellowship stipends?" "Should fellowship recipients be permitted to accept optional internship opportunities which pay a support stipend?"

Summary

All of the problems discussed so far have no readily apparent or easy solution. Yet the answers given to each will have a basic effect on the extent to which the fellowship program meets its defined objectives. Unfortunately, too, decisions are made must be uniformly applied to all schools and all applicants, yet such application invariably renders arbitrary and apparent inequities in the program.

The diversity in academic programming throughout the nation, even within a well-defined field of study, is frequently so great that rules reasonable and germane for one school's academic program inevitably will appear arbitrary and illogical when applied to the program from some other school. Nevertheless, the implementation of the program requires that decisions be made and applied.

Despite such substantive uncertainties, the existing record would indicate that HUD's Urban Fellowship Program is making an important contribution: it has been a success insofar as sending graduates into the urban public service is concerned. Despite this record, however, the Fellowship Advisory Board remains uneasy about the extent to which the existing program benefits are being maximized, even within the fiscal restraints imposed by Congress. In part, this is a healthy feeling: the fellowship program is still relatively new, so new that a questioning approach to its operating policies is essential to its ultimate maturation. In part, this uneasiness is a natural by-product of the administration of national programs. But, in part, too, it might also be traced to questions about the utility of fellowships as the most effective mechanism for the task of attracting people to the public service.

Related Problems I: The Role of Internships

Students today claim that their academic instruction does not prepare them for the jobs they will eventually take. Yet, students have always made this claim, and they always will because everyone has different expectations regarding the educational process. Public administration courses have long been assaulted for not teaching more techniques: for not teaching how to fill out budget forms, prepare a job description, or process a purchase order. More recently, these courses have been assailed for not focusing upon public policy issues, such as the Vietnam war or racism. Yet the challenge of public administration is far more complicated than form processing, and few novice public administrators are assigned the task of developing new national policies on subjects such as Vietnam or racism.

This is not to suggest that students should play no role in curriculum design. Students have a vital stake in curriculum content and a perspective too important to be ignored. But theirs is not the only perspective that is relevant, nor is it necessarily the most relevant. Given their choice, for example, most students of public affairs and administration would minimize – or even avoid altogether – such subjects as statistics or quantitative administrative methodology. Yet graduates without grounding in these subjects are already functionally obsolete.

Four perspectives need to be reconciled in curriculum development. One is that of the students, for they are the recipients of the education, and it is this education which provides them with essential life capabilities. A second is the perspective of the profession for which students are being trained: this should be rooted in the profession's background of experience. A third is the educational program's alumni, for these people can make judgments after having experienced both the student's and the professional's perspectives. Finally, the academicians, if they are competent, also have a perspective based upon a lifetime of experience in preparing persons for professional careers.

Today, student claims have some validity: their perspective has not been adequately acknowledged. On the other hand, however, their claim has often been overstated and poorly expressed.

Internship experience and classroom work are two different kinds of instruction designed to do different tasks. Which should be emphasized depends upon the objectives and purposes for which the education is being undertaken.

The internship is an experience in which the participant gains his first exposure to actual job techniques – to paper processing, project execution, decision-making. Hopefully, too, it is an arena in which classroom concepts can be observed and applied. Its applicability to career goals is glaringly apparent; hence its value is frequently overstated.

As already noted, classroom work could teach these same skills, but the typical student will learn them anyway during his first months on the job. It is more important that the classroom deal with the implication of the techniques and methods used in administrative operations. These implications are insights into administration that the administrator might learn on the job – or might not. Typically the administrator is so busy coping with the volume of facts, questions, and paper crossing his desk that he has little time to stop and reflect about the implications of what has been happening.

City managers, typically, are experts at this kind of reflection. They do it all the time while they are driving from one job to another. But while they are on the job, they don't take time to sit and think about where they are and where they are going. A recent International City Management Association survey showed that the single function most neglected by managers is that of sitting back for reflection and planning.

If the classroom can provide students with a social science background to which human behavior on the job will be more relevant and can acquaint students with the human dynamic of organizational behavior, then those students should be much more able to guide and direct the human interactions which are the "stuff" of administration.

Education has to be balanced: both kinds of knowledge have to be imparted. Academic instruction, for instance, must cover the processes of decision-making. Such processes are actually easier to teach than the more intangible concepts relating to the dynamics of human interaction.

Processes such as decision-making can, in part, be learned in the classroom. Students can be taught how to define the parameters of a problem, identify alternatives, gather pertinent information, assess possible consequences, and apply decision-making rules. But, in part, the process must be learned through actual experience. A medical student can be taught the steps of an operation, but he won't have mastered the lesson until he has taken the surgical tools in his own hands and actually performed the operation a number of times.

For the administration student, the internship is the most common device used to provide actual, monitored experience in the application of administrative processes. But the internship, without accompanying classroom training, is a much more barren experience.

Related Problems II: Internships versus Training

Some have alleged that the quality of existing government employees could best be improved by cutting back on fellowships and internships. Since many of the limitations and shortcomings seem to be traceable to a lack of adequate educational preparation for the positions government employees hold, short courses should be offered.

Funds to sponsor such short courses have been available under Title VIII of the Housing Act (administered by the Department of Housing and Urban Development) and under Title I of the Higher Education Act (administered by the Department of Health, Education and Welfare). Furthermore, most colleges and universities have extension and continuing education programs that would be willing, and often eager, to assist such activities. So the capability for developing such programs has been available without resort to fellowship and internship funds.

The courses of this kind that have been held, however, have had an apparent lack of consequential impact. There are several reasons for this, but principally it is due to the difficulty of getting an audience: most such programs literally go begging for an audience. The audience that does come, furthermore, is generally composed of those persons that least need the training. It's like the problem of the minister on Sunday: he lectures on sin to those persons who are usually least guilty of it.

The paper talks about how haphazard the decision-making process about careers really is for young people. Once the career is tentatively chosen, its development is also haphazard, particularly in local government. A young person starts as an administrative assistant, but where is the next step? A number of young fellows in Kansas City have reached that first step and don't know what is next. A guy can go to work for Procter and Gamble and see it — he can see it all the way up to the vice-presidency.

This hits upon one of the most basic problems of public service at the local government level. It is a problem, not only for the person in the service, but also for young people contemplating a career in local government. They not only can't see a ladder of advancement, they can't find an entrance portal. It would be very useful if all the local governments in a particular area would get together and open up a store front career office where young people could get information about career opportunities and job applications procedures for *all* the governments in the area.

One of the reasons for the invisibility of career ladders is that, frequently, there is no ladder. There is no ladder because the career system is horizontal: the difference between the bottom and the top is one, two, or at most three steps. In other words, many young people start out as an administrative assistant to a city manager or as an assistant planner and the next step up the line is city manager or planning director. Thus it is entirely possible today for a person to become a city manager before his thirtieth birthday. From that point on, his career development consists of undertaking similar assignments of an increasingly challenging nature.

What a young person must understand is that he is entering a profession, not the employment of a particular city. His next job is not in Kansas City, but it's an assistant manager's job in Arlington County, or finance director in a suburban community, or the executive director of a council of governments in another state. Professional development, in other words, requires geographic mobility.

To be sure, there is a critical need for mid-career development programs. Yet, as already noted, existing programs have trouble drawing an audience. In part, then, what is needed is some means of assuring such programs of an adequate audience.

There are several problems here. For one thing, there are not that many people in local government who are receptive to training. For instance, a very high percentage of local government administrative personnel are within a few years of retirement: one-third of all active city managers will be eligible for retirement within the next ten years. Such people are not viable candidates for professional upgrading.

Second, local governments themselves have mixed feelings about mid-career development. While generally recognizing the value of such training, these governments also fear that, as soon as they invest money in developing an employee, that employee will take a better job elsewhere. Even offering an employee more money upon completion of a course is not a guarantee against his departure: he may feel that a new pasture is a better place in which to practice his newly acquired talents and insights.

Finally, programs calling for the temporary reassignment of personnel for educational purposes have limited attractiveness in local government because there is not the personnel depth in most agencies to backstop the people who will be away from their desks for any extended period of time. Large agencies can participate in exchanges such as those contemplated by the Intergovernmental Manpower Act; small governments cannot.

These problems do not justify de-emphasizing mid-career training; they simply point out the hurdles that must be met in providing such training. All too often the resulting approach is the two- or three-day seminar. Such seminars have their value, particularly when well designed and executed, but all too often they are not. Even when they are, they are a disjointed, noncoordinated, and severely limited tool for mid-career training.

It is patently evident that neither mid-career training nor intensified recruitment and education of new personnel will, alone, solve local governments' manpower problems. Both have their place and must be maximally utilized. Another path to the solution of manpower problems, which is also being utilized increasingly, is the reassignment of functions, transferring from professional persons the routine tasks which can be adequately handled by properly trained paraprofessionals, and leaving the professional more time to cope with the more demanding aspects of his work. This technique is useful and demands further development, but it too is subject to inherent limitations.

Related Problems III: The People Perspective

Some people say that the problems of organizations today are not technical ones, but that they are people problems because, too frequently, solutions to technical problems will not be accepted by the people involved.

The valididty of this premise depends in large part about the time frame involved. Kansas City wants a superroadway built to its new airport. The road can't be built this year because of technical constraints: there is no money available. Over time, however, the financial problem can be solved through new tax levies, authorized borrowing, intergovernmental grants, or reassignment of priorities in existing public expenditure patterns. All of these solutions require the support of a political consensus, and the task of getting such a consensus is definitely a people problem. Similarly, in the long run, most problems are more human than technical in nature.

This is related to the point being made when I asserted that American society can't make hard decisions, can't bring itself to deal with difficult issues. The society is wealthy enough to eradicate poverty as presently defined — and to do so without dropping the average person's standard of living down anywhere near the living standard of people in Japan, West Germany, or the Soviet Union. But the American society is, or has been, unwilling to make the requisite decisions.

It has long been the practice, of course, to have such persons administering the agencies devoted to their professional specialization. Thus, for instance, professional policemen administer police departments; doctors of medicine administer public health departments; civil engineers usually administer public works departments; and the corporation counsel administers the law department.

What is needed is not an expansion of this practice, but rather educational programs which would provide such persons with the requisite administrative insights and skills. This has long been a major theme of Professor Frederick C. Mosher. Such forward looking federal agencies as the National Aeronautics and Space Administration (NASA) are doing this: the University of Alabama at Huntsville has an MPA program in which almost all of the students are NASA executives who have already earned doctoral degrees in the natural and physical sciences. Professor Mosher argues that such training should be provided people in other professions during, not after, their training in their own professional school.

This trend is encouraging. As a result, the generalist is becoming more rather than less important because an increasing number of governmental problems have general social and political implications. The generalist's particular skill or contribution in the administrative setting is the variety of perspectives he can bring to bear upon a particular problem. Too often, for instance, the specialists — the engineers — in the public works department are concerned only with building as many miles of streets of high quality with as few dollars as possible. Yet street construction must also consider the impact of that construction upon adjacent property, upon other street utilization, upon neighborhood living patterns, upon land values, upon local political conditions, and upon a host of other factors. If the generalist has any particular skill, that skill is his comparatively greater ability to anticipate, analyze, and reconcile this broader range of concerns into a more satisfactory policy outcome.

If, in fact, this is the kind of person to whom reference is made by the term "generalist," then the need for generalists is definitely increasing, and will continue to increase, as the complexity of society and the interdependency of public problems and issues become more pronounced.

Conclusion

There is undoubtedly a need for a vast increase in the supply of professionally educated manpower available to the nation's governments, and particularly to its state and local governments. The present situation of imbalance between supply and demand has reached such critical levels that token responses by government can no longer be viewed as either adequate or acceptable. What is needed is not a national internship program or a national fellowship program, but both of these devices, working in conjunction with aid for the development of new and stronger programs of education for the public service.

In other words, the nation will not make satisfactory progress toward the amelioration of its social and economic problems until it has a pool of professional manpower adequate to meet the staffing requirements of new public programs and of existing governmental agencies at all levels. A coordinated national attack on these manpower problems, involving the efforts of national, state, and local governmental units, and involving fellowships, internships, and other recruitment and educational tools, must be synchronized and brought to bear upon the problems.

Finally, all of this must be done sooner, not later, for the nation's opportunity to remedy its fundamental problems is continually and dangerously eroding away.

7

The Emergence of State Management Internships

LARRY HUGHES AND
THOMAS P. MURPHY

One of the prominent themes in American public administration during the twentieth century has been the move from political domination of public business to professional management. The federal government acted first through gradual implementation of the Civil Service System. Next to feel the impact of professionalism was the local level. Major cities, which became the focus of population migration and the resulting problems, became the second target of professionalization drives; the zeal of some of these city level reform campaigns resulted in the decline of the big city bosses. Much later a number of counties undertook to reform their personnel systems, although many still have not done so. State governments represent another level of public service in which professionalism has finally become a trend. This trend in states, however, is much less developed and in some states still is subject to regular political interventions. The relatively recent emergence of professionalism at the state level can be directly traced to the shift in representation in state legislatures from rural counties to urban and suburban counties, and on federal pressures in behalf of professional state management.

These trends at the various governmental levels have manifested themselves in the development of internship programs. Internships at the federal level are widely utilized and almost institutionalized. At the local level, primarily in cities, internship programs involving students for urban and state universities and colleges have been enthusiastically welcomed. In some cases, professional recruiting bulletins reflect that agencies and governments are indicating as a prerequisite for employment a specified number of years of experience or an internship.

Internships of various types and durations have developed, and a considerable body of knowledge about them has accumulated. At the same time educational opportunities for federal and local interns have expanded significantly as agency supervisors have developed skills in using and training interns.

Extensive use of state level internships, on the other hand, is a fairly recent development. Various political and executive initiatives have been undertaken to upgrade the capacity of state government to the point where it can serve as a partner in public problem-solving. One of the essential elements in the revitalization of state governments is in changing the level of qualifications of

95

the people who fill the decision-making and support ranks of the agencies that will implement state programs and policies. As Frank H. Bailey has put it, "a significant measure of the success of state government in the future will be its ability to attract, recruit, train, and maintain competent professional, administrative, and technical personnel."[1] The goal of the much touted "New Federalism" is to slow and even reverse the transfer of power to Washington and cultivate a viable federal system involving effective governments at the national, state, and local levels. However, this will require recruiting more capable managers to state government.

The increasing demands for state government effectiveness and increased participation in intergovernmental programs have led to increased attention to recruitment and training of managers for state government. States have sought to improve their system through a combination of in-house state-training staffs, university programs, and the use of training consultants. One of the tools which has been applied to recruitment and the development of managers at the state level is the internship. However, most of these programs have not yet approached the level of sophistication found in the city and federal government. In fact, at the state level, legislative internships as discussed in chapter 9 have received more attention than management internships.

California and New York State Internships

The state management internships seem to have reached a high level of sophistication only in a few states. The two most populous states — California and New York — stand out in this respect. These same two states also were ranked first and second, respectively, in terms of their legislative capabilities in an evaluation by the Citizens Conference on State Legislatures. The ranking was in terms of minimum performance standards and not the ideal.[2] Nevertheless, these states have clearly shown offical concern in both the legislative and executive branches with the problem of management. Based on information available, New York currently has the strongest state internship program. However, with adequate funding, the Public Service Internship Program adopted by the California would also offer great promise.

The nature of management internships in state government and their development as a training tool is perhaps best characterized by the view of R.P. Everett, state training officer in California, which has one of the more aggressive state programs. He indicated that the goals of state internships in California are still at the level of a tool by which the message of management problem-solving and research needs is relayed from the state government to campuses. States must draw the eyes of professors and students from the glamor and clamor for programs in the cities and federal government to the much less publicized problems of the state.[3] Thus for this official, immediate training and recruitment of young collegians was not considered the primary objective of the program. Rather, the goals were longer range and included aspects other than direct recruiting.

The California State Legislature passed a "Public Service Internship Program" in 1970. However, the State Scholarship and Loan Commission has been unable to develop the program since it has not been funded as of fiscal year 1972.[4] It has become a case of promising enabling legislation with insufficient interest to secure an appropriation. However, the potential of the law is evident from the goals and objectives set forth in its first chapter:

A public internship is a student assignment with a governmental jurisdiction or public agency, the purpose of which is to provide the student with a learning experience designed to provide exposure to and understanding of the environment and tasks of government and of particular agencies and functions. In contrast to a specific job or work task, the internship affords creative opportunities for the intern to participate in various phases of a planned training program developed jointly and implemented cooperatively by governmental agencies and institutions of higher learning.[5]

Becoming more specific the Public Internship Program legislation lists the following objectives:

1. To acquaint students with the opportunities for challenging careers in public service and to stimulate the interests of students in particular functions and agencies.
2. To enable public jurisdictions to attract students of high ability and achievement potential to government and thereby improve the overall quality of the public service.
3. To induce students to seek careers in fields of public employment where critical shortages exist and where future personnel needs will be great.
4. To develop closer relationships between educational institutions and government agencies of the state by fostering better understanding of each jurisdiction's respective problems and needs.
5. To extend and improve existing legislative and administrative internship programs throughout the state, programs which have already made a major contribution to the quality of state and local government.
6. To cooperate with agencies of the federal government and quasi-governmental and private organizations in building more effective state and local internship and training programs.[6]

Those who drafted the bill included the key elements of an internship experience: participant observation, project experience, research, and academic supervision. The law emphasizes academic and professional managerial interaction in article 3 of chapter 3 which provides that "any intern selected by a government agency must maintain an academic affiliation with a college or university during the period of internship."[7] Further, the internships are to be tailored to meet the respective academic levels from undergraduate to doctoral and professional levels. The bill declares "the type and level of education and training shall be based upon the academic advancement, work experience and maturity of the intern."[8]

The California law approaches a model piece of legislation as far as internships at any level of government are concerned. Perhaps the provisions are too model since funding has yet to be delivered by the legislature or even requested by the governor in his FY 1972 budget request. Unless it is extended, the act will expire at the end of FY 1973.[9] Whether the general budget crunch being experienced by all public agencies is the moving force behind the failure to appropriate money for this program or whether the public disenchantment with "the universities" is the cause can only be speculated. While this centralized internship program has not been implemented, various other internships are available through individual departments of the California government. Further, the governor's Advisory Coordinating Council on Public Personnel Management has begun to use Intergovernmental Act grant funds to begin to implement certain phases of the Public Service Internship Program.

One of the more advanced state public administration programs is in New York State. Established in 1947, one-year internships are available to master's degree candidates from any state. The 1971-72 program announcement capitalized on some of the prominent public administration experiences available in New York:

The capital of one of the most populous and cosmopolitan states affords an ideal laboratory for the study of public administration. The size and the resources of New York State, the variety of its problems, the pioneering efforts in public policy, and its far-reaching relations with local and federal systems, afford the student a comprehensive view of American government in operation.[10]

The program is structured to maximize the options available to potential interns. That is, any one who qualifies may select his agency and to a large degree the nature of his projects. The experience is optimized by the offering of training institutes for the interns during the course of the internship.

The New York program reflects a relatively long experience with internships. The appointment of interns is centrally coordinated by the State Civil Service Department. However, each department, bureau, or agency that wants an intern submits specifications to the Civil Service Department which in turn recruits the interns and attempts to place them in programs in which they are interested. The range of internships available in New York for the 1971-72 internship period ranges from general administrative assignments such as those in the Budget Bureau and General Services Department to specialties such as narcotics addiction control and environmental conservation.

The state openly indicates the desire to recruit the public administrators it trains. The announcement states "on successful completion, interns are offered permanent appointments with a salary increase, to the first professional level in New York State service."[11] In that same spirit, interns are not required to complete the one-year internship before they move into a regular service position. They may take a civil service examination before the end of their internship and qualify for a professional level position and salary. The appointment would not necessarily have to be in the agency where the internship was taken.

The selection and salary aspect of the internship tend to indicate that the program is a good deal more than an internship. In fact, it is an entry level position in professional state administration. Selections are made on the basis of an "oral examination" which is comparable to the interviews and unassembled examinations used by most agencies. Further, the oral examinations are open to students across the country. Interns start at a salary just over $10,000. This is a significant aspect of the New York program as most internships provide a stipend instead of a salary. The major difference in these two terms is that the stipend is usually considerably less than the value of the talent represented by the intern and is usually not a major recruiting factor.

The unusually high salary paid for the internship raises another question involving some of the philosophical aspects of internships. The purpose of an agency providing any stipend at all is to give the organization some investment in the internship and thus some interest in seeing that the intern is used on assignments which will provide him a challenge. Interns who provide significant services to the agency can then receive feedback in terms of their management judgment and effectiveness. The salary offered by the New York State program goes quite a bit beyond this and, in fact, the agency has a significant commitment to the intern. In fact, the salary here is so high that it could deter the intern from taking calculated risks in developing proposals and recommendations as well as in reacting openly to the administrative environment he experiences. With a salary near $10,000 the intern may approach his internship in the state so intensely that much of the growth opportunity in the internship could be set aside in favor of building himself into a job, in blissful ignorance of the fact that effective interns usually grow into organizations and are asked to stay on.

New York State offers fifty-seven internships annually in forty-four agencies, including the full range of departments, the State University of New York, the legislature, and the State Health Planning Commission. The state publishes an annual catalogue listing each of the fifty-seven internships, the office, the supervisor, and a brief description of the assignment.

While not currently committed to internship programs on a New York or California scale, Maryland has had several imaginative pieces of legislation in recent legislature sessions. House Bill No. 666 proposed setting up executive or management internship programs as well as legislative internships. It qualifies as model legislation for such a program. The bill sets four goals for state executive internship programs:

1. To provide training in, and develop a realistic understanding of, executive process public policy formation for graduate and professional students attending colleges and universities.

2. To provide assistance for key departmental officials in the executive branch of state government.

3. To develop academic interest in state government with an emphasis on the executive branch.

4. To deepen the political and governmental involvement of graduate and professional students.[12]

The importance and high expectations of the program are reflected in the location of the program in the governor's office. This proposed legislation would provide an executive internship under the direct supervision of the governor's chief of staff. The potentials of the program to meet the goals set forth in the legislative proposal are given a fairly good chance of success by providing that interns would serve "as special assistants to key officials and departments of the Executive Branch of State government."[13] The opportunities for both the state and the intern to benefit from the internship are optimized by calling for a one-year internship. Salaries would be set in accordance with state personnel policy, with academic credit to be determined by a selection committee composed of state personnel, academicians, a citizen-member-at-large, and representatives of the college or university sponsoring the intern. The bill also broadens the state internship program to allow it to function "as a complementary part of federal and local internship programs."[14]

American Political Science Association Interns

In addition to individual universities and state governments, national organizations also have taken an interest in the development of state management internship programs. Two of the most prominent have been the Ford Foundation and American Political Science Association (ASPA), which has conducted a state and local government internship program since 1967 under the financial sponsorship of the Ford Foundation. By 1970, 105 interns from twenty-seven political science departments had been sponsored as interns.[15]

Table 7.1 has been developed from data contained in a report of that program. It shows the significant dominance of local management internships over state management internships and of state legislative internships over state management internships. Further, the category of state management internships includes internships in the offices of the governor, lieutenant governor, and other elected officials, and the research topics assigned to the interns are weighted toward the study of legislative and political behavior. Local management internships, on the other hand, tended to include areas such as air pollution, emergency services planning, program administration, planning, and program evaualuation. It would be expected that the research areas pursued by APSA interns would naturally be oriented toward political behavior while research topics selected by interns from professional organizations such as the International City Managers' Association would be oriented toward administrative behavior and analysis.

Table 7.1 reveals that a majority of the APSA interns who went to state government for their internships probably did so for one of two reasons. First, most of the interns were from state-financed universities and contracts with state officials might be greater than with local officials. Second, state government – both executive and legislative – represents a more political atmosphere than local government, which has tended to become more professionalized. Also the emphasis by APSA on state government internships is compatible with national trends to revitalize state government. Achieving that goal requires research to discover not only what changes need to be made, but the most likely way in which to effect those changes. The emphasis in the APSA program is on research vis-à-vis administrative or political experience and often results in a dissertation or thesis. Some universities in the program, such as the University of Iowa and Iowa State University, have only state level interns. They were placed in the administration, in political parties, in pressure groups, and in the legislature.[16]

Table 7.1. Assignments of 104 APSA Interns[a] – 1967-68, 1968-69, and 1969-70

	1967-68	1968-69	1969-70	Total
Local Management[b]	8	16	15	39
Local Legislative	1	3	2	6
State Management[b]	3	12	12	27
State Legislative[c]	7	10	15	32
Total	19	41	44	104

[a] Only 104 interns are included in the APSA data.

[b] Including elected executives.

[c] Including legislative councils.

Source: American Political Science Association, THE STATE AND LOCAL GOVERNMENT INTERNSHIP PROGRAMS OF THE AMERICAN POLITICAL SCIENCE ASSOCIATION, report to the Ford Foundation for 1967-68, 1968-69, 1969-70, pp. 10-20.

The APSA report also includes subjective evaluations of various individual interns and their success and problem areas. Some of the most valuable of the intern criticisms presented thoughts from which future interns could profit. For example, while one intern was lauded for his success in working himself into the office, the depth of his involvement became apparent in his research papers and created professional-ethical problems for the city manager. The topic of the paper in itself revealed the sensitive nature of the area he was probing: leadership requirements of the city manager. The evaluation of the university types who were reviewing the intern's program indicated, "there is question . . . in our minds as to whether the intern was not given too much access to too many phases of city operation. He may have proved a little too stimulating for the blood of an effective, but generally conservative, administrative situation."[17] If the research paper by the intern created the magnitude of difficulty indicated, the issue is not whether the intern received "too much access," but whether the intern had sufficient maturity to recognize the degree of confidence placed in him.

One of the goals of an internship is to develop the kind of open relationship implied. If the intern violates the relationship, he undercuts his stature in the agency and reduces the learning opportunities of future interns. This is not to say interns should not rock the boat, for internships are a time when the student is stretching his interests and abilities. The goal *is* to pursue growth, but not at the expense of co-workers, agency missions, and future interns.

In addition to professional kinds of feedback related to behavior in the specific assignment, students often receive other constructive feedback on their skills. For example, interns have been evaluated in terms of their ability as academic writers, their skills as administrative-political analysts, and their ability in separating and integrating theory and practical observation. Interns have indicated that the experience in these various agencies and legislatures became a feedback mechanism for their respective academic programs. One of the APSA interns in an urban public health department indicated, "the knowledge I have acquired this summer has significantly supplemented my academic program. It has provided me with a much greater background to continue my formal studies. I will return to the university seminars in political science with an intense interest in seeking answers to new questions about how a political scientist can professionally contribute more effectively in the development and conduct of public policy."[18]

Some of the assignments directed toward state interns reflect the need for greater professionalism and the shortage of qualified professionals in state management positions. One intern was assigned a job of assembling from the various state departments a check list of information that was required by the governor's office to establish the required comprehensive federal grant review process. "In addition to simply collecting information he was entrusted with the responsibility for recommending, as the complexities of a general grant review process became clearer, what information was most needed to be collected, and he assisted in framing the questionnaires for both initial and continuing survey."[19] Not only was the intern maintained as an employee after the internship but his project also represented the groundwork of a Ph.D. dissertation. Still another intern was assigned responsibility for establishing the procedures for setting up a law enforcement management information system.

Some interns have shown a real propensity for establishing close rapport with their supervisors. The degree of this rapport is often indicated both by the nature of the assignments and by the degree of responsibilities surrounding the assignments. One intern was so effective that the governor of the state where he was interning asked him to stay on the staff to prepare his legislative program. Another intern to a governor developed a relationship which led to his appointment to recommend the disposition of patronage problems and to provide the governor with analyses of legislative proposals and recommendations. Still another intern in a governor's office established a relationship with his supervisor which the intern summarized in the following way: "From the beginning, he included me in all staff meetings and did not refrain from giving me information which was classified for within the walls of the office. Without full participation, I feel that the intern suffers greatly. He must be a part of the staff if his experience is to go beyond the level of a research assistant."[20]

The high expectations of internships are not only limited to the interns and their professors. West Virginia Governor Hulett C. Smith said, "The need for this type of program has long been evident. The development of needed managerial and executive talent for state government has been a goal of this administration. Through this pilot program we might be able to train additional competent and well-qualified individuals, who will, in turn, train people for government service."[21]

The Changing Role of Governors

Probably one of the more significant misconceptions about state government centers around the executive branch and more specifically the chief executive or governor. Popular conceptions of the governor generally give him credit for much more power than he actually has. Until recent years, a governor's primary role has been that of "keeping his legislature in line, politics, and part leadership."[22] Recent years have seen a rather drastic change in the role of the governor from that of a politico to that of a public manager. This change in roles has been spread over several decades as most major governmental reform movements are. The new demands of governmental effectiveness, scientific management and technology, and public pressure to deliver services have led to a general strengthening of the governor's hand in securing the tools necessary to establish "unity of command, effective coordination, internal responsibility, and administrative leadership."[23] However, in spite of the constitutional and judicial limitations on the powers of the governor, every governor has some control over appointment of personnel, the budget, and supervisory powers. These three vital management areas coupled with "the political strength, personal appeal, or custom," centered in the person of a given governor could well indicate the availability of wider and more effective powers than may be specifically granted.

In addition to these real and potential powers of management, governors have acquired powers of executive initiative and support for legislative proposals. At the same time most state legislatures have not been inclined to criticize governors for overextending their powers in such areas. While jealous of their powers legislators have been experiencing the same kinds of pressures as the governor to produce greater effectiveness and efficiency of government programs and policy development. Further, most legislative decision-makers have neither the time nor the staff to perform the kind of watchdog role over the governor and executive branch they would like to; this factor is accentuated in states where legislatures are convened biannually or when called into special session by the governor. In the latter case, the governor has specific powers over the legislature.

As the executive and administrative demands on the governor have been increasing, the time he has available to devote to these kinds of duties has been decreasing. More and more, governors are finding it absolutely essential to delegate management decision-making to departmental executives in order to provide the time necessary for state-wide leadership and policy issues. These demands have become so pressing in recent years that as described by Grant and Nixon,

the lack of previous experience in public administration makes some analysts doubt whether the elective governor can perform effectively as the general manager of state administration. The most frequent proposals for improvement are to increase the governor's professional staff assistants to make his time count for more in the administrative field, or to create an office of assistant governor. This official would be, in effect, a highly paid director of administration responsible to the governor. Occasionally the state manager plan is proposed along the lines of the council manager plans for cities.[24]

All of these demands and proposals lead to the conclusion that in order for state government to assume the position in public policy and service delivery demanded by state constituencies and required to meet federal program guidelines, increased managerial effectiveness is needed in state policy and program areas. Thus the response, in addition to internships, has been the widespread establishment of state management training and executive development programs for upgrading the existing management and support of staffs.

State Management Internship Survey

Internships have become a hallmark of relevant academic and professional public management training programs. A survey of state internship programs conducted by the author in 1972 indicated that thirty-seven of the forty-four states responding have established some form of management internship in the respective state administrations. Each state shows some propensity for uniqueness in its approach to internships by introducing different elements. This means that at this stage of internship development in the states, generalizations are elusive and far from definitive.

The most striking observation is the diversity of structure apparent from state to state. For example, Alabama, Florida, Ohio, Oregon, and Pennsylvania respondents indicated that the internships at the state level were available on a scattered, ad hoc basis. In these states there is no central state-level coordination either among schools or the agencies. Often internships are arranged between individual professors and department or division heads. These internships may be offered regularly or only when a particular course is offered by a particular professor. When the course is offered, the instructor calls his contact at the state level to arrange an internship or two. Thus the specific structures represented in the states vary widely. Qualifications, pay, duration, and credit may vary among individual students in the same class depending on projects and goals.

On the other hand, several states have highly organized and centralized internships available to students in various learning and financial situations. Massachusetts. for example, has centralized internships in the Division of Civil Service where a catalogue of generalist and specialist internships is developed (including local-level internships). While these internships claim the goals of participant observation for the student, the primary goals enunciated in the announcement document are (1) financial support and (2) recruitment. Massachusetts emphasizes the financial aspect of the internships somewhat more by requiring that nearly 90 percent of the interns have financial needs sufficient to qualify for the work-study program.[25]

Thus internships in state government are an expanding part of state administrative organizations. State management internships probably are developing rapidly to make up for lost time and to meet growing public demands for results at the state level. Further, by their definitions of their state programs the respondents have shown the split in academia over the issue of the role of internships in academic and professional training. Just over one-half of the states for which there are responses indicate they grant academic credit for internships. In seven of the twelve states where credit is offered, the programs are partially or fully summer programs, indicating some reluctance to commit real classroom time to the participant-observer approach to learning. The requirements of the various programs in terms of papers or theses varies too. Some states require subjective, impressionistic reports while others require in-depth, analytical research projects.

There is also some ambiguity in terms of whether the program is to be administered by the state or by the university. This uncertainty is indicated in selection, administration, and the whole question of pay vis-à-vis credit. Part of the ambiguity undoubtedly is generated by the historic independence of the university from the state and the sometimes grudging attempts in recent years on the part of the universities to accept an active role in governmental problem-solving. The real and imagined myth of the "ivory tower" also had to be overcome. If the universities have been reluctant co-workers, so have the states. While often pronouncing their eager acceptance of *any* help the universities could offer and speaking of the great stores of knowledge and research skills available, the state legislators and administrators have been slow to invite real university involvement. The Intergovernmental Personnel Act discussed in chapter 16 should act as a facilitating mechanism in advancing this interaction.

Internships have provided a tool for building a bridge to break down the isolation. For governments, new resources have been made available at a bargain-basement price. For the universities, real data and opportunities to be involved in real problems have become accessible. The third and most important element, the intern, has become more informed and has been given inputs necessary to raise the right questions in his academic setting.

Conclusion

State management internship and development programs are growing at the same time the public administration role of the state is growing at an ever-increasing rate. Caught between pressures from federal agencies and local governments, states are responding. This response is evident in the acceleration of state reorganization movements since World War II. As early as 1952 thirty-three states had established "little Hoover" commissions to propose reorganization plans that would lead to more effective state level administration.[26]

At the same time state governments were reemerging, the academic community also has been seeking new avenues of application and experimentation. It has been found that some of the most significant learning and developmental experiences occur when the ideas of the classroom mix with the practicalities of the real administrative world. Thus the universities are moving toward experimentation precisely at the time when the states are reaching out for new talent and ideas.

Many states have been able to take advantage of these two trends. Significant internship programs have taken firm hold in several states. At the same time training and development programs have been expanding into executive development in addition to clerical and traditional production employee training. Revenue sharing requirements will result in additional pressures on state governments to improve their management systems and upgrade their personnel.

Notes

1. Frank H. Bailey, "State Manpower and Training Needs," *Civil Service Journal,* April-June 1970, p. 4.

2. Citizens Conference on State Legislatures, *Report on an Evaluation of the 50 State Legislatures,* Kansas City, Missouri, 1971, pp. 27-28.

3. Telephone conversation with E. P. Everett, California State Training Officer, April 1, 1972.

4. Interview with Mrs. Nanette Blandin, Assistant to the Director, California State Scholarship and Loan Commission, January 3, 1973.

5. California, *State Education Code,* Division 23, Section 35000, September 2, 1970.

6. Ibid., 35001.

7. Ibid., 35200.

8. Ibid., 35106.

9. Ibid., 35255, Section 2.

10. New York Department of Civil Service, "Public Administration Internships, June 1971-June 1972," p. 2.

11. Ibid., p. 6.

12. Maryland House of Delegates, House Bill No. 667 to be added to Article 41 of the Annotated Code of Maryland as a section of "Governor-executive and administrative departments," subtitle "Executive Internship Program" Section 430, subsections 1, 2, 3 and 4, March 1, 1972.

13. Ibid., Section 431, subsection d.

14. Ibid., Section 431, subsections c, g, and i.

15. American Political Science Association, *The State and Local Government Program of the American Political Science Association,* report to the Ford Foundation, for 1967-68, 1968-69, 1969-70, p. 1.

16. Ibid., pp. 21-23.

17. Ibid., pp. 25-26.

18. Ibid., pp 26-29.

19. Ibid., p. 39.

20. Ibid., pp. 48, 52, 58, and 60.

21. "State Plans Government Intern Plan," Charleston Gazette, Charleston, West Virginia, December 17, 1967, cited in APSA report, appendix D.

22. Daniel R. Grant and H. C. Nixon, *State and Local Government in America* (Boston: Allyn and Bacon, 1968), p. 319.

23. Ibid., p. 320.

24. Ibid., p. 334.

25. Bureau of Personnel and Standardization, State of Massachusetts, *Handbook of Student Internship Program,* pp. 2-3.

26. Grant and Nixon, *State and Local,* p. 340.

8

State Legislative Internships

THOMAS P. MURPHY

In the past decade a number of studies and books on state government have pointed up the need for upgrading legislative staff work. The latest to be written is a comprehensive report under the auspices of the Citizens Conference on State Legislatures, which attempts to evaluate and rank the fifty state legislatures in terms of their capacity to enact effective legislation. This legislative evaluation study was based upon factors deemed valid in measuring the potential of the legislature to do its job. General factors used in the analysis were: functionality, accountability, information-handling capability, independence, and representativeness. The top ten states in the ranking were California, New York, Illinois, Florida, Wisconsin, Iowa, Hawaii, Michigan, Nebraska, and Minnesota.[1]

The need to upgrade state legislatures is evident, but the problems in the legislative process are not confined to the halls of legislatures. Various surveys and reports indicate that slight attention is paid by our universities and colleges to social science courses dealing with the state government. Improving the state governments will not be possible without adequate support from our educational institutions, upon which rests the task of improving the level of staff services in the state legislatures. Increasingly the nation's universities are finding a contribution to be made which is of benefit to both the legislature and the campus. This contribution is the legislative internship program. Currently two-thirds of the states have some form of internship available to university students, even if only on an informal basis. While some twenty-one states maintain programs that are predominantly, if not wholly devoted to undergraduates, it cannot be denied that all such programs provide the legislature with at least some brief acquaintance with the benefits of receiving staff services.

Results of a state-by-state survey by the author of legislatures and associated private and state universities indicate that only nine states have neither experimented with internship programs nor shown any official desire to do so. These states are: Alabama, Arkansas, Louisiana, Mississippi, Missouri, Nebraska, New Mexico, South Carolina, and Wyoming. Five of the nine ranked between 42nd and 50th in the Citizen Conference analysis. In some of these states it is expected that this record may be subject to change as other more vital refinements are undertaken and achieved. All forty-one remaining states have at one time had or currently operate a legislative internship program.

109

Figure 8.1. Geographic Distribution of Legislative Internship Programs

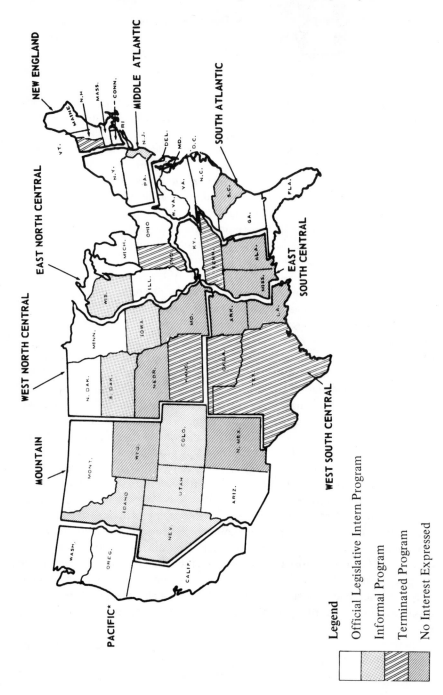

Legend

Official Legislative Intern Program

Informal Program

Terminated Program

No Interest Expressed

Figure 8-1 indicates the present pattern of program adoptions and non-adoptions. All areas in white have an "official" legislative internship program, while those areas shaded with dots currently maintain an informal program, often on an individual basis with specific state legislators. Other shadings indicate program terminations or nonadoptions.

Apparently internship programs are most favored by those states having a predominantly urban orientation, or located in one of the major urban corridors. Most of the more active states are located on the East or West Coasts, and the big-city states of the central Midwest — Illinois, Michigan, and Ohio — also have programs.

Many of the more successful programs, such as those in California and New York, were origianlly begun with assistance from the Ford Foundation beginning in 1957. Twleve states and the commonwealth of Puerto Rico have hosted Ford programs and at least two other states — Florida and Wisconsin — have internship programs as a result of spinoff from the Ford Foundation effort.[2] Those programs that have failed to produce were located in the heartland of the nation where apparently the crunch in legislative staff services is not yet being felt. In a few instances, however, competent staff services have already been developed through other mechanisms. Kansas was the first state in the union to develop a legislative research council, and Indiana converted its internship program into support for permanent staff services.

Benefits and Objectives of Legislative Internships

While no cause and effect relationship between internships and legislative "professionalization" has ever been shown, most observers feel that some valid correlation exists between the initiation of university sponsored programs and the upgrading of legislative staff services, particularly with regard to research activities. The joint efforts of university and state to remedy both academic and legislative deficiencies have resulted in the development of legislative internships in thirty-nine states since 1957.

Legislative internship programs contribute to both academic and legislative environments. The opportunity to be in the processes of state government from the perspective of the legislator is a tremendous educational experience for budding political scientists and lawyers. The very weakness of traditional legislative staffing has provided an opportunity for aggressive young interns to fill a need in performing at levels for which they never would have been hired. As these students carry their experiences back to the classroom the educational system itself is enriched by the pilot programs of the legislature. Many students who might never have considered an internship or career position with government have been favorably impressed with the pride of experienced interns as well as with the scope of the problems they have had the privilege of resolving. This has led many of the newer students to follow the path to public service.

Although legislative employment patterns are leveling off, many interns hired in the early years of state programs have had the good furtune of being retained in a professional capacity following the conclusion of their internships. Such occurrences have not been a surprise to knowledgeable legislative observers. Where else could a legislature find such experienced and interested young people to serve its needs? Aside from the professionalism they lend, the interns – now full-time employees – have through their nonpartisan employment been able to lend stability to the legislative leadership during periods of interparty shift. Heretofore, legislatures were generally at the mercy of fortune in securing qualified legislative staff personnel, inasmuch as those personnel who did reach a level of high achievement were often replaced in the event of party turnover.

A further dividend to the legislature has been the provision of standards for employment of legislative staff. Many states report that before the inauguration of an internship program, few legislators had any particular idea as to the nature and quantity of service they should be receiving from their staff. Interns, on the other hand, have provided the touchstone of quality upon which to base the hiring of other personnel. So important has been the impact that in fact many interns who began their experience as casual observers became in the normal course of events indispensable to their respective offices.

The degree of success in recruiting experienced interns for staff positions has not been well documented, but a few states have sustained intern programs long enough for suitable observations to be made. In California many of those in the early intern classes were immediately pressed into service within the California Assembly. "Nearly half of the interns in the first five years of the program subsequently served as full-fledged members of the Assembly staff."[3] The most famous alumnus of the California "class of 1957" is Chief Clerk of the Assembly James Driscoll. As these early interns moved into positions of responsibility, less room was available for the oncoming graduates; however, widespread professionalization of the assembly staff has made these positions all the more desirable. By 1965 more than one-third of the eighty-eight interns who had served in the program were in government at one level or another. Consequently the intern program is now operating very successfully on the basis of its reputation for placing qualified persons in government.[4]

The objectives of legislative internship programs tend to vary slightly from state to state: however, most may be said to contain more similarity than difference. Many of the early programs, including those of California, Wisconsin, Illinois, and Oklahoma were programs supported through the grants of the Ford Foundation. Due to this commonality of funding, most internship programs list three major purposes: to demonstrate the value of staff services for the state legislature, to strengthen academic programs in the training and "practical" education of students in the legislative process, and to foster research in the area of legislative studies. The wording of the statements of program objectives is characteristically couched in idealistic terms. Florida, for instance, speaks of providing graduate students "with an opportunity to become actively involved in legislative activities,"[5] while Georgia claims to provide "a meaningful and realistic experience for college students in the legislative process."[6] New York seeks "to provide intensive and practical training in the processes of legislation and public policy formulation for a selected group of graduate students."[7] Each of these statements makes certain assumptions as to the success of student involvement in the legislative process. However, as inquiries with experienced interns have shown, the intensity of the experience may be somewhat less than that which might be presumed from the above statements.

On the other hand, statements of objectives as they pertain to legislative benefit generally manage to avoid overstatement. Usually it is matter-of-factly mentioned that the program intends to provide professional staff assistance or otherwise provide a genuine service for understaffed legislatures. From this comparison one might question whether legislative internship programs assume a greater prospect of success for academic as opposed to legislative interests. On these terms it would have to be stated that research objectives are given the least chance of realistic success inasmuch as they receive by far the least attention of the three program objectives.

Advantages to the student from the legislative internship program will usually include in addition to the intangible benefits of experience the granting of stipends and academic credit. Stipends currently appear to vary anywhere from $100 total to $600 per month, depending upon the design of the program. States such as California, Illinois, New York, and, surprisingly enough, North Dakota provide the higher compensations for intern assistance. Generally these programs assume a certain degree of professional talent on the part of their interns and provide proper motivation in exchange for demanding time expectations. Undergraduate programs, by contrast, may seek only to cover the costs of transportation for the students. In these cases the stipend will vary according to such factors as the amount of money available and the quantity of expenses generally incurred per intern. But dollar compensation is of course only one of the returns to the intern.

In addition, the intern receives experience, contacts, "practical" education, and is often times provided with academic credit upon completion of a research paper or other assignments in conjunction with satisfactory completion of an academic seminar and a satisfactory work evaluation. The pattern of academic credit may vary according to the prevailing academic system, and it ranges from three semester hours of graduate credit in many states to fifteen semester hours of undergraduate credit in Kentucky. Where more than one academic institution is involved, it is not uncommon for each individual institution to grant its own credit on its own terms. Credit granted is usually based upon the length of assignment as well as the requirements placed upon the intern for academic "production."

Financing

As has been observed, most of the outside funding for state legislative internship programs has been provided by the Ford Foundation. In fact, almost all of the programs begun prior to 1967 were initiated with Ford support. All in all, the foundation had provided assistance to twelve states and Puerto Rico by December 1966, and even though most programs were funded only for the duration of the first several years until the program reached maturity, the foundation still carried five states in its books as late as September 30, 1968.[8] By that date California's nine-year grant had expired. The Ford financing pattern was somewhat erratic, due to the reliance placed by Ford upon personal persuasion of potentially amenable state and university officials as well as by proselytizing from California and, later, other Ford program states. Also highly critical, of course, were the changing political climates of the several states. Many legislatures proved hard to convince, and support even eroded in a few established programs.

Some states drew other private support. For example, Connecticut began its program in 1969 with the combined support of the Sears, Roebuck and Company ($2,500), the Connecticut League of Women Voters ($200), Pratt and Whitney Aircraft Corporation ($400), the Bridgeport Hydraulic Company ($100) and the Connecticut Education Association ($100). As this money became exhausted, the financial requirements of the internship program were met through state appropriations, as is the case in most other states. In 1970, the amount appropriated by the Connecticut legislature came to $10,000 with $6,400 used to pay salaries, $3,500 used for administrative costs and $100 allocated to overhead.

Another state with private financing is the state of Florida. This program began in 1967 on a much larger scale with support being provided by the American Political Science Association through the Ford grant for state and local government internships. Under the current arrangement, APSA provides $1,000 per year for each intern hired after the first six, which are wholly supported by the state of Florida. To illustrate how this works, Florida employed nine interns in 1968, twelve in 1969, and eleven in 1970; APSA grants for these three years were $3,000, $6,000, and $5,000 respectively. In program year 1970 the total budget for the Florida program approximated $70,000 total of which the $5,000 grant from APSA was but a small part.[9]

Other states considered donation and contributions by private colleges within the state to be "outside" support. An example is the state of New Hampshire, where Dartmouth College provides 45 percent of the total operating fund for the program. The other participating colleges in the New Hampshire program are state supported, and thus the state contribution is said to be 55 percent. North Carolina, which initiated a program in 1962 under state support, has since 1965 received operating funds from participating colleges.

Differences in funding levels by states are often accounted for by the breadth of individual programs. For instance, California and New York, which only maintain programs in one house of the legislature, would undoubtedly be head and shoulders above all other states in terms of budget if their programs operated in both houses of the respective legislatures. Another factor is the time for which interns are employed. Kentucky and Connecticut maintain programs only during the spring semester, while most programs are apparently run on a nine- to twelve-month basis. Recently Ohio has adopted an internship program that runs for the duration of a two year master's degree schedule. Georgia, Iowa, New Hampshire, and North Dakota are states that operate their internships concurrently with the legislative session. Thus it is futile to compare program budgets until the duration of the program and the number of interns employed in each state has been reduced to some comparable level of study.

Selection and Placement of Interns

With regard to selection criteria, Don Herzberg is of the opinion that much more than an acceptable level of academic attainment is necessary to make for a good intern. He states, "it is these requirements — a greater degree of extrovertism, an enhanced ability to write clearly, succintly, and under pressure, a commitment to politics, and an appreciation of the role of a politican — that are rarely reflected in the present criteria governing the selection of academic fellows."[10] Respondents in several states, most notably Florida, indicated that they experienced difficulty in predicting the potential of an intern during the selction process. Perhaps these problems are a function of traditional reliance upon grade point averages as tools in the selection process. Florida points out that selection is extremely crucial because it is very difficult to eliminate an intern from the program after he has started work. This is in part due to the complications that would result academically.

On the brigher side, North Carolina indicates that the prime reason for program success has been the effectiveness of the selection process.[11] North Carolina has apparently had extremely large competition for the twenty available internship positions and this had made it possible to select top-flight interns. North Carolina uses a selection committee composed of five faculty members from participating educational institutions to screen applications and determine who should be interviewed. The committee also conducts the interviews and makes the final choices. It found the most success in "looking not especially for the student with the highest academic record, or the longest list of extra-curricular achievements, but rather the student with a good mind, demonstrated leadership ability, broad interests, and a desire to tackle the problems facing the people of North Carolina."[12]

Interns for the California program are selected by a board including academic and legislative members, plus two staff members from the Assembly Rules Committee. In addition to a review of the student's academic record, the selection process includes an extensive interview. Victor Jones of the University of California at Berkely, while serving as chairman of the Executive Committee of the California Legislative Internship Program, stated: "There has been no appeal from nor overruling of, the interviewing committee, although on very infrequent occasions, the interviewing board has recommended that an applicant be subsequently re-interviewed by other persons within the Assembly, or its staff.[13]

Placement is also a careful process in California. During the orientation period, committee chairmen are provided with background data on the interns and are asked to select interns for their committees. Of course the placement process also considers the assignment preferences of interns. Jesse Unruh stresses the need to make prompt assignments of new interns so that their enthusiasm does not wane while a decision is being made. Finding suitable assignments is sometimes difficult, "Not only because the interns, with some exceptions, are usually not specialists in the matters with which committees deal, but because personalities may well clash between highly individualistic legislators and a 'newcomer from the outside.' "[14]

The assignment process is especially important in those programs where the interns are not frequently rotated. Unruh expressed the opinion that it takes an intern three or four months to become adjusted to a particular office and that if an intern is later transferred this process would then have to be repeated. He adds, "furthermore, the most valuable experience the intern has is in 'living with' a piece of legislation or a program of legislation from its formulation through its progress in the legislature, and this chain may be broken by reassignment."[15]

The specific assignment mechanisms in the various state internship programs fall into one of three categories:

1. Assignment by a chief legislator or a representative of the legislature
2. Assignment by the educational institution with the cooperation of the legislature
3. Assignment by a committee composed of legislature and academic representatives

In any of these cases, the availability of positions for assignment depends in large part on the needs of the legislature at that time as well as the preferences of individual interns.

Program Control

The successful faculty advisor must have the capacity to identify situations in which his intervention is necessary. While the faculty advisor should generally intervene as little as possible, on occasion, "because of a mismatch of intern with job, a clash of personalities or a complete misunderstanding of the role of an intern, problems do arise that require tactful but fast action." Usually a discussion between the advisor and the intern supervisor, rather than direct intervention, will correct a problem or misunderstanding. "The advisor is the buffer and he must often be available to both the student and the agency."[16]

In the final analysis, the success of a program often depends upon the creation of successful relations among legislators, interns, and the faculty advisor. The faculty advisor must insure that the legislator fully understands the nature of the program so that the may accurately interpret program objectives to members of his staff who will be dealing with the intern. More importantly perhaps, if a busy legislator does not fully comprehend the importance of the program, chances are that he will not sacrifice his personal time to cultivate relationships with the interns. Under such adverse circumstances the program is bound to suffer, and other students may lose their opportunity to serve if the program should be curtailed.

Regarding the importance of proper coordination, a report to the Ford Foundation prepared by journalist Whitman Bassow suggested in 1968 that the part-time arrangement of so many program faculty advisors was hurting the operation of internships by allowing inexperienced students to enter a full-time job without providing adequate supervision.[17] Students became disgruntled when no one was available to give advice. Legislators, many of whom felt too busy to offer their time, still became dissatisfied to see improperly supervised interns "waste their time." A full-time coordinator would remedy much of this malfunctioning, but closer attention by experienced faculty would also serve to alleviate much of the current unhappiness.

Thus an important decision involves the choice of the right person to be the program faculty advisor. To be effective, the faculty advisor must have the respect of his colleagues and of the personnel of the agencies with which he deals. Donald Herzberg and Jesse Unruh assert, "Ideally, he should be both a scholar and a man who may have had some experience as a governmental or political advisor himself."[18] The faculty advisor must also exhibit a high degree of sensitivity towards people. To insure the success of the legislative internship program, the faculty advisor must also exhibit a high degree of sensitivity towards people. To insure the success of the legislative internship program, the faculty advisor must discuss the specific goals of the program with his counterpart in the legislature. Failure on the part of the legislators to understand the objectives of this program will decrease the effectiveness of the program and lead to its termination.

A further responsibility of the faculty advisor is the administration of a regularly scheduled academic seminar. Herzberg and Unruh express the view that "given the diversity of the job experiences the interns are likely to have, it takes a great deal of ingenuity to arrange a seminar that will be helpful and meaningful to the interns."[19] The faculty advisor must accurately perceive the needs of the students when constructing the seminar format. For example, do they need exposure only to the operation of their particular state legislature or should they have broad exposure to the legislative process? And "should the thrust of the seminar rest on the bringing in of a stream of outside speakers, such as legislators, staff people, budget officers, and other representatives of the executive branch?"[20] If the seminar is given for credit, the faculty advisor must determine how much time should be devoted to reading and research, but without assigning so much that the intern is unable to complete his staff assignments. All of these considerations make the faculty advisor and program control the key to effective legislative internships.

Program Variations and Evaluations

As indicated in table 8-1, thirty-three legislative internship programs were in operation in 1971. Programs vary from state to state depending upon the size of the program, the university participation, whether the state has annual or biennial sessions, and whether graduate or undergraduate students are involved. These distinctions and the institutional and historical differences can best be pointed up by reviewing a number of sample programs, including a Ford-sponsored program which succeeded, one which failed, and a number of non-Ford programs which achieved varying degrees of success.

Certain shortcomings have been identified within the Ford programs and it might do well to keep some of these in mind. The 1968 Bassow report, besides pointing to poor coordination on the part of university advisors on part-time appointment, also noted inadequacies in the areas of academic seminars, staff utilization of interns, the recruitment process, low stipends, internal communication, and minority group hiring.[21]

The academic seminars were uniformly felt by students to be too removed from the day-to-day concerns of the interns. The Bassow report, however, has not been the first to air this allegation about seminars. Currently the battle appears to be not over reform of the seminar, but rather the complete rejection of the seminar as a teaching technique. In many states the seminar is losing out, but warns Professor Victor Jones: "Without the seminars, the internship becomes just another job."[22]

Another Donnybrook has formed around the recruitment process, which many persons have felt to be too informal and subject to chance. In too many instances states have complained that not enough students applied for positions and too few of these included the highest caliber students at the participating schools. Three states that discontinued internship programs subsequent to termination of Ford financing reported insufficient applicants.[23]

California

The state of California was the first in the nation to initiate a modern legislative internship program. It has been perhaps the most successful of all current or past such programs. Starting in 1957 the Ford Foundation, through the University of California at Berkely, began to channel grant monies on a 50-50 matching basis into an internship program operating within the California State Assembly. The program was intended to serve three principle purposes:

Table 8.1.   Status of State Legislative Internship Programs, 1972

	Currently Operates Program	Program Now Terminated	Ford Foundation Grant[b]	Legislature to Implement, Revive, or Expand Internship Program
Alabama	--	--		--
Alaska				Expected to implement in House of Representatives.
Arizona	Yes			
Arkansas	--	--		--
California	Yes[a]		1957-65	
Colorado	Yes			
Connecticut	Yes			
Delaware	Yes			
Florida	Yes			
Georgia	Yes			
Hawaii	Yes		1962-68	
Idaho	Yes			
Illinois	Yes		1961-67	
Indiana		Yes	1961-67	
Iowa	Yes			
Kansas		Yes	1962-70	
Kentucky	Yes			
Louisiana	--	--		--
Maine	Yes			
Maryland	Yes[c]			Passed 1 house; died in closing minutes of 1972 legislature
Massachusetts	Yes		1965-69	
Michigan	Yes[a]		1963-69	
Minnesota	Yes			
Mississippi	--	--		--
Missouri	--	--		--
Montana	Yes			
Nebraska	--	--		--
Nevada	Yes			
New Hampshire	Yes			
New Jersey	Yes			
New Mexico	--	--		--
New York	Yes		1961-66	
North Carolina	Yes			
North Dakota	Yes			
Ohio	Yes		1963-68	
Oklahoma		Yes	1961-68	
Oregon	Yes			
Pennsylvania	Yes[a]			
Rhode Island	Yes			
South Carolina	--	--		--
South Dakota	Yes[c]			Formal passage killed in 1971 Session
Tennessee		Yes		Reinstatement subject to addition of physical space and better coordination
Texas		Yes	1964-69	
Utah	Yes			
Vermont		Yes		
Virginia	Yes		1961-68	
Washington	Yes			
West Virginia	Yes			
Wisconsin	Yes			
Wyoming	--	--		--
TOTALS	33	6	12 (& Puerto Rico)	2 (implementation)

[a] In House only.   [b] Operating years.   [c] Informal operation.

1. To provide training in the process of legislation and public policy formation for graduates and graduate students
2. To provide assistance to the members and committees of the state assembly as a supplement to the staff services already available
3. To foster research on the legislative process.[24]

As such, the program provides practical training in the legislative and policy-making processes. The program's application brochure describes its internships as being "designed especially for those who expect to follow careers in teaching, law, journalism, and public service."[25]

The program is a joint effort involving the state assembly with professional and graduate programs in the social sciences housed within various California educational institutions. In terms of career training, the program has proven to be an excellent source of practical experience for California graduate and professional students. "Of 136 interns who participated in the program during the first 13 years of operation, 50 accepted staff positions with the Assembly for brief or extended periods following completion of the internship."[26] Additionally, many students have found teaching positions within the state or accepted employment with district attorneys or county councils, leading in either case to a valuable enrichment of the ranks of public servants.

Besides being the first legislative intern program in the nation, California also holds the distinction of being the first legislative intern program to graduate to independent funding status. Since 1965, the program has been financed fully from state funds, with the current budget approximating $70,000. The program runs from September 1 through June 30 of the following year and generally employs an average of ten interns recruited on a roughly equal basis from graduate schools and law schools. Students are expected to be California residents with plans for future careers within the state.

The responsibility for recruiting interns into the California program is assigned to an academic and legislative board of directors called the Executive Committee. This committee is composed of six representatives from the public and private universities and colleges. A member of the assembly and two staff members from the Assembly Rules Committee are the legislative representative on the Executive Committee. The annual selections are based on the intern candidates' overall and specialization grade point averages, as well as personal interviews. The selection process is well ordered, with a specified application period running from early October until late January for the internship period commencing with the following fall. Documentation required to accompany an application includes the following: recommendation by a department head, transcript of academic record, essay or short statement concerning the candidate's motivation, plus three letters of recommendation from college instructors or others of similar stature.

Although no records have been kept regarding the number of applications for the available internship positions, it is said that California's program is one of the more popular. Not only does the intern receive academic credit for the successful completion of his internship with some colleges and universities, but the level of compensation for services rendered is also one of the highest in the nation for positions of this kind. In September of 1970 the stipend for the state assembly internship was raised from $440 to $600 per month, with this figure to be further raised to $650 per month for the 1971-72 internship period. The original 1957 stipend paid only $400 per month. All accredited private and public universities and state colleges may participate in the internship program.

Internship assignments are made cooperatively between the intern and the program director on the basis of individual interest and legislative need, with final approval for assignments being granted by the staff members of the Assembly Rules Committee. As the program has matured, increasing emphasis has been placed upon intern placement for maximum effectiveness. More care in assignment has been necessitated by the complexity of legislation and the increasingly specialized interests of the interns. It has been the practice to assign one intern each to the majority and minority parties for use either with individual leadership or with the prospective caucuses, with the balance of the interns being assigned to major policy committees. As in most other states, internship responsibilities are divided between research and administrative support.

The California program begins with a ten-day orientation for new interns covering a tour of facilities, an explanation of legislative organization, and an explanation of legislative procedures. Beyond this basic orientation to legislative activity, the interns are introduced to the functions of, and assembly relations with, lobbyists, the legislative council, the governor's office, the legislative analysts, and controller, etc. Throughout the program regularly scheduled discussion seminars are held for the benefit of interns. Although the submission of an essay or research paper was in the past required for successful completion of the internship, this practice has been dropped inasmuch as not all interns need to receive academic credit for their period of service. Presumably the individual academic institutions granting such credit still may require completion of scholarly assignments as an indication of educational advancement, although the program itself no longer requires such work. As a matter of record, interns are not now required to be registered students. Orientations and seminars persist, however, as a means of tying together the varied experiences of the interns with discussion of relevant political science theory vis-à-vis current political and legislative problems.

Like most successful internship programs, the California program contains a regular evaluation of program effectiveness. Annually the Executive Committee holds a session to review, criticize, and suggest improvement in the program. Members of the Assembly are queried as to their views of the program effectiveness and intern questionnaires are reviewed for their suggestions and criticisms. In addition to the successive annual reviews, the state's evaluation is supplemented by a Ford Foundation report carried out as a result of an agreement reached following the conclusion of their assistance to the program in 1966.

As reported by Mr. L. H. Lincoln in *State Government,* the program was patterned after the Congressional Intern Program of the American Political Science Association which had been operating since 1953.[27] According to Lincoln, past speaker of the California State Assembly, "the popularity of the Washington program among Congressmen and the keen competition among students stimulated the adoption of the program in the California State Assembly."[28] Credit for the successful initiation of the program is largely due to Professor Joseph Harris of the University of California at Berkeley, who successfully guided the initial phases of the program from his post as professor of political science. Professor Harris later worked with Mr. Matthew Cullen of the Ford Foundation to carry the success of the California Legislative Internship Program to other states in the middle and far west.

Following a celebrated Conference on Streamlining State Legislatures held in 1955, the University of California at Berkeley had assumed leadership for the development of a program to alleviate complaints by legislators of the lack of competent legislative staff. The university, naturally, found in this complaint an opportunity to provide graduate students with practical experience in an important segment of California political life. After fourteen years it is now self-evident that the resulting arrangement has been mutually beneficial for both legislative and educational communities.

A 1967 review of the California Legislative Internship Program compiled by Victor Jones, chairman of the Executive Committee of the California Legislative Internship Program, noted that "almost all interns felt that both their personal goals as well as the formal goals of the program had been achieved."[29] However, certain difficulties had arisen over the course of a decade of experience. Notable mention was given to the fact that legislative personnel and members of the Executive Committee had brought into question the caliber of the interns being recruited, inferring perhaps that the more outstanding students from university programs were not being actively solicited. Other mention was made of the fact that out of the first 101 interns appointed to the program, only 5 interns had received training outside of the fields of political science, journalism, and law. Furthermore, in the first nine years of operation the program had recruited only seven from institutions not represented on the Executive Committee. Nevertheless, a solution has not yet been found to alleviate this problem.

The same report brought to light that several selection committee members have in the past raised strong objections to the interviewing process. One assembly staff member was quoted as believing that " 'the interview really does not show much about the applicant' and that 'no one could effectively hire help on such a basis.' "[30] An academic member of the selection committee was remembered as having expressed the opinion that "the interview process reminded him in intensity of the Ph.D. qualifying exams."[31] Happily, the report was able to state that the quality level was such that even several interns who were originally selected as alternates and who later were accepted into the program have on the whole performed well.

Other topics of the Jones report dealt with the placement and work assignment of interns once selected for the internship program. As previously indicated, the program has experienced something of a "shakedown" in arriving at an effective method of intern placement. Significant adjustment problems were also experienced in determining an appropriate "mix" of legislative activities. Transfer of placements has presented an additional difficulty which has yet to be successfully resolved. Two hazards are present here: the risk that the intern may experience future interpersonal strain if he requests transfer and is not granted a secondary placement, and the risk that his transfer may reflect unfavorably upon him if someone is "blamed" for the difficulty. Yet a more ominous note was sounded in the report with the statement that "no intern group in any year has uniformly believed that his access to political and policy formulation has been high."[32]

Despite these and other problems, reaction to the program has been highly favorable. Most interns have regarded their experience as well worth the effort expended, while the assembly has benefited from the availability of professional staff assistance. The California program has now evolved to the point that it must bear slight resemblance to its original format. With luck and innovation, its excellence will continue. Not all programs have been so fortunate.

Oklahoma

The history of the Oklahoma program was somewhat unique. Inaugurated on December 1, 1961, by the State Legislative Council, policy decisions of the program were set by the council itself with only advisement coming from the cooperating graduate colleges and universities.

The general program objectives were threefold:

1. To provide practical and responsible experience in the legislative process for selected advanced students in the institutions of higher learning

2. To supplement research and general staff services to the Legislature

3. To develop through pilot projects new techniques in securing citizen participation in the lawmaking process[33]

The program was not directly fashioned after that of any other state. However, the impetus for the program came from one Dr. Joseph P. Harris of the Political Science Department at the University of California at Berkeley, who, as chairman of the Executive Committee of the California Legislative Internship Program, wrote to the executive director of the Oklahoma State Legislative Council in December of 1959[34] with information as to the California program and an offer of personal assistance in exploring the possibilities of beginning such a program under a grant from the Ford Foundation. The result was the establishment, under the guidance of the three chief officials of the Legislative Council, of a Special Committee on the Ford Foundation Internship Program which was to study the feasibility of such a program over the course of the next two years.

The Oklahoma Legislative Internship Program was thus a Ford Foundation program in its initiation, but unfortunately the program did not continue following expiration of the Ford Foundation grant. Most accounts of the program's failure mention specifically the failure of the recruitment process to attract enough qualified applicants. However, it should also be made clear as some have recognized that faculty participation in the program was limited because of legislative dominance. The program began in 1961 with a total of three interns and reached a peak employment of seven interns in 1964. Unlike the California example where matching funds were provided on a 50-50 basis by the Ford Foundation, Oklahoma's program was funded on a 35-65 basis with the Foundation picking up the larger share of program expenses. Most of the state contribution was of an in-kind nature. The Legislative Council was designated the sole participating sponsor.

Interestingly, while the Ford Foundation grant for the Oklahoma internship program was to cover a grant period of six years, only about $73,000 of the $117,000 grant was expended during the life of the grant. A measure of the lack of aggressiveness of the Oklahoma internship program is provided in the comparison between the total disbursement of Ford Foundation funds for the first five years of the Oklahoma program with the current expenditure of the California Assembly for its program, which rests at the $70,000 level. Local matching funds in Oklahoma totaled only a mere $10,250 per year, hardly enough to strain legislative budgets.

Duties of the Oklahoma interns included research and administrative support activities for committees, officers, and central research agencies of the legislature. During interim periods between legislative sessions, interns were assigned directly to the Legislative Council and its committees. It was intended that each intern, to the extent possible, be allowed to participate in all major phases of the legislative process, from research and bill-drafting through legislative enactment.

Like the California program, the Oklahoma internships were recruited from the ranks of graduate and law school students. Qualifications for intern positions included an acceptable personal interview, a specific academic rank, and a background within a specific academic discipline. Application for the twelve-month internship was relatively informal with a transcript of academic record and a short statement of personal motivation to be included with the candidate's completed application form for acceptance no later than September 1 of each year by the State Legislative Council. No academic credit was given for completion of the internship as no cooperation was ever effected between the Legislative Council and universities. Salaries provided were particularly anemic for a twelve-month program, resting at $300 per month. Interestingly enough, although no academic credit was given and although the compensation for services was exceedingly low, a uniform requirement for the submission of a research paper related to internship experience was included as a part of the program.

These conditions of the intern program might also help explain why the Legislative Council found it necessary to terminate the program following the lapse of the Ford Grant. Not only was Oklahoma operating under the premise that $3600 per year would secure the services of a promising graduate student, but it was trying to accomplish this without academic credit attached to the program. And yet, "it was anticipated at the outset that there would be little difficulty recruiting seven interns for the initial year of the program."[35]

Considering the circumstances it was not surprising that results did not measure up to expectations. The difficulties of the Selection Committee were outlined as follows in the first annual report of the project:

There was a plethora of applicants but very few met the minimum requirements set up by the selection committee. They were either not currently enrolled in school, or if enrolled, were not enrolled at a graduate level. By October the committee came to the conclusion that for the pilot year of the program they would have fewer than the seven authorized interns if the minimum qualifications were to be maintained. It was the unanimous opinion of the committee that the program would be better served with fewer interns possessing higher qualifications rather than lowering the qualifications for the sake of quantity.[36]

From a review of the applications, it was determined that only three applicants met minimum requirements. Following interviews, all three were appointed to the program. Of these three, one was forced to resign early in the program due to hospitalization for severe stomach ulcers, while a second intern took a teaching position in Kansas after two-thirds of the year had elapsed. This left one intern to complete the first year of the program. If morale were not bad enough, the Internal Revenue Service, contrary to practice in California, declared in a tax ruling that interns were employees of the state and as such were required to pay Federal Income Tax on their stipends. When the internship program was finally put to rest in 1968, the major reasons cited for the failure to assume responsibility for funding from the Ford Foundation were the lack of full university participation and the inability of the program to recruit enough qualified people.

In retrospect it is surprising that an oil-wealthy state such as Oklahoma could not find it feasible to afford more than $10,250 per year for semiprofessional staff assistance. Even with a limited amount of funds available, a workable program could have been salvaged by halving the number of internships so as to allow stipends to reach the level of $7200 per year of appointment. Role conflicts cited by the first annual report of the program suggest that some legislators might have regarded the experiment as either a "giveaway" or a "slave-labor" resource, each suggestion being equally unfortunate.

To the regret of those who favor the internship as an avenue to direct student participation in public affairs, many legislators have apparently underestimated the potential contribution of interns. It has usually been only through the favorable showing of the interns themselves that the program has progressed to a higher status within the eyes of legislative leaders. Witness the comment of New York State Senate Secretary Albert J. Abrams:

Our original idea was to send the interns back to academia with a realistic idea of the legislative process. We didn't expect help from them. We were simply trying to subvert the political science community. We got some good leg work and research out of them. Then a reappraisal developed and we decided to keep them on as staff. We also looked on them as a base for professional staffing of standing committees.[37]

The conclusion to be made from the Oklahoma program is simply this: that all good programs stand of their own accord, and that programs undertaken with less than full commitment will usually yield less than full success. Apparently the Oklahoma program did not gain the favor of any nucleus within the legislature. Nor did it enjoy the prominent support of a single individual, such as Speaker Jesse Unruh in California's State Assembly. Without this kind of support, and with the initial program impetus coming from outside the state, it is not surprising that the program was doomed to failure.

Miscellaneous non-Ford Internships

Having considered the California case, where strong legislative support carried a matching grant program, and the Oklahoma case, where legislative support was not enough to meet the challenge, let us now consider the case of the self-supporting, state-inspired internship program.

The Rhode Island legislative internship program is one of those that has recently been initiated without external funding support. This particular program began in 1969 in both houses of the state legislature. It had derived from experiments beginning in 1967 under the aegis of the Rhode Island Legislative Council, at which time twenty interns were employed. This number has remained stable in succeeding years and state funds for the program now amount to $6,000 per year with $4,000 of this money earmarked for intern stipends. The modest funding provided for the internship program may be explained in part by the duration of the internships. Each fall and spring interns are selected for a twelve-week internship, during which time academic credit may or may not be awarded upon completion. Whether credit is received depends upon the individual institution, as in many other states. Undergraduates as well as graduate students are selected for the internship positions, and it appears from this data plus the nature of the internships and explanatory material provided by the program that the major interest is academic rather than employment-oriented as in other states where intern programs are encouraged primarily as a means of updating legislative professional staff services.

Significantly, Rhode Island's program was not patterned after the experience of any other state, and this may explain the uniqueness of the program and its apparent strength. The fact that a need for a legislative internship program was perceived and acted upon within the state indicates that sufficient interest exists for the successful maintenance and possible expansion of this program.

Currently the program reflects its academic orientation. Applicants for intern positions must attend school at cooperating universities or colleges, these being thirteen in number, and must have sufficient academic standing within their school. Each of the thirteen universities or colleges has its own program coordinator, and recruitment of intern candidates is handled through these colleges separately. Each applicant must have in addition to his completed application form, a statement of motivation, as is required in other states, and a recommendation from his department head. Inasmuch as two separate intern programs are held each year, there are two separate application periods each year. An academic committee within the legislature is responsible for selecting interns, who receive $100 for the twelve-week internship period. The program is seemingly successful inasmuch as the number of applicants reached sixty students in 1970, or a 3 to 1 ratio of applicants to positions available.

Assignments are made on the basis of need as determined by the academic committee and including, of course, personal preferences of the interns. Interns are assigned to both house and senate research agencies, as well as to individual members of both the house and senate. Other departments of government are also assigned interns. Regular discussion seminars are held each week during the internship and provide a broad orientation to the legislature. Intern evaluations have been requested each year, and it appears that changes are forthcoming in the program.

Another program similar to Rhode Island's is that of the state of Georgia. Like The Rhode Island program, Georgia's legislative internships have always been completely financed from state funds, and place their primary emphasis on undergraduate education. Georgia's program, begun in 1970, employs approximately the same number of students, although the stipend at $350 per month for the duration of the legislative session is noticeably larger by comparison. This program demands large interest, with fifty and sixty interns having applied for the first two years of the program.

Although the program has been pronounced a success after its first year, several changes are being suggested by the program initiators.[38] In the first place, it has been noted that the senate and house had different intern programs, and the results indicate that consideration should be given to developing a common program between the chambers. Secondly, more attention is being given to selection and placement of interns, with selection choices to be made earlier in the year by each participating school operating independently. As interns are chosen, it is recommended that additional opportunities, such as placement within the Ways and Means and the Appropriations Committees, be offered to the most capable candidates. Further attention is being given to supervision aspects of the program with daily coordination being suggested as the best alternative among existing options. Much of this new emphasis has been inspired by intern comments to the effect that they have been underutilized in the first program year.

In this respect Georgia's program is not only like that of Rhode Island, but also represents the concerns of new undergraduate programs generally. Besides the Rhode Island and Georgia programs, roughly eighteen other states have predominantly undergraduate-oriented legislative internship programs. It is significant perhaps that of those programs having been initiated by the states themselves almost all have concerned themselves with undergraduate education. Of further interest is the fact that none of these programs has met with difficulties of a magnitude that would require termination or professionalization of the program as has been the case with several graduate and law student programs. The difference perhaps is that undergraduate programs are usually "home grown," and therefore less subject to divisive controversy.

Whether graduate programs are more difficult to administer is open to conjecture, but some indication exists that graduate students may tend to put more strain upon their sponsoring legislators. Whereas undergraduate students are content with only moderatly responsible duties and an occasional chance to observe the legislative process, graduate students by contrast are often found to be too aggressive in their pursuit of academic and personal challenge. Aside from their more aggressive maturity, graduate students are often operating under pressures placed upon them by peers and relatives, who in supporting the intern's endeavors may place upon him too much expectation to produce results. However, graduate students as well as undergraduate students often find it difficult to mesh properly within the traditional framework of legislative operations. Graduate students in particular can become bitter as they find themselves without any substantial duties or responsibilities.

The Outlook

A lesson to be learned from these observations may simply be that new internship programs must not try to expand too rapidly. Where too much has been expected of a program, and too little effort has been expended in laying program foundations, strains upon interns, legislators, and academic advisors alike may prove to be too heavy a burden to bear. On the other hand, those programs that begin modestly and persevere through the initial pangs of birth may in the long run outperform and outlast the more glamorous programs.

Currently there are a number of revisions in the academic programs which are being considered in various states. Many interns have complained about their dual responsibility in attempting to please their employers while at the same time completing academic requirements. In some cases changes in the format of the seminar are being considered in response to suggestions received from the internship questionnaire responses. In some states, though, academic institutions have gone so far as to drop academic credit entirely. This decision may or may not tend to prove fruitful, inasmuch as the level of expectation generally drops on both sides when the granting of academic credit is terminated. Furthermore, graduate students who are pressing to complete their degrees may not be willing to contribute additional time towards an internship without receiving their just compensation within the academic system.

In retrospect the Ford Foundation's programs experienced considerable success. Table 8.2 shows that in 1960 one state had an internship program, by 1965 there were fourteen, and in 1970 there were twenty-nine. The trend is clear. It is also clear that a foundation can serve effectively as a catalytic agent. The greater challenge now is to the universities to make the programs work.

The twelve states in which Ford triggered the program have produced over 600 legislative interns out of the total of about 1,200 as of 1970 (see table 8.2). However, Massachusetts with 154 and California with 142 account for half of the Ford-related total. Seven of the twelve Ford states have maintained continuous operation of internship programs, while Hawaii recently revived its program. Those that canceled the program, in addition to Oklahoma, were Texas, Kansas, and Indiana. While the termination in Texas came as a surprise, particularly because of the enthusiastic support of popular Democratic House Speaker Ben Barnes, the deaths of the Kansas and Indiana programs were not altogether unexplained inasmuch as both states opted for fully professional staff services. In Kansas, where a Legislative Research Council has existed for almost forty years now, opposition apparently developed within the council against the amateur status of the internship program and, perhaps more importantly, against the Lt. Governor of that period, who was a chief advocate of the program but was also a Democrat competing aggressively with the Republican party which controlled the legislature. Indiana, on the other hand, apparently suffered from a distrust of the interns as well as the program. Speaking of the questionable political loyalty of interns, a leading member of the Indiana Senate who did not choose to be quoted commented: "Interns are better than nothing, but not much."

What criteria could be used to determine the effectiveness of a legislative internship program? Presumably, one gauge would be whether the program has served as a mechanism for attracting future state legislative staff employees or even legislators. The data indicate that a well-run program has every chance of providing an avenue into state government for ambitious young researchers and managers. The California example has proven this to be true. As for legislators, time enough has not passed to judge, but Whitman Bassow does report that some former interns have run for public office with success.[39]

Another measure would be any indirect effect the program had on raising the level of staff services in the legislature. The Indiana case may be of interest here.

Table 8.2. Number of Legislative Interns Trained

	1960	1961	1962	1963	1964	1965	1966	1967	1968	1969	1970	1957-70 Total Interns Trained	1957-70 Total Returning Full-Time
California	45	12	13	9	10	8	10	8	10	8	10	142	50
Colorado[a]									4	12	16	32[b]	18[b]
Connecticut[a]										6	16	24	1
Florida									9	12	11	32	6
Georgia[a]											15	15	1[b]
Hawaii			3	4	4	4	4	4	0	0		23	0
Illinois	2	2	6	6	4	4	13	0	14	12	16	77	20
Indiana	2	2	3	4	4	4	3	3	0	0		24	5
Kansas[a]			3		4		3	1	2	3		16	5
Kentucky[a]									30		20	50	0
Massachusetts[a]						14	14	14	14	44	54	154	3
Michigan				4	4	9	8	8	8	3	3	47	9
Minnesota[a]										6		6	1
Montana[a]								4		5		9	0
Nevada[a]										12		12	0
New Hampshire[a]										14		14	0
New Jersey[a]											20	20	0
New York		5	5	5	5	5	5	5	5	5	5	50	16[b]
North Carolina[a]						3	0	10	0	10	0	23	0
North Dakota												6	0
Ohio					5	5	0	10	4	6	10	40	10
Oklahoma	3	5	6	6			4	1	1	6		31	—
Oregon[a]	6		10			15		20		30		81	0
Pennsylvania[a]								9	9	9		32[b]	—
Rhode Island[a]							20	20	20	21		81	2
Texas					7	2	11	0	13			33	10
Utah						6	2	8	3	8	5	32	1
West Virginia								4				4	0
Wisconsin						4	4	8	8			24	2

[a] Primarily undergraduate or informal.
[b] Estimated.

Despite the antagonism expressed by some toward the internship program, it remains to be shown that the program did not in fact contribute the necessary stimulus to the professionalization of staff services within the legislature. Cause and effect is always difficult to demonstrate in such cases but, the reform having been achieved, does it really matter now how it actually came to be?

Yet, while there is no conclusive proof that internship programs will raise the professional level of state legislative staffing, it would appear that states putting a relatively high value on professional staffing are most likely to be receptive to internship programs. For example, of the ten top-ranked states in the Citizens Conference study, nine have internship programs, Nebraska with its unicameral legislature being the exception. Perhaps even more instructive, five of the bottom ten states in the Citizens Conference evaluation have internship programs (Montana, Arizona, Georgia, North Carolina, and Delaware), although three of these have begun since 1969. As table 8.3 shows, four of these five ranked considerably higher on their evaluations in "functionality" and "information-handling capability" (the two rating factors in which professional staffing was evaluated), then they did in the overall evaluation.

Table 8.3. Bottom Ten States in Citizens Conference Evaluation

State	Overall Rank	Functionality Factor	Information Handling Capability Factor
Montana	41	26	31
Mississippi	42	46	45
Arizona	43	11	38
South Carolina	44	50	39
Georgia	45	40	36
Arkansas	46	41	46
North Carolina	47	24	44
Delaware	48	43	47
Wyoming	49	42	50
Alabama	50	48	49

Source: John Burns and Larry Margolis, THE SOMETIME GOVERNMENTS, New York: Bantam Books, 1971.

This chapter suggests that, as with internships in executive departments, the value of an internship experience will vary considerably. In addition to differing institutional environments, there are personality differences among elected officials, interns, and university personnel which can make or break an internship. One must be careful, therefore, not to reach premature conclusions as to the relative potential efficacy of an internship in a high versus low rated state legislature. The evidence to date suggest that the internship experience offers opportunities that a study of political process would be well advised to pursue, regardless of the relative ranking of the legislature.

Notes

1. John Burns and Larry Margolis, *The Sometime Governments,* New York: Bantam Books, 1971.

2. Whitman Bassow, "The Legislative Internship Program: A Report to the Ford Foundation," (unpublished report) October 1, 1968, pp. 7-8 and Appendix 1.

3. Robert Seaver, "Internships and Legislative Staffing," *State Legislatures Progress Reporter,* 2, no. 3 (December 1966), supplement, p. 2.

4. Ibid.

5. Sponsoring Committee for Legislative Staff Internships, "Statement of Policy Governing Florida Legislative Internship Programs," p. 1.

6. Georgia House of Representatives, "Faculty Report and Recommendations, Legislative Internship," 1970 Legislative Session, p. 2.

7. New York State Legislative Internship Program, "The Internship Program: 1961-1966," p. 3.

8. Bassow, *"Internship Program",* appendix 3.

9. Sponsoring Committee for Legislative Staff Internships, *"Statement of Policy",* p. 3.

10. Donald G. Herzberg and Jesse M. Unruh, *Essays on the State Legislative Process* (New York: Holt, Rinehart, Winston, 1970), pp. 89-90.

11. Ray Ferris, "Internships for Leadership in North Carolina," *State Government* (Winter 1964), p. 43. See also Preston W. Edsall, "North Carolina's Legislative Internship Program," *State Government* (Summer 1968), p. 176.

12. Ibid.

13. Victor Jones, Chairman, Executive Committee of the California Legislative Internship Program, *Review of California Assembly Internship Program,* (February 27, 1967), p. 6.

14. Jesse M. Unruh, "Califronia's Legislative Internship Program," *State Government* (Summer 1965), p. 157.

15. Ibid., p. 158.

16. Herzberg and Unruh, *Essays,* p. 93.

17. Bassow, *"Internship Program,"* pp. 26, 27, 38.

18. Herzberg and Unruh, *Essays,* p. 92.

19. Ibid., p. 94.

20. Ibid.

21. Bassow, *"Internship Program",* pp. 26-33.

22. Ibid., p. 29.

23. Ibid., pp. 31-32.

24. "The California Assembly Internship Program: 1971-1972," 1970 (mimeographed brochure).

25. "California Assembly Internships for 1971-1972," 1970 (poster).

26. "The California Assembly Internship Program."

27. L.H. Lincoln, "California's Legislative Internship Program," *State Government*, (January 1958), pp. 12-13 ff.

28. Ibid., p. 12.

29. Victor Jones, "Review of California Assembly Internship Program," Memorandum to the Honorable Jesse Unruh and others, February 27, 1967, p. 18 (mimeographed).

30. Ibid., p. 10.

31. Ibid.

32. Ibid., p. 13.

33. Phil Smalley, "First Annual Report of the Oklahoma State Legislative Council," a report on the Legislative Internship, Training and Research Program, December 1, 1962, p. i (typewritten).

34. Letter from Joseph P. Harris, Professor of Political Science, University of California, Berkeley, to Mr. Jack Rhodes, Executive Director, Oklahoma State Legislative Council, Oklahoma, December 18, 1959.

35. Phil Smalley, *"First Annual Report"*, p. 2.

36. Ibid.

37. Bassow, *"Internship Program,"* p. 10.

38. David M. Olson, "Faculty Report and Recommendations," Georgia House of Representatives Legislative Internship, 1970 Legislative Session, August 1970 (typewritten).

39. Bassow, *"Internship Program,"* p. 19.

Part 3
Federal Internships

9

An Overview of Federal Internships

STEPHEN JOEL TRACHTENBERG
LEWIS J. PAPER

At the beginning of the Cuban missile crisis in 1962, after the Central Intelligence Agency had discovered that the Soviet Union was installing offensive missiles in Cuba, there were numerous meetings at the White House to determine what the response of the United States should be. At one of these meetings, President Kennedy outlined for those present the grave implications which the Soviet move had for America's security, noting in particular that the situation could well lead to a nuclear confrontation between the two Cold War adversaries. At this tense moment, General David M. Shoup, commandant of the Marine Corps, said to Kennedy, "You are in a pretty bad fix, Mr. President." Whereupon Kennedy replied quickly, "You are in it with me."[1] Which all goes to show that, even at the highest level of government, there are lessons to be had through on-the-job training.

Internships enable an individual to work closely with government officials in their day-to-day operation for a short period of time, ranging usually between a few weeks and a year. Like state and local internships, federal internships serve three basic purposes. First, such internships provide a tool to educate the intern in the actual dynamics of government operation — a significant goal in view of the fact that there is often a wide gap between the theories and the realities of government operation. Second, internships enable the government host to benefit by the service of the intern — a purpose with considerable potential since many government offices are understaffed and overworked. Finally, internships are a potential means by which the government host can actually screen and recruit prospective job applicants.

All internships do not serve these three purposes to the same extent or in the same way. Differences within each internship program result from the nature of the work performed by the government host, the educational level and competence of the intern, the interpersonal relationships between the government officials and the interns, and many other factors. In the first section of this chapter, these variances will be explored by examining two broad categories of internships: those for undergraduate and high-school students, and those for graduate students and career professionals. The second section will consider the politics of selecting and retraining interns. On the basis of these two sections, some conclusions will be offered concerning the advantages and disadvantages of internships.

Internships for Undergraduate and High School Students

Most federal internships for those who don't have a college degree consist of summer programs or projects of less than six months' duration. Summer programs usually provide a stipend, as do those operative during the academic year even though these latter programs also involve academic credit for the work.

Congressional Internships[2]

Congressional internships hold a special attraction for the student interested in political affairs. These internships enable a student to spend a whole summer working in the office of a congressman or senator, performing a host of different tasks — from the humdrum work of responding to constituent letters to drafting speeches and, in some cases, legislation.

Congressional internships are something of a recent phenomenon, having been introduced only after World War II. Perhaps the primary factor which inspired the development and expansion of internships on Capitol Hill is the extended sessions of Congress in recent years. Traditionally, congressional sessions were expected to adjourn on July 31 of each year. Since the beginning of World War II, however, they have gradually lengthened, with the 91st Congress concluding on January 2, 1970, the very eve of its retirement. The first congressional internships involved only a small number of students. In the 1950s, some congressional offices had local college students working on a volunteer basis to meet the staff needs imposed by the lengthened sessions. By the late 1950s, some colleges, notably Wellesley, arranged limited internship programs which allowed their students to work in the House and Senate. In the summer of 1959, there was a significant expansion of internship programs because the House was studying labor racketeering problems in great depth and needed assistance to help answer the sharp increase in mail inspired by media coverage.

There were few attempts to establish formal intern programs until the early 1960s when political and educational groups throughout the country sensed the benefit to the Congress and to the student in arranging broader internship programs. Among the first groups to recognize this benefit were the Republican Conference and the Democratic Study Group, both informal congressional organizations. The first steps taken were, to say the least, modest. These two partisan groups initially scheduled seminars for the volunteer students with members of the congressional staffs. This marginal program was well received and encouraged some of the innovators to take bolder action.

Shortly before the summer of 1966, Representative Donald Rumsfeld (R-Ill.) and Robert Ellsworth (R-Kan.) persuaded House Republican Leader Gerald Ford (R-Mich.) of the need for the House Republicans to conduct a structured intern program for undergraduates. With Ford's blessing, (of prime importance since the program required the expenditure of GOP funds), Rumsfeld convened a group in early 1966 to consider establishing close ties between the Republican leadership and the interns. A three-part program was developed: (1) a lecture series featuring noted political personalities; (2) seminar sessions consisting of a series of small gatherings (10-15 interns per group) with Republican Congressmen; and (3) a social program that included an ambitious welcoming reception given by the party leadership.[3]

Rumsfeld's efforts coincided with a growing awareness within Congress of the value of college internships. This interest was reflected in the adoption of a House resolution introduced by Representative John Brademas (D-Ind.) which provided that in 1966 each congressional office could pay $75 per week over a ten-week period to one intern.[4] Approximately 350 congressional offices participated in the resulting program during the summers of 1966 and 1967. William Kendall, administrative assistant to Representative Peter Frelinghuysen (R-N.J.) directed much of the undertaking. He created two working committees of interns: a program committee which served an advisory function, suggesting speakers and issues for the lecture and seminar discussions; and a social committee which managed the hospitality schedule.

The political activism on the college campuses in the 1960s did not spare the congressional internship program. Few students came to Capitol Hill and left their political views at home. This was, of course, to be expected, but few members of Congress anticipated that congressional interns would use their opportunity to further their political views. Many interns had different expectations, and so a conflict was, to some extent at least, inevitable. The confrontation emerged in the summer of 1967, when student protests against American involvement in the Vietnam War were reaching a crescendo.

Sometime at the beginning of the summer, an idea evolved among the interns to initiate an antiwar petition. A student intern in Senator Jacob Javits' (R-N.Y.) office allegedly launched the first one, an effort which reportedly resulted in several others reflecting positions for, against, and neutral on President Johnson's Southeast Asia policies. The *Washington Post* gave these petitions considerable coverage, and this publicity inspired a group of student activists to organize an "independent" House program for interns.[5] This group, called the House Interns Speakers Forum, invited a putative draft-card burner, David Miller, to address them and reserved the Caucus Room of the Cannon House Office Building for the event. When Speaker John McCormack (D-Mass.) learned of the proposed guest's identity, he withdrew permission to use congressional facilities. The House Interns Speakers Forum was not to be discouraged by McCormack's action. Possibly as a spoof, this same group then asked Representative Joe Poole (D-Tex.), a conservative member of the House Unamerican Activities Committee, to speak. Poole agreed to come and then lectured the students on the merits of American involvement in the Vietnam War. His remarks were greeted by profuse hissing and booing. The interns' colorful activities soon earned them the criticism of some members of Congress.

Among those offended was Representative H. Michel (R-Ill.), who called the student group a "federally subsidized dove's nest under the eaves of the Capitol."[6]

The criticism of interns reached a climax when a scheduled intern meeting with President Johnson was quietly cancelled by the White House after the antiwar interns threatened to boycott the session and march on Pennsylvania Avenue instead of attending the White House affair. As a result of these events, the college interns had few champions in the following session of Congress. In 1968, the House Legislative Appropriations Subcommittee eliminated funds for interns from the Legislative Appropriations Bill with hardly a protest from any member. Apparently, most of the members thought it best to give the program a rest. The Republican leadership program was similarly reduced to a token exercise administered by one of Representative Melvin Laird's (R-Wis.) staff.[7]

With the election of a new President in 1968 and the convening of a new Congress in January, 1969, the concept of the internship program was revived. Early in 1969, largely through the industry of William Kendall and Dr. Donald Robinson, administrative assistant to Representative Henry S. Reuss (D-Wis.), the Bi-partisan Intern Committee was formed with Speaker McCormack's approval and with the two House leaders agreeing to act as co-sponsors. Robinson and Kendall were named co-chairmen and twelve House staff people were appointed to the Committee. The Bi-partisan scheme, designed to give interns an overview of Congress and the Executive Branch, had the following features:

1. Interaction with well-known Washington figures in and out of government.
2. An ambitious off the record seminar program which, in response to a lengthy questionnaire determining the interests of the interns, considered such topics as urban problems, and the ABM rather than such traditional topics as parliamentary procedure and legislative drafting.
3. An advance reading list, consisting of books, speeches, bills, and articles that had been suggested by the Speaker or the seminar committee.

In all, there were fifty-seven seminars with a total of sixty-six speakers on twenty-five topics. Of the 950 interns in the Bi-partisan program, approximately 650 participated in the seminars.[8]

Because of the program's success, congressional sentiment favored the formal reinstatement of an internship program for 1970 (the 1969 program was not established pursuant to a resolution and did not use appropriated funds) — citing in particular the need for better communication between the Congress and the university community. The legislative subcommittee of the House Appropriations Committee subsequently did restore the resources needed to implement the Brademas resolution. Members were then able to hire one intern in each office for a stipulated summer period.[9] As a result of this action, the Bi-partisan Committee was free to conduct another program for 1970 which proved even more rewarding than its predecessor.

One reason for the program's improvement was the establishment of the Institute on Legislative Affairs by the Bi-partisan Committee and the George Washington University School of Public and International Affairs. Through the Institute, the university offered academic credit for a Capitol Hill intern course – essentially a scholarly seminar on the legislative process emphasizing the questions of power and influence within Congress. While Capitol Hill summer internships were still arranged by students directly with their congressmen, enrollees were now expected to participate in the activities and seminars sponsored by the Bi-partisan Committee. The Committee in turn assumed primary responsibility for educating the students about Washington in general and the Hill in particular. The Committee also agreed to serve as a communications link between interns and members as well as between interns and full-time congressional staff. The latter responsibility was of considerable importance because interns occasionally found that staff people were somewhat antagonistic toward them. This tension was understandable to some degree. Professional personnel sometimes resented what they felt were self-styled "whiz kids" who they belived were at times too willing to advise the congressmen on how to vote but were a bit reluctant to do routine office work.

Although genuine prima donnas among the interns have been rare, the Committee has sought to help interns avoid early frustration and disillusionment with their assignments by offering an extensive practical orientation. It has also recommended that interns have at least a rudimentary background in American government before coming to the Hill and attempted to suggest meaningful tasks for interns once they arrive. In a memo to staff entitled "The Care and Feeding of Summer Interns," the Committee has cited examples of useful work which interns have previously done and can do in a member's office.[10]

One goal of the intern program – to provide a meaningful educational experience for college students – has assumed greater importance over the past ten years. The Bi-partisan Committee now feels that one of its chief functions is to integrate "government courses" and practical politics. The Committee's hopes seem justified by the confidence which it now enjoys within Congress and the growing number of applicants. At this time, the program promises to have the continued advocacy of the leadership of both parties and of congressmen who have encouraged their staffs to become involved in the activity.[11] Nevertheless, these congressional internships differ substantially from the congressional Fellowship program discussed in chapter 11 and from the Washington Semester programs involving both executive and legislature internships such as are presented in chapter 13.

Student Internships in the Federal Bureaucracy

Like congressional internships, internships in the governmental bureaucracies are a relatively recent phenomenon. In the 1950s, college students could acquire summer employment in the federal government by passing a special examination. The success of this program inspired the implementation of a formal internship program in the federal government which, even today, remains distinct from the summer employment opportunities available to college students who pass a special examination. Many of these federal programs have now been in progress for a number of years and have proved to be a model for the creation of similar internships at other levels of government.

The most comprehensive federal internship program for undergraduate students is provided by the U.S. Civil Service Commission, the supervisory agency which is generally responsible for staffing the federal bureaucracy.[12] During the 1960s, the Commission administered a test for undergraduates who were interested in summer employment (usually as a typist/clerk) in selected (and generally non-controversial) federal agencies. This program was received enthusiastically by the nation's college students. Moreover, participating agencies reported that the students provided valuable services and injected some new blood into a bureaucratic system not known for its dynamism.[13]

Accordingly, in 1969 a formal internship program was inaugurated so that promising students could become more closely involved in bureaucratic decision-making. Thus was born the Executive Intern Program of 1969, in which seventy-five undergraduate (and graduate) students were offered an opportunity to work with high-level federal officials. All four-year colleges and graduate schools in the nation were invited to nominate students for positions created by participating agencies. Applicants were selected on the basis of scholarship, leadership, interpersonal relationships, and participation in extracurricular activities. In 1970, the number of internships in the program increased from seventy-five to 250, and by 1972 there were 410 participants. The program has not been an unqualified success. Often the interns complained that the promise of involvement and excitement described in the brochures was replaced in actuality by a tedium of routine tasks in which the individual talents and interests of the intern were ignored. In response to this criticism, the project, renamed the Washington Summer Intern Program, made special efforts in 1971 to match job assignments with the intern's background and career ambitions. An additional effort was also made to ensure that the periodic seminar discussions – a feature of the internship program from its inception – offered the interns an opportunity to evaluate their experience with high-level government officials.

Other federal agencies, notably the Social Security Administration and the U.S. Information Agency, have independent summer internship programs similar to those established by the Civil Service Commission.[14] Programs such as these, of course, can and often do provide students with insight as to how the government really operates and as to whether a vocation in governmental decision-making offers a career consistent with the intern's abilities and interests. Regardless of whether the student is inspired to seek a career in government, however, there is no question but that internship programs provide a potentially valuable tool for educating the college and high school student about the realities of the political process. The Civil Service Commission is also responsible for the full-time employee "Management intern" program evaluated in chapter 10.

Internships for Graduate Students and Career Professionals

Internships for graduate students and career professionals are in many ways similar to internships provided for college and high school students. Indeed, some internship programs are available to undergraduate as well as graduate students. The differences between internship programs for undergraduate students and those for graduate students and career professionals, to the extent there are differences, are generally twofold. First, the graduate or professional intern will usually find a greater opportunity to engage in the substantive task of shaping and administering government policy. This difference reflects the basic fact that many graduate students and career professionals have a certain expertise and experience which, it is believed, qualifies them to perform the substantive tasks.

Second, internships for graduate students and career professionals, more so than those for undergraduate students, are viewed by the host agency as a valuable means to recruit new staff. An individual examining the brochure of the Internal Revenue Service internship program for graduate and law students, for example, will learn that, among the program's five objectives, three involve talent search:

1. To give outstanding college men and women a true picture of employment with the IRS so that they will better understand the advantages, challenges and rewards of Federal employment.

2. To interest these men and women in a career with the IRS upon graduation.

3. To demonstrate IRS interest in colleges and students by providing employment and compensation and help meet the cost of continued education.

4. To accomplish substantial amounts of necessary and productive work.

5. To improve our collective recruitment efforts through contacts which participating students have with their fellow students, faculty and administration.[15]

This emphasis on recruitment is to be expected. Graduate students and career professionals are actively looking for jobs. They are more likely to accept an offer for employment in the immediate future; in fact, many graduate and professional interns view their experience as a means to explore available employment prospects. In contrast, many undergraduates intend to do post-graduate study and are not prepared to enter the job market for at least a few years. Consequently, most undergraduates view internships merely as a means to round out their college experience.

The distinctions between graduate and undergraduate interns are not always clear — in part because the distinctions frequently arise in the attitudes of the administrators rather than in the program descriptions. Nonetheless, the distinctions between graduate and undergraduate internships can be appreciated more fully by an examination of the more prominent graduate and professional internships.

The White House Fellows Program

This program was originally conceived by John Gardner in the early 1960s, when he was president of the Carnegie Corporation. The program was first implemented by President Johnson in 1964, ten months before Dr. Gardner became Secretary of Health, Education, and Welfare. In general, the White House Fellows Program is designed "to provide gifted and highly motivated young Americans with first-hand experience in the process of governing the Nation and a sense of personal involvement in the leadership of society."[16]

The program offers these talented young people perhaps the best interning year available. The Fellows learn about government from the top, serving as assistants to Cabinet-level officials as well as to the President and Vice President. Most cabinet members are delighted to have the Fellows as staff members. The Fellows usually have a special expertise, work hard, and frequently go virtually everywhere with the cabinet member. Fellows are expected to be versatile, have an ability to grasp new situations, and have considerable leadership potential. Ages of eligibility range between twenty-three and thirty-five, and the salary scale now ranges up to $28,692, depending on educational background and experience (although some of the men and women selected may absorb a cut in pay to accept the opportunity). Fellows are not required to leave government when their fellowship expires, and, in fact, many do elect to remain in public service for an extended period.

Needless to say, this program has met with considerable success. It is not unusual to have more than 1,000 applications in a given year for fifteen to eighteen positions. This program is discussed in more detail in chapter 12.

The U.S. Office of Education's Career Development Project

Under this federally sponsored program, selected educators are invited to spend a year in the U.S. Office of Education in Washington, D.C. OE originally intended to invite only people from the state departments of education. Indeed, at its inception in 1965, the program was funded by appropriations authorized to improve the quality of personnel in state departments of education.[17] But it was often difficult to persuade such personnel to leave their jobs (and the "promotion track") for an intern year. Despite reassurances to the contrary, these state educators were frequently concerned with the possible loss of seniority and felt that, if they left their jobs even temporarily, they would slip several rungs down the ladder of career success. University people, on the other hand, generally seemed less troubled by such matters; most of them seemed to believe that a program such as OE's would enlarge their professional options. OE therefore decided that university professionals also should be eligible to participate in the program, and made state university personnel eligible for consideration along with employees of the state departments of education.[18]

The scope of the OE program was subsequently widened further to include not only state university and department of education personnel but also people from private universities.[19] In line with this innovation, OE has begun to view its internship program as an opportunity to exploit the potential of promising young graduate students and professionals. The program's brochure, for instance, speaks of the changing spirit of the program — instead of merely "recognizing" educational leaders, OE seeks affirmatively to develop the potential of those who show a capacity for constructive leadership. This forward-looking philosophy enables OE to select as interns individuals who may not have fully blossomed, but in whose future contribution to society OE is willing to invest.

Washington Interns in Education

Another internship program in education was launched in 1964 with a three-year grant from the Fund for the Advancement of Education. Washington Interns in Education (WIE) has since continued with funds from the Ford Foundation, the Office of Education, and other government and private agencies (which numbered thirty-one in 1970). The program exists to develop leaders in education, seeking out approximately twenty action-oriented people each year who have the following common characteristics:

1. past academic and professional experience in which they demonstrated initiative and responsibility;
2. a demonstrated commitment to American education.[20]

Interns selected are usually engaged in some form of graduate or professional work in education and use their internship to concentrate on some specialized area of education such as "higher education administration," or "recruitment and retention of Mexican-Americans in universities." The group spends one year in Washington, with about three-quarters of the time devoted to working in congressional offices, federal agencies, or national educational organizations. The remaining time is spent on an "educational element," which includes group meetings, field trips, attendance at educational conferences, and group projects (all selected by democratic procedures). Emphasis is on "self-education" and maximum opportunity for participation in the decision-making process is encouraged.

According to WIE, a primary benefit of the program is that it has established a community of individuals who can help each other professionally and have a collective impact on education. For instance, the program bulletin states:

These people have at their disposal a network, as close as their telephones, made up of ninety other present and past interns with a common tie to WIE and, in varying ways and to varying degrees, a common commitment to changing the educational system. The network also extends to past and present members of the advisory board, sponsoring agencies, clinical faculty, and other 'friends' of WIE.

How is the network used? On the most basic level it is an information system almost beyond comparison. Through this system, questions can often find an answer very quickly: Is a certain program really working? Who's the man to see about a particular problem? What does the funding picture for education look like this year? What key spots are opening up, and who are the best people to fill them?

The network can also have a more important output function. That is, it can serve as a force for change . . . it could involve all interns applying pressure at their own levels aimed at producing the same changes — such as in teacher certification requirements, funding procedures, or the concept of a school.[21]

Although the selection process varies from program to program, most interns are between twenty-five and forty. As a general rule, it makes sense for agencies to use internships as a means of recruitment. A man or woman of twenty-five may be easier to train and then place than someone who has already crossed many professional bridges.

A detailed description of all graduate and professional intern programs is beyond the scope of this chapter. It should be stressed, however, that there is a wide variety of intern programs for the graduate student and career professional, with most of them centered in Washington.[22] In recent years, a growing number of such intern programs have been inaugurated in other places, often with considerable success.

The Politics of Selection and Retention: The Art of Being Chosen

There is no simple description of criteria employed to select interns from the thousands who apply to the vast number of available programs. Nonetheless, some general observations about the selection process can be made.

To begin with, the prestige of the applicant's institutional affiliation is not necessarily a determining factor in selection. A man or woman from a small and obscure college can be chosen over someone from Stanford, Harvard, Michigan, or Duke. The qualities of the individual, the energy and imagination with which he or she and their institution present his or her case for selection, generally predominate. This is so, in part at least, because most intern selection committees seek a geographical, sexual, racial, vocational, and age balance in their choices.

The search for diversity, in fact, is common to most federally sponsored internship programs. Much of the explanation here is simple politics. If, for example, after a federal intern program has operated for a couple of years and nobody from the less populous states has been selected, the senators and congressmen from those areas want to know why. Private groups may have less immediate concern for geographical spread, but it is usually one factor which is considered. A more broadly based group of participants, it is argued, makes a program more enjoyable as well as more educational. Nothing could be more stultifying for those involved, experience suggests, than filling a national program with interns of similar background from the same geographical area.

Institutional support also can help an applicant in the selection process. However great the respect for individual achievement, the applicant sponsored by an educational institution is usually one giant step ahead of his or her unsponsored competitors. For an institution's sponsorship not only adds stature to the applicant's "paper" qualifications; of equal, if not greater significance, is the fact that an institution sponsoring an applicant will often undertake measures — such as letters of recommendation and phone calls to well-placed individuals in the host agency — to enhance the probability of the applicant being selected.

This brief description indicates that the politics of selection can often be a complex business. The experience of one government intern program — which must remain anonymous — is illustrative. When the program was first formulated, those in Washington who designed it, limited in their experience with such matters, tried to select the enrollees. In their innocence they relied on their professional friends, colleagues, and acquaintances for references. While every effort was made to be fair and impartial, the result was frequently (though inadvertently) a paradoxical combination of unconscious nepotism and kindly deception. A reference might recommend someone whose work he liked and wanted to reward; or in the rare case, he might suggest someone whom he wanted to remove gracefully from the environs.

Another problem in the selection process concerned the provincial base from which the interns were chosen. Most of those considered belonged to a small circle of friends, acquaintances, and colleagues. New inputs were minimal. After a year, a change was made. A decision was made to rely on regional committees established throughout the country. The committees, in turn, secured applications, held interviews in regional offices, and then sent the names of their selections to Washington. Unfortunately, the revision did not improve matters as much as had been hoped, because a few of the regional officials seemed to use the new opportunity to satisfy their own political, professional, and even social obligations. The result was that selection was often more a matter of politics than a matter of merit.

The present system (the efficacy of which has not yet been tested fully) requests agency personnel located in different regions to select four or five promising applicants from among those who apply and send their rated files to Washington. In order to encourage regional cooperation, the central office in Washington appears to have an unwritten agreement to choose at least one applicant from each region. Complications may arise, of course, if the Washington office wants to select an individual other than the one given the highest priority by the regional officials.

In essence, the process of choice, particularly among many qualified applicants, is exceedingly complicated, subject to change in needs and emphasis. Anyone who ventures an application for an internship should first review the history of the particular program to determine those factors and pressures likely to contribute to the selection committee's deliberations. In addition, the most current criteria and application forms should be obtained. Internships are variable creatures subject to constant change. New regulations are issued; deadlines and requirements sometimes change from year to year; programs die or lapse; new ones are created or spun-off to deal with particular areas. Researching internship opportunities is hard work. Many small programs do not have national visibility and are easily overlooked. This is especially true with respect to state and local options, which normally do not command wide publicity but which often offer most exciting and innovative experiences.

The Politics of Selection and Retention: The Art of Hanging On

A perennial debate in some agencies sponsoring internships centers on the question of whether it is possible, and desirable to retain an intern whose scheduled tenure with the agency expires after a year or less. The answer to this question is frequently a matter of emphasis. Should a program seek those with already demonstrated professional talents, or should it find and invest in potential leaders? Should the agency concentrate its efforts in educating the intern, or should it concentrate on offering the intern a substative experience which will induce him or her to remain with the agency after the internship has expired (assuming the agency is satisfied with the intern's work). There is, in effect, a strain between recruitment and development. The dilemmas were once framed in this way by an official in an agency which had made a substantial investment in an internship program:

The . . . Fellow is not a regular employee of the office and therefore, there are a number of questions from those in the executive office that should have answers. First the Fellow is paid by a sponsor institution, with funds sent to us four times a year. That was one of the devices we used to make the sponsoring institution feel that the employer was our office. We said, "O.K., we won't put this Fellow on our payroll at all. Keep him on your payroll. We'll send you the

money and you send the money to him. He becomes an ... employee."
Secondly, by his not becoming an ... employee, we save ourselves a lot of
internal headache. We made it possible for the [people] ... to get themselves an
extra pair of hands without losing a personnel line. There were fifteen men
appointed at first, fourteen plus an intern. In the new system, they get fifteen
plus the intern, so that there will be sixteen. So the people, instead of rejecting
interns, are scrapping like mad to get them.

Secondly, since the Fellow is not an employee of the office, he doesn't have a
timekeeper, he doesn't have a time card. He works out informal methods of
accountability, so that if he wants to take a couple of days off and go to a
research program, he can do it. In the old days, he was holding down a job. They
needed him there to do whatever he was doing. . . . Fellow is not counted in the
job ceiling. The ... Fellow should not be given any position title. He is simply
a ... fellow in the respective office. What used to happen in the old days was
that when he came in on Mondays he was an intern. Tuesdays he was a program
officer for ... He suddenly became a program officer of ... and forgot he was
a ... fellow. And another man wants the job. It was corrupting the whole
purpose of the program. The policy of not offering any ... fellow regular
employment in the ... until the close of his fellowship year has been reaffirmed.
Implications of this policy however, will be reviewed this year.[23]

This was the thinking of this particular agency in September, 1969. In
February, 1970, the recommendations were finally adopted. A later internal
memorandum states that there is nothing illegal in offering a permanent position
to a Fellow at the end of his internship, and that no legal constraints prevent the
intern from accepting. Hence, the current agreement does not prohibit the
agency from offering a permanent position to a Fellow, and provides that a
Fellow may accept a position if offered. But the agreement does not indicate
whether a permanent position *should* be offered. So the question ultimately
resolves into one of discretion. As one official argued:

Whether they should be hired is an internal program matter, which would take
other important factors into account. The conclusion that they may be hired is
derived from the exceptional cases. I recommend that it is not in keeping with
the nature and purpose of the program that they be hired.[24]

He then lists the reasons for this view:

You're in an agency and you know you're going to be there for a year and it's
not going to offer you a job no matter how likeable and lovable you are.
Chances are, you're not going to be a "yes" man. If you're up in some state
agency and you'd really rather work in Washington, you may turn out to be a
"yes" man or may turn up a way to settle a permanent job. So that's one of our
concerns. We want these fellows coming in partly because we want to get them
experienced, but partly because we want fresh blood. The fellow should not be
absorbed by the bureaucratic reality of ... and program policy should in no way
contribute to these possibilities ... In addition, the sponsor institution should
understand that we're not poaching on their ground.[25]

This individual really hopes to have interns work in the system, but not become a part of it. In short, he seeks to isolate the intern from the "bureaucratic attitudes" — which experience shows may unfortunately be assumed even without clear prospects of being hired.

In the end, there are two operative perspectives in determining whether an intern should be retained after his internship has expired. On the one hand, the host agency must determine — aside from whether the individual intern has the requisite qualifications to fill an available position — whether a general policy of retaining interns will undermine the very purpose of the intership program. For if the intern does remain with the agency, then the benefits of his internship are lost — at least for the immediate future — to the institution and community from which he came. Moreover, a policy of retaining interns may cause the intern to be less venturesome and inquiring if he or she feels that such initiative may make his or her retention less attractive politically. And this, in turn, may lead the agency to lose the benefit of all the intern's abilities.

On the other hand, the intern himself should also determine whether it is desirable for him to extend his stay with the host agency after the internship expires. In making this determination, the intern should first consider whether the politics of the host agency are consistent with the intern's politics — although in some cases (particularly in the federal government)[26] political homogeneity is a prerequisite to being accepted. In deciding whether to extend his stay with the agency, the intern should also consider whether a continued stay will add to his education as well as offer a meaningful opportunity to make a contribution toward the attainment of desired goals.

Whatever the benefits of remaining with the agency, the intern should also consider whether his interests would be better served if he returned to his original environs to share the learning experience with colleagues and the community. For if experience and expertise remain centrally located in the governmental bureaucracies, a principal purpose of the internship concept — an attempt to expose those *outside* the governmental network to the workings of the political system — will be compromised.

Conclusion: Blessing or Curse?

Most internships have the potential to offer advantages to aspiring young students and professionals. Career advancement is one clear advantage which may accrue from an internship. This is due in great measure to the visibility a program may provide for the intern's talents and the professional people they enable him or her to meet. Being selected for an internship program can lead to some collateral benefits as well. For example, when a professional is chosen for a congressional internship, he might later elect not to return to his former position unless he were offered a promotion. The institution from which the intern left may expect this to happen, because if the intern has performed well on the Hill, the senator or congressman might ask the intern to extend the term of service. To recapture the wavering intern, the institution may attempt to improve on the congressional opportunity. In a way, the intern could find that his or her employment options have increased.

Similarly, under another internship program, the young Ph.D. in academic administration might return home from his or her year away to become a "baby" dean or professor, or perhaps even an executive officer in college administration. Indeed, a study of participants in the Academic Administration Internship Program (AAIP) revealed that 83.2% of the former interns were involved in some phase of educational administration, mostly in higher education.[27] Moreover, a random sampling of ninety-five former interns and sixty competitors who did not receive internships showed that 76% of the interns had become educational administrators whereas only 20% of the competitors had become educational administrators.[28]

The graduate and undergraduate students can benefit in a like manner from internships. Aside from any educational benefit, internship exposes the student intern to people who may ultimately become career allies, providing guidance as well as exposing the intern to professional opportunities once the student has completed his or her course of study. Over and over again, interns find that fraternal relationships formed during internships supplement the more traditional means of talent search and career development — especially in times when the demand for challenging jobs well exceeds the supply.

Internships, however, are not without costs and risks. Indeed, many interns — but especially student interns — find their experience disillusioning. Officials in the host agency sometimes are uncooperative or patronizing, and unwilling to assign the intern any substantive task. More than one congressional summer intern, for example, has returned to his or her campus to tell only tales of stamps licked and pages xeroxed. In these circumstances, the internship may not only result in professional frustration; sometimes it can also breed contempt for the governmental process and those who participate in it, a contempt which may survive later experiences. There is, in addition, the cost of undermining independent and rigorous thinking which many interns bring to their venture in government. Often an intern develops professional and social relationships with government personnel which inhibit the critical thinking which is indispensable to improving the political processes.

Few, if any, of the costs of internship programs are inevitable. Almost always they are a product of the personal and political dynamics of the government in operation. For this reason, both the host government agency and the prospective intern should consider carefully those dynamics in designing and applying for internship programs. Otherwise there will be a substantial risk that an internship will become, as Oscar Wilde once remarked of experience in general, "just another name for our mistakes."

152

Notes

1. Robert F. Kennedy, *Thirteen Days,* (New York: W.W. Norton & Co., 1969), pp. 36-7.

2. While the congressional internship program described here is for undergraduates, college graduates can also be congressional interns under a variety of other programs. See especially Chapters 11 and 13.

3. William Kendall and Dr. Donald L. Robinson, cochairmen of the House of Representatives Bi-Partisan Intern Committee, *Letter* dated February 18, 1971 to Stephen Joel Trachtenberg.

4. House Resolution 416, 89th Congress, 1st Session, June 19, 1965.

5. Aaram Latham, "The Long Sad Summer for Congressional Interns," Washington *Post,* October 1, 1967.

6. Kendall and Robinson, op. cit.

7. Ibid. and conversation with Representative John Brademas, July 12, 1972.

8. Ibid.

9. Ibid.

10. Bi-partisan Intern Committee, "The Care and Feeding of Summer Interns," Summer 1970. The office is located in Room 2162, Longworth House Office Building, Washington, D.C.

11. Internships are also available with the U.S. Senate but these are less structured and are not supported by enabling legislation. The kind of experience offered and payment arrangements are determined by each senator.

12. The U.S. Civil Service Commission owes its genesis to a disappointed federal job-seeker who assassinated President John Garfield in 1881. President Garfield's successor, Chester Arthur, quickly saw the advantages of a system in which government employment was based on objective criteria rather than on the spoils system. In 1883, the Pendleton Act established the Civil Service Commission and charged it with the basic responsibility of staffing the federal government through use of an objective merit system. The current legislative authority for the Civil Service Commission is found in Title V of the U.S. Code (1966). There is some controversy as to how successful the Civil Service Commission has been in implementing this "meritocracy" (especially since the President is still empowered to fill the higher levels of government with his own appointees). Ralph Nader's Public Interest Research Group published a report, *The Spoiled System: A Call for Civil Service Reform* (1972), which was highly critical of the Civil Service Commission. The Civil Service Commission, in turn, attempted to refute the Nader group's analysis. See CSC, *Analysis of the Nader Reports* (1972).

13. At the program's peak in 1968, the federal government employed approximately 12,000 college and high school students in summer position.

From an interview with John Jones, College Relations Division, U.S. Civil Service Commission, January 9, 1972.

14. Because the Civil Service Commission generally assigns interns to agencies who wish to participate in its program, most other federal agencies — if they do wish to have undergraduate interns — choose to rely on the Civil Service Commission rather than establish an independent program.

15. Available through the Public Information Division, Internal Revenue Service, U.S. Department of the Treasury, Washington, D.C.

16. See President Lyndon B. Johnson, "White House Fellows Program Announced," *Weekly Compilation of Presidential Documents,* October 3, 1964.

17. The Office of Education's Cooperative Development Project with state universities, state colleges, and state departments of education was authorized by the Elementary and Secondary Education Act of 1965, Title V (Public Law 89-10).

18. As described in an April 17, 1968 internal memorandum, the Office of Education viewed the objectives of the program as follows: 1 — provide fellows with an opportunity to gain an understanding of federal-state-local relationships; 2 — help them to become knowledgeable about the role of the Office of Education; 3 — provide the Office of Education with the views and skills of trained educators; and 4 — build continuing relationships between Office of Education staff and future leaders of American education.

19. U.S. Office of Education brochure, "Cooperative Development Project," U.S. Government Printing Office, 1967, GPO 884-544.

20. See *Washington Interns in Education Bulletin I 1969-70* 3 (1971).

21. See *Washington Interns in Education Bulletin 2 1969-70* 28 (1971).

22. Some of the more established internship programs in Washington include the following:

The American Political Science Association's Congressional Fellowship Program. Initiated in 1953, this is probably one of the most widely known and respected internship programs. It enables political scientists and journalists to spend a year as staff specialists with congressional committees or members of Congress.

The National Association of Secondary School Principals has a program which brings secondary school principals to Washington so that they can spend a year in governmental planning agencies and also visit high schools throughout the country in order to gain new perspectives on national developments in secondary education.

The National Institute of Public Administration's Career Education Awards Program reaches into the Federal Government to identify career civil servants who attend one of several major universities for an academic year to study public administration and related subjects.

The Securities and Exchange Commission has a Student Assistant Program for those who have completed two years of law school and are interested in law and securities.

The National Labor Relations Board operates a limited internship program for those who have completed two years of law school and are interested in labor law.

The American Society of Public Administration has an internship program for minorities. Its aim is to encourage minority group members to consider a civil service career. Graduate students are brought to Washington for a three-month period for service in a government agency.

The Brookings Institution's Economic Fellowship Program is designed to bring young public administrators to Washington. The interns spend a year at Brookings in some phase of economics and its relation to federal government policy and programs.

The American Political Science Association and the U.S. Civil Service Commission sponsor an executive internship program on congressional operations. This program enables promising civil servants to work for members of Congress, alternating six months with a member of the House and six months with a senator.

The American Association of College Teachers internship program enables educators from developing countries to spend some time in Washington and elsewhere to learn about college administration.

The American Council on Education (an association of institutions of higher education) provides an internship program for Ph.D.s interested in college administration. The intern first spends some time in Washington and is then assigned as an assistant to a president of a university.

23. The specific name of the agency is not published at the request of the author of the memorandum. The material is taken from an internal federal agency memorandum dated September 18, 1969. The memorandum is in the possession of Dean Stephen Joel Trachtenberg, Boston University, 755 Commonwealth Avenue, Boston, Massachusetts.

24. Ibid. and another memorandum dated February 17, 1970.

25. Ibid.

26. In fact, it was reported recently that one government intern in the Nixon Administration made the mistake of explicitly identifying this prerequisite to employment. As the article in *Science News,* (vol. 97, 1971, p. 572) stated:

To further compound the apparent politicalization of science appointments, on March 18, [1971], Thomas Kelly, described as an HEW intern, sent a letter of recruitment to a score of university deans asking for nominations for the position of director of health evaluation. Candidates, he wrote, "must display a willingness to work with and for the incumbent Administration, which would best be indicated by Republican registration or, at the least, by the absence of opposition registration."

Deputy Under Secretary Malek denies that party affiliation is a prerequisite to employment, except for predefined political jobs, and says "Kelly simply made a mistake." A letter of apology and correction was subsequently sent out, but critics suggest that Kelly's only mistake was putting an established policy into black and white."

27. Dobbins & Stauffer, *Educational Record* (Fall, 1972); see also *Higher Education & National Affairs* 8 (Nov. 10, 1972).

28. Ibid.

10 The Federal Management Interns

JAMES P. JADLOS

The Management Intern Program of the federal government is designed to attract, train, and retain carefully selected and highly qualified college graduates for positions of responsibility in federal management. It is a means by which government organizations seek a continued input of vitality into middle and top management positions. Individual agencies generally describe the purpose of their programs as one of a number of steps to develop a manpower reserve of people with leadership ability to assure continuity of competent management and operations. There are indications that the program tends to achieve these objectives.

The Management Intern Program has become an auspicious way for an ambitious, articulate, capable young college caliber person to begin a federal government management career. Persons selected for the program are those whose records suggest that they have the potential to progress to high level executive and senior staff positions. Over the past fifteen years an efficiently run screening process and promising career opportunities have attracted almost 4,400 of these people to positions in every major federal agency. By virtue of their having passed through a multiphased screening process, management interns receive special treatment for developmental opportunities and receive a "success" stamp which may stay with them throughout their careers.

There is evidence that management interns as a group progress faster than others hired into entry level administrative positions. Of the approximately eighteen thousand young people hired by federal agencies each year, management interns are among the most sought after as potential occupants of mid-management and higher level management positions. Starting salaries for management interns during 1971 were $8,852 (interns hired at the GS-7 level) and $10,470 (interns hired at the GS-9 level). Many of these management interns can expect to earn $15,000 and $17,500 in three years, by 1971 compensation rates.

Though management interns constitute an important source of manpower for higher level positions, it must be recognized the Management Intern Program was not designed as the primary source of federal managers. Of all employees (ages 44 and below) in grades GS-15 and above, only 7 percent started their government employment as management interns; of all federal employees (ages 44 and below) in management occupations in grades GS-15 and above, only 20 percent started their government employment as management interns.[1]

The Origins of the Management Intern Program

Today's Management Intern Program is the successor of other programs that have attempted to identify and develop potential managerial talent. The first such effort was the Junior Civil Service Examiner (JCSE) examination given in 1934 and 1936.[2] Before this time there was no concerted federal effort to recruit college graduates. This examination was for persons with bachelor's degrees in all but certain scientific and professional fields. The depressed economy and the high rate of unemployment over this period were primarily responsible for the demise of the JSCE. The absence of career planning was also a factor; highly qualified persons often found themselves performing clerical duties with little hope for greater responsibilities.[3]

A later evaluation of the college recruiting situation led to the development of the Junior Professional Assistant examination in 1939. Successful competitors in the JPA were placed on lists of eligibles, or "registers," with separate registers established for different courses of study. While a great many specialized registers were established, many persons with liberal educations were omitted from consideration for jobs.[4] The Junior Administrative Technician examination, an option of the JPA, then opened up a channel of entry, but the onset of World War II interfered, giving the program little chance to prove its worth.[5] The JAT examination was reannounced in 1947. It was, however, discontinued by the Civil Service Commission when just 15 of 3,000 eligibles were appointed to jobs.[6] It is widely believed that the small number of appointments was due largely to agencies being reluctant to hire returning disabled veterans who, despite very low test scores, were given preference for employment and placed at the top of the list of eligibles. They had to be selected for employment before those lower on the list could be selected.

At about the same time, from 1934 to 1949, the Laura Spellman Rockefeller Foundation supported a National Institute of Public Affairs program to place college graduates in the federal government. This NIPA program is the source of many of the present-day Management Intern Program methods for recruiting, selecting, and training interns. NIPA worked closely with colleges and universities to identify candidates for the program. Particular attention was given to the academic records of applicants, their extracurricular activities, and recommendations of professors and others in a position to judge their capabilities. These recommendations included information on each candidate's objectivity, accuracy, thoroughness, integrity, physical vitality, originality, initiative, emotional stability, cooperativeness, and personal adjustment. The interviewing committee would then take a first-hand look at the candidates by meeting with three or four of them for about an hour. Those who passed this final screening became interns.

Training in the NIPA program was primarily learning by doing, learning through diverse assignments, coming in contact with distinguished administrators, and working with well-qualified supervisors. There were also a number of tuition-free educational opportunities available at American University, George Washington University, and the U.S. Department of Agriculture Graduate School. Periodic progress reports also afforded experience in writing and organizing materials. A number of program flexibilities allowed interns to move ahead at their own pace. In 1949, after NIPA had trained and helped place 521 interns, the U.S. Civil Service Commission assumed responsibility for such training and the NIPA program was dissolved.[7]

Beginning in 1948, the Junior Management Assistant Examination (JMA) became the focal point for college recruiting in the management field, succeeding the Junior Civil Service Examiner examination and the Junior Administrative Technician examination. More importantly, it employed many of the recruiting and training methods developed in the NIPA program. From the outset of the JMA, responsibility for its administration was placed in an interagency committee, members of which were officials of all the participating agencies.

The committee did the recruiting, developed examination announcements, passed on minimum qualifications, arranged and conducted interviews and reviewed tests. The Civil Service Commission developed and administered the tests. This joint relationship was intended to give agencies the opportunity to participate in organizing and conducting the program and to gain support for a continuation of the NIPA success.

In the JMA, tests were more extensive than those required of other Civil Service job applicants. Candidates were required to pass the basic examinations and one of two other three-hour written tests of seventy questions. The first test was one concerned mainly with administrative problems. A "public affairs" test covering social sciences was introduced later and then a few current events questions were added. Those who passed the written examination then competed in individual and group oral interviews where they were rated on factors such as leadership ability, character, and personal bearing. Confidential personal references were also considered.

The selection procedure included a significant departure from previous practice; all eligibles were considered equally qualified when presented to agencies for selection. Agencies could select any of these eligibles. Previously, agency selections had to be made according to the "rule of three," that is, from among the three persons standing highest on a ranked list of eligibles.

JMA training programs varied in length from a few weeks to a year or more. Length and content of individual programs were determined by participating agencies. Rotational assignments were a regular part of the training as was academic work related to the job.[8] Many highly qualified college graduates were recruited through the JMA program, but wide-scale use was not possible because of its involved and highly selective character. Universities lost interest and this combined with other factors, contributed to its revision and expansion.

In 1956 the Federal Service Entrance Examination (FSEE) was introduced with a Management Intern option.[9] The FSEE is a single examination designed to fill a wide variety of administrative and professional entrance level positions from among applicants who have a college education or equivalent experience. It is not the only examination used to screen college caliber people. Separate application procedures are used by those interested in highly specialized and professional positions such as engineer, accountant, librarian, nurse, architect, and others. The FSEE provides broad opportunities for capable young people to begin federal careers. The two-and-a-half hour examination consists of a general test of verbal abilities and quantitative reasoning. By passing this one examination, applicants can receive early consideration for appointments to more than 200 kinds of jobs which do not require a specific technical degree.

Administration of the Intern Program

The United States Civil Service Commission and federal agencies share responsibility for the Management Intern Program. The commission's responsibility is basically one of staff direction, operation of the selection process, and program monitoring. The agencies are responsible for the actual selection of interns and the operation of the program. Until relatively recently, the Civil Service Commission has emphasized the preemployment portion of its responsibilities. The commission's primary association with agency program operations has been through its review and approval of training agreements, which are agency-prepared documents describing in general terms the purpose and content of the management intern programs and how the programs will be conducted. The Civil Service Commission's Bureau of Personnel Management Evaluation has also been involved, to a limited extent, in reviewing problem areas of intern programs on their periodic evaluations of agency personnel management which are conducted at three-to four-year intervals.

In June 1969, the Civil Service Commission established an Inter-agency Management Intern Committee to consider the many issues important to the operation of management intern programs. Agency designees on this committee are persons who coordinate management intern programs and have direct contact with interns and their supervisors. In agencies where there are several programs, a coordinator of one of the programs is usually chosen by the agency as its representative. Prior to the establishment of this committee, there was no forum for the systematic exchange of information concerning important aspects of management intern programs, and there was no single readily available source of information on these programs. Some five Civil Service Commission offices have responsibility for various parts of the Management Intern Program, and they rarely have reason to communicate as a body with the participating agencies. The establishment of the interagency committee has provided an opportunity for discussions on such topics as career progression of management interns, the history of the program, turnover of management interns, methods of sharing information on interns, evaluation of management intern programs, the

Management Intern Lecture-Seminar Series, the screening system for management intern applicants, and the preparation of management intern-training agreements.

Perhaps the most significant accomplishment of the committee has been the preparation of fact sheets on each agency's management intern program. The thirty-two departments and agencies that have participated in the Management Intern Program in the past few years answered forty-seven questions divided into six categories: program in general, intern characteristics, assignments, training, supervisors, and evaluation.[10] Originally compiled in late 1969, these sheets were updated in 1971. They have proved a valuable source of information for agencies seeking to improve their programs.

Selection of Management Interns

The present method used by the Civil Service Commission in screening applicants for the Management Intern Program consists of four main phases. First, applicants must pass the FSEE with a score of 95 or better. From 1968 to 1971, persons who obtained a combined score of at least 1300 in the Graduate Record Examination Aptitude Test were also eligible to proceed to the next phase in the screening. GRE scores are no longer used, as the Education Testing Service objected to their use, contending that the GRE does not purport to measure one's potential for success on the job as does the FSEE.

Until 1968, management intern candidates were also required to complete a two-hour test on administrative problems and public affairs. This was a more rigorous examination than the FSEE. Only those candidates who first scored well on the FSEE were informed of their management intern test scores. Civil Service Commission officials eliminated this special examination because it failed to make any finer separation of those with more potential than did raising the management intern qualifying score on the FSEE.

In addition to the FSEE requirement, management intern candidates are evaluated through a review of their education and experience records. Past supervisors, faculty members, and other persons who have first-hand knowledge of the candidate's abilities and characteristics are then asked for their evaluations. Candidates appear for oral test/interviews held throughout the country where, typically in groups of four to seven, they are judged by two examiners on their performance during a discussion of problems assigned to the group as well as during an individual interview with both examiners. Important factors on which candidates are judged include:

> Bearing and manner
> Social adjustment
> Oral expression
> Problem-solving ability
> Motivation and maturity
> Leadership qualities

The oral examiners are responsible federal program management and general management officials who take time away from their jobs to be trained by the Civil Service Commission for this task. They can approve for selection those candidates who: (1) clearly show exceptional personal qualities or potential, (2) give every evidence of being generally outstanding, and (3) can be expected to progress eventually to high level executive and senior staff positions in the federal service.

Persons who pass through this final phase of the process and whose references and past record are likewise of a very high quality are referred to as "MI eligibles." They are presented to hiring agencies by the Civil Service Commission. Agencies contact any of the MI eligibles who seem to hold most promise to them as future managers and invite the candidates to interview for internships. Some agencies send their selecting officials across the country to interview the best eligibles.

To give the reader a better appreciation for the extent of this selection process, the following figures are presented:

From its beginning in 1956 through 1969, almost 360,000 applicants, mostly recent graduates of American colleges and universities, competed for management internships. Of this original number who were tested by the separate management intern examinations or more recently by the FSEE, 42,600 achieved a score sufficiently high to compete in the oral portion of the examination. Just 10,573 of these people were found eligible on the oral examination and according to Civil Service Commission figures, 4,372 were selected by Federal agencies.[11]

What this means is that approximately 11 percent of the written test takers score 95 or above on the FSEE. Only 25 percent of these are successful in the interview portion. Only 3 percent of the original test takers are MI eligibles. Slightly better than 1 percent of the original competitors are selected for management intern positions.

One of the most serious problems with the selection process is the very low number of minority group members who become MI eligibles. People who receive high scores in the written test tend to be well educated, young, and Caucasian. Few other candidates achieve even a passing score of 70. The FSEE score of 95, necessary to qualify for the MI oral examination, is many times more difficult to achieve.

There is some provision for appropriately qualified people who are not MI eligibles, but who have other important abilities not measured by a written test, to become management interns. Once hired by agencies, any appropriately qualified employee can be selected for an internship based on the quality of his work performance. There are various methods of hiring in federal agencies which permit the use of this provision. Most agencies have undertaken large recruiting programs to predominantly black colleges, particularly those located in the South. Recruiters have been assisted by a Civil Service Commission regulation which encourages employment of college graduates who graduate in the upper

10 percent of their class or with a high grade point average in undergraduate courses.

A number of the large users of the Management Intern Program, including the Departments of Housing and Urban Development and Health, Education, and Welfare, select many of their present employees to participate in the regular Management Intern Program. Agency selection process of present employees is highly competitive and is very similar to the one conducted by the Civil Service Commission with the exception that the written test score is used as one of many rating factors and not as the basic "in or out" standard. Such flexibility is, however, a stop-gap measure, as the following quotation suggests:

In an informal survey among several different cabinet level departments and independent federal agencies this past spring, only one agency could claim a better than 10 percent representation of minority group members among its interns, and that agency relies heavily on internal recruitment to achieve its racial-ethnic balance. Selection of the in-house candidates — because they do reflect more accurately a cross section of cultures — has brought a needed new dimension to the program, but it further spotlights the inequitableness of external selection procedures.[1][2]

Action taken thus far encouraging the employment of "minority group" members do, however, constitute a very significant first step.

Recruiting the Right Number of Interns

The Civil Service Commission makes every effort to provide what is considered an appropriate number of management interns for agency hiring needs. However, this is not a simple procedure. The budget cycle is such that federal agencies cannot be certain of the exact number of management interns they can afford to hire until after college commencement exercises. For budgetary and other reasons, their estimates in the fall of the preceding year may be far from the number they finally hire. Yet, the schedule for management intern oral examinations must be arranged in the spring of the year prior to the time when interns will enter on duty with agencies. This has contributed to an examination and recruiting program somewhat out of phase with agency hiring needs.

On occasion the frequency of written and oral examinations has been adjusted in an effort to produce a proper number of MI eligibles. When agencies were hiring a large number of management interns in the accelerated hiring years (1964 through 1967), just two sets of oral examinations were given. The commission, anticipating continued hiring of management interns at an accelerated rate, then doubled the frequency of oral examinations and eventually increased the number of management intern eligibles. As table 10.1 reflects, the number of jobs available for management interns has been decreasing since 1967.

Table 10.1. Number of Management Intern Eligibles and Selections by Year

Year	Eligibles	Selections
1956	623	139
1957	289	147
1958	318	188
1959	355	167
1960	321	133
1961	625	271
1962	459	234
1963	686	305
1964	516	245
1965	639	311
1966	1005	506
1967	1240	577
1968	1094	521
1969	1664	365
1970	739	263
Totals	10,573	4,372

Source: TREND OF COMPETITION AND SELECTIONS, 1956-1969, U.S. Civil Service Commission, Washington, D.C. (updated through interviews in May 1971)

During the peak hiring years, every management intern eligible who wanted a management intern position was virtually assured of one job offer. Civil Service Commission literature to MI eligibles also held promise of great opportunity:

Because of the unprecedented number of management internships available today, you may well find yourself forced to make a difficult choice from among the attractive programs offered by a number of agencies. The material sent to you previously furnishes preliminary information about the various agency programs. More detailed information will be available from individual agencies considering you for appointment. Study their offers carefully, and take advantage of your attainment by accepting the one which excites you the most.[13]

This message remained a part of the Civil Service Commission's letters through most of 1968, though job opportunities were decreasing in relation to the number of eligibles.

Early in 1971 there were unprecedented numbers of management intern eligibles ready for hiring and more being added to the list at quarterly intervals. Minor adjustments were made in commission literature to remove some of the former promises. Agencies were provided with a much larger pool of interns from which to select. The larger pool, however, has led some critics to suggest that the oral interview portion of the screening process now fails to distinguish the best qualified from some lesser qualified applicants. Agencies continue to interview large numbers of interns for fewer positions and 1971 data indicates that trend is continuing.

Advance Development of Management Interns

Most of the thirty management intern programs currently in operation follow the same general pattern. Though the length of the training programs varies from one to four and a half years, most cover one year. The purpose of the training is to give the intern a working understanding of his agency's organization and functions, its relationship to the total governmental structure, and to improve his managerial knowledge and skill. During the training period, interns sample and learn from a number of different job assignments, perhaps as many as six to ten, in their agency. Rotation from job to job usually occurs in the first six to twelve months of the program. Various combinations of lectures, seminars, special projects, outside reading and study supplement the work assignments.

The training and assignments of management interns are usually broader in scope and greater in depth than those given people who enter the federal government through other methods. The size of agency programs varies considerably, from agencies with a single intern to others that hire forty to eighty management interns a year. Most interns begin their federal careers in Washington, with approximately 20 percent training in locations outside the Washington area.

Agency program coordinators usually plan and administer the training and developmental phases, but most do not have a major role in deciding who the agency will hire as interns. That decision is frequently made by other officials, perhaps recruiting officers. There is lack of coordination in some agencies between hiring officials and program coordinators. Most coordinators have a number of duties in addition to program coordination, and there have been many instances of interns attracted to the federal government only to find a program coordinator who considers his management intern duties to be of a low priority in relation to his other duties. While in most agencies directing the management intern program is a substantially full-time activity, a great many intern programs change hands from year to year. From 1969 to 1970, eighteen of thirty programs had new coordinators.

Though agencies may profess to seek management interns with specialized backgrounds or specific majors, they hire people with a great variety of backgrounds. Most management interns hold degrees in the social sciences and humanities, political science and government, and business administration and economics.[14] The range of positions for which the program is supposed to prepare interns is equally diverse. Many interns have gone into various program management positions. Most others have gone into these career fields:

Property management and disposal	Automatic data processing
Personnel staffing	Operations research analysis
Budget analysis	Supply management
Systems analysis	Employee development
Management analysis	Financial management

The selection of permanent assignments is usually a cooperative venture at the end of the training program, with the intern, his coordinator, and management officials taking part. A number of agencies, however, select target positions or at least occupational or organizational targets near the beginning of the intern program.

Agencies evaluate the success of their overall programs in an informal manner based on unstructured written reports and meetings with supervisors and interns. Most agencies do not have an overall evaluation system, but tend to rely on retention rates of interns, their progress in the organization, and occasionally some measure of their constructive contributions to agency mission. Some agencies do not keep even basic retention and progression data on their interns and are unable to say with certainty how many interns they hired as recently as three years ago and what jobs they currently hold.

Agencies tend to point to continued use of the Management Intern Program and its general acceptance by management officials as evidence of its worth. Except in rare instances, there is no evaluation comparing the Management Intern Program with alternate means of developing young managers. The evaluation aspect of these programs could stand strengthening.

Promotion Patterns

Management interns normally receive annual promotions to the GS-11, 12 or higher levels in most agencies. Some management interns have risen rapidly to the GS-15 level and beyond. It is generally true that management interns advance at faster rates than others who enter the federal government at entry levels.

The first comparative data on this subject was made available by a 1969 survey which drew on the Executive Inventory developed by the Civil Service Commission's Bureau of Executive Manpower. The inventory contained information on managers in grades GS-15 to GS-18 or equivalent (lowest starting salary $25,251). The files were searched to determine how many managers had entered the government through the Management Intern Program and how many had entered through regular FSEE positions since the inception of the program in 1956. For each of the two categories a cut-off date was established to exclude people who had not been with the government long enough to reach these grades. Adjustments were also made to allow for the fact that management interns enter at GS-7 and GS-9, but FSEE's enter at GS-5 and GS-7. Table 10.2 shows the results of that survey.

Not surprisingly, it suggested that it is thirty times as likely for a management intern than an FSEE executive to progress to a GS-15 position or higher. It must be recognized, however, that this information is not complete since the study measured only those persons who had recorded their former management intern status in filling our their Inventory Record Forms. About 20 percent of the total in the inventory left their question unanswered.[15]

Table 10.2. MIs and FSEEs in GS-15 to GS-18 Positions

GS	MI	FSEE
15	85	101
16	16	12
17	4	2
18	3	— —
Special Rates	2	— —
Number of those who could be eligible for these grades	3,800	107,700

The study also suggests that the management intern selection process may have considerable validity and that it does, in fact, identify those most capable of performing high level managerial duties in the federal government. There may, however, be other explanations such as the following:

1. The vast majority of management interns begin and spend a large portion of their careers in Washington, D.C., where jobs at GS-15 and above are more plentiful and where promotions at lower levels may come more rapidly.

2. The psychological advantage of being cast as "one of the chosen" probably endows the management intern with additional motivation and confidence to do his best.

3. Management interns are usually hired into career fields with good possibilities of rapid advancement to the GS-12 and GS-13 levels.

4. Management interns generally receive more systematic and in-depth training than FSEE trainees.

5. Management interns receive assignments at levels of organizations where they work with top officials able to influence favorably a person's progress.

6. Some managers consciously look for former management interns in filling key jobs.

7. Ninety-seven percent of recent management interns had at least a B.A. degree whereas approximately seventy percent of the FSEE's had at least a B.A. degree.

Intern Criticism and Suggestions

The most consistent critics of the program are management interns themselves. The interns frequently go through a multistage process of socialization which may result in their working less efficiently and even leaving their agencies. This process often begins in the recruiting phase where interns are told the many virtues of agency management intern programs. The initial shock frequently occurs in the second stage when the intern discovers that the expectations raised in the recruiting process cannot be approached in the program. Assignments are less challenging and have less responsibility than first suggested. Managers often have little time for interns and do not begin to devote enough attention to developing them. In the third phase, a souring of intern attitude frequently occurs. Although a good many interns rise above the circumstances, others succumb at some cost to themselves and at great cost to their agencies.

About four months into the intern year there is an outpouring of derogatory comments concerning the Management Intern Program. This outpouring coincides with the Management Intern Lecture-Seminar Series, when interns from different agencies gather together for formal training during which they may compare notes and find that they have had similar experiences. The criticism apparently has a cathartic effect since bitterness tends to decrease after the feelings are expressed. The criticisms are often well founded, and occasionally organized intern groups take the concerns to those in a position to act on them. There is some continuity from year to year in the outpouring of dissatisfaction.

In 1967, U.S. Civil Service Commission Chairman John W. Macy, Jr. addressed the interns assembled in Washington, D.C., and heard these points among several others raised by members of the group:

1. Agency program operation tends to place graduating management interns in staff and support jobs. There is less opportunity for interns to develop into program managers.

2. Though executives have a great many opportunities for interesting training courses, there are few courses for those aspiring to program management positions.

3. Agencies do not widely announce government-sponsored training opportunities for interns and refuse to fund training courses for interns that exceed forty hours.

4. Agencies do not assign meaningful work to interns, but too often serve them routine and artificial assignments.

5. Supervisors do not understand the management intern program and because of their lack of understanding are unwilling to give their best efforts to the interns.

During the 1969 Lecture-Seminar Series, a group of twenty interns presented the series director with their list of problems surrounding the Management Intern Program. Included in their list were these items:

1. Very few interns know the purpose or function of their training agreement. Those who do know about training agreements have not had the opportunity to comment on the agreements during periodic revisions.

2. Interns in some agencies have little meaningful work; this correlates with a lack of management interest in those agencies.

3. Many interns receive a succession of short rotational assignments and this contributes to job dissatisfaction.

4. The Civil Service Commission does not give proper attention to monitoring training agreements in order to detect violations.

These two lists of concerns point up major problems interns have with their programs. The reasons for these problems or their validity are less important than that they are perceived by interns to be of major importance. Progress has been made on some of these points, such as the offering of additional training opportunities for interns and the approval of training which exceeds forty hours in a single program. The majority of these problems and many more like them, however, remain in several management intern programs.

Intern Training

A wide variety of training opportunities is available to management interns in their first years of government service. As part of their internships, agencies enroll interns in formal training ranging from single agency courses to subject matter programs conducted for all interns by the Civil Service Commission to after-hours academic courses at universities.

Generally, interns have attended the week-long Management Intern Lecture-Seminar Series early in their internships and later one or more specific programs oriented to their agencies or occupation. The purpose of the Management Intern Lecture-Seminar Series has varied. In the early days of the Management Intern Program there were lectures to the plenary group. Later, monthly seminars were added and the "lecture-seminars" format developed under sponsorship of the Brookings Institute in the late 1950s. The Office of Career Development of the Civil Service Commission assumed responsibility for the lecture-seminars in the early 1960s. The series has gone through many changes conditioned by changes in society generally, and particularly by the youth movement.

The modern-day series was usually presented to enable all Washington-based interns to meet together for a single week to hear noted authorities discuss subjects of interest to the interns and to serve as an introduction to processes of government. The usual format with certain variations was one week of auditorium lectures in the morning and seminars in the afternoon.

The backgrounds, interests and needs of the interns are such that constructing a single lecture seminar series of value to all attending was an almost impossible task. A good number of interns selected each year were recent college graduates with no work experience. A large number had previous experience on full-time jobs. Many interns studied political science or public administration at the undergraduate or graduate level, but many had little or no understanding of government processes. There were interns greatly interested in discussing national issues and others who preferred discussing management techniques directly related to their jobs.

As a consequence, the series was considered by some to be too long, repetitious, boring, irrelevant, and a waste of time. Plenary sessions were replete with interns reading the *New York Times* during lectures, dwindling attendance by week's end, and occasionally disgruntled interns making their feelings known during the sessions to speakers and program coordinators alike. Often those who conducted the series one year were disinclined to take the challenge the second year or had gone to other jobs when the next year's series was being organized.

Lecture-seminars in past years have concentrated on managing various federal programs and presenting the various sides of national issues. Additional work-group sessions have enabled participants to discuss and develop ideas for eventual presentation to highly placed agency managers. Until recently, speakers had included a wide assortment of agency heads, special assistants to presidents, congressmen, noted academic figures, governmental, civilian, and military leaders, and newspaper reporters.

In the fall of 1970, emphasis was shifted somewhat to include high-level career civil servants, many of whom were alumni of the Federal Executive Institute in Charlottesville, Virginia. These relatively young officials discussed various facets of life in the federal bureaucracy, but the previous difficulties once again appeared. The program failed to consistently meet the diverse needs and expectations of the interns.

The Civil Service Commission's Bureau of Training reconstructed the training program. Beginning with the fall of 1971, the commission has offered management interns an integrated group of short courses, usually of three days in length, dealing with various areas of interest to the interns. A management intern lecture-seminar series will be presented to give the interns an overview of the Management Intern Program, its place in the entire scheme of developing managers, and some of the major issues of concern to the federal government. An additional series of short courses to be conducted for small groups in a classroom setting will include:

> The Dynamics of Government
> Introduction to Public Administration
> Seminar on Modern Management Theories
> Fundamental Management Techniques
> Management Introduction to ADP
> Financial Management in the Federal Government
> Scientifically Based Approaches to Management
>   in the Federal Government
> Federal Personnel Management — An Orientation
>   for Government Interns

All of these courses serve not to prepare one for a career in budgeting, personnel, ADP or other specific disciplines, but to make available brief presentations of subjects important to future managers.[16] Though certain of these courses were offered in the past, part of the new-look offereing is that the courses are presented as a package of training opportunities with sections specifically redesigned for future managers new to the government.

Recent Research

The Management Intern Program is a favorite subject for study by present interns, particularly those engaged in after-hours graduate studies in Public Administration at universities in the Washington area. Though interest is high, it is apparently short-lived, as few studies of note have been published. The better studies are those conducted by the Civil Service Commission as part of its continuing responsibility to monitor the program. Even these studies leave much to be desired due to limitations of scope. The primary concern of these studies has been with quantitative aspects of the management intern program. For this reason, the studies have been less geared to identifying the reasons for employee turnover or the rate of MI progression, and there is no continuing mechanism to collect even basic data on intern retention and advancement rates. When interpreting the studies below, it must be remembered that they occurred at different times, and that the employment outlook, attitudes of society, current events and other factors influenced the findings. For instance, the abundance of jobs for college graduates in the mid-1960s accounted in part for a much higher employment turnover rate than one would likely find in the 1970-71 intern job market.

1966 Survey

A 1966 survey took a random sampling of better than one-third of those interns appointed in 1956 and 1957 and those appointed five years later in 1961.[17] The survey revealed that 66 percent of the interns appointed in 1956-57 and 68 percent of those appointed in 1961 were still federal employees. This suggested that perhaps turnover decreased sharply after the first five years of employment. The survey was also interpreted to indicate that government retention was comparable to that reported for business and industry at the same time. But, the business-industry survey counted turnover as occurring when a person left his original company. The government survey considered interagency movement not as turnover but as continued employment with the same employer. While this is conceptually true, the government retention figures would doubtless have been much lower had each agency been considered a separate employer, as 41.5 percent of those interns still with the government during this survey had served with more than one agency.

1967 Survey

A later Civil Service Commission study of management interns appointed in 1965 and 1966 indicated that as of September 1967, when 9 to 33 months had lapsed since the date of appointment, 83 percent of the appointees were still employed.[18] The study also indicated:

1. Twenty-nine agencies hired interns; 11 hired over 25 interns and 6 hired from 10 to 20.

2. One hundred twenty-six or 21 percent of the interns were women.

3. At the time of application for the examination, half of the applicants were students; 19 percent were in private employment; 13 percent were federal employees.

4. Fifty-eight percent had the A.B. degree only, 36 percent M.A., and 1.6 percent Ph.D.; 1.4 percent had no college degree.

5. Of the 128 persons who left the federal service, about one-third left to return to school, another one-thrid went to private employment, and the remainder gave other or no reasons.

1969 Survey

The most comprehensive survey by far was conducted late in 1969.[19] It included all 1,915 management interns selected by federal agencies from 1965 to 1968. The first finding of this survey was surprising in that 384 or 20 percent of those offered management intern positions had apparently never been employed as management interns. This number of management intern eligibles, though selected for employment decided against accepting management intern positions; yet they continued to be included in the statistical summaries of management intern selections. The figures, while not absolutely accurate, are probably close enough to serve as indicators for the kinds of conclusions being drawn from current studies. Table 10.3 shows trends on retention, quite different from those found previously.

Table 10.3. Intern Retention

Years appointment since	Percentage in government remaining
1	79%
2	72%
3	55%
4	55%

These figures, particularly for those appointed three and four years ago, were substantially below retention rates presented in previous surveys. The study included additional data on:

1. Retention by sex (increasingly lower for women after the first year)

2. Reasons for leaving federal employment (21 percent to return to school, 17 percent to work in private employment, 12 percent to enter military service)

3. Location during management intern period (78 percent in Washington)

4. Retention rates at various ages (rates increase consistently with increasing age at appointment)

5. Promotion rates by sex (slightly lower promotion rates for women than for men)

6. The average age at appointment by sex (female management interns are younger)

7. Agency changing (less than one in ten interns still with the government changed agencies during the first four years of employment)

As part of the most recent Civil Service Commission survey, follow-up forms were sent to 206 people who left the federal government after having been employed as management interns. This portion of the survey was intended to uncover attitudes about government employment and MIs' perceptions of their internships. Survey forms were returned by more than half of the former management interns. These responses indicated:

1. Seventy-four percent would be willing to return to the federal government in a position comparable to or higher than the one they previously held.

2. Eight-five percent would recommend the Management Intern Program to a friend seeking employment

3. Only 10 percent said they would not recommend the Management Intern Program to a friend seeking employment

Narrative responses to the inquiries were varied but included the following anonymous three:

1. I felt that the position I held . . . had very little relevance to the mission of that installation and that the mission of the agency had very little relevance to what I considered to be the most pressing needs in the U.S. (Just so it won't appear that I criticize the Government unfairly, I would like to say that I have since come to feel the same way about my subsequent job in private industry. Thus I am now looking again.) My experience as an MI has led me to believe that most Government agencies have a very parochial view which leads them to fight for money which they cannot use effectively, thus resulting in distorted priorities within the Government. But this is probably unavoidable in any position lower than the highest policy-making levels. Since I cannot work effectively without "believing," Government is probably not for me.

2. I left the Federal service to return to college and work on a Ph.D. degree with the ultimate goal of teaching history and American studies in a university. Part of the reason for abandoning my intern position was the conviction that the true administrative positions are not open to females despite all the rhetoric to the contrary. My experience convinced me that as long as you wear skirts you are expected to smile pretty, answer the telephone, and be helpful, but to stay out of the way when important administrative matters are under consideration. I am fully aware that I could have stayed with the Government service and fought for 'equal rights' but I, frankly, do not desire to expend all my energies on a feminist campaign. There are, in my opinion, more important worthwhile things to devote my time and talents to in this world.

3. The Management Intern program offered me wonderful opportunities for personal advancement and personal improvement — Federal Service in general, including the MI program, did *not* offer opportunities for public service equal either to public needs or the desire of the intern to meet those needs. The bureaucracy is not responsive to change or public needs, and generally wastes the talents of its employees. The MI program tries to recruit talented young people — from my experience it succeeds. The question is, what happens to these people? They are generally interested in (1) decision-making and (2) outputs of the Federal bureaucracy. Since it is highly unlikely that these young people can or should be placed in actual decision-making positions, I believe the interns should be placed in field positions where (1) they see and participate in the actual output function of the Government and (2) they have the opportunity to deal with people and relate their work in terms of its worth (or lack of) to people, not machines, or divisions of the Government bureaucracy.

Evaluation Considerations

The Management Intern Program is the result of almost forty years of development and changing philosophy about how best to fulfill the government's need for managers. Additional changes are required, however, to keep the program viable. There are many issues to be joined and steps to be taken before the program will meet government's current needs. Some of these steps are government-wide in scope and others are measures that should be taken by individual agencies.

As the first step, agencies should reevaluate the purpose of their programs and decide what kind of impact they should have. The purpose of most intern programs is stated in vague terms. Few agencies express a clear concept of why they host management intern programs; some may do so simply because they always have for twenty years. Few have identified precise needs (e.g., provide key replacements for an aging work force, provide an intake of specific kinds of people for the work force) they intend to satisfy through the program. Too few programs are conducted with the main purpose of bringing about organizational change or improving the organization's management. Too few agencies conduct their programs as if they realize that an intern program is an excellent way to inject new talent, enthusiasm, and philosophy into an organization.

There is also a need for a more systematic means of involving supervisors in management intern programs. This contributes to part of the adjustment problems many interns experience. Some portion of supervisors are highly placed middle-aged officials who have sons and daughters in the same age bracket as management interns. Problems in communicating with offspring may be replicated in their dealings with interns. With very little effort, agencies can compile lists of articles on supervising young college graduates or booklets answering frequently asked questions or misunderstood facts about the program. Supervisors of management interns must be properly briefed.

More progress on current proposals and new program alterations are needed to identify more minority group members who should pass through the testing screen and qualify for internships. As it stands now, minority group members, particularly those from predominantly black colleges, have great difficulty achieving a qualifying score on the Federal Service Entrance Examination. Alternate measures to substitute for the test score must be found to permit members of minority groups to compete in the oral interview portion of the examination. Among the alternatives considered but not adopted by the Civil Service Commission are class standing and academic average. Perhaps a more aggressive stance by the Civil Service Commission strongly encouraging other means of attracting minority group members to internships will be the most effective method in the short run.

Methods used to evaluate the Management Intern Program are in general need of improvement. The fact that few agencies maintain even rough records on their former interns suggests the degree of evaluation sophistication. Additional consideration must be given to evaluating intern programs on factors such as constructive contributions made to the hiring agency, cost-benefit relationships, and retention and turnover rates only to the extent that the reasons for high or low rates are identified. A statement made to personnel officers in 1969 by the executive director of the Civil Service Commission is still true today:

Basic data on management interns must be collected and interpreted. There is still no mechanism for gathering periodically the figures which would reveal intern progression and turnover. To date, all management intern surveys have been one time efforts, whereas a continuous study is needed if the long-range effectiveness of the program is to be gauged. This also obviates trying to root out the career history of each former intern every time a survey is made.[20]

A comprehensive study comparing the relative worth of management intern programs with alternate methods of recruiting and developing young managers would be a worthwhile addition to available information. The cost of the recruiting and development phases may be too high in relation to the 55 percent of management interns who remain with the federal government three to four years after their appointment. Some portion of the turnover may occur in organizations which should not use the management intern program as a source of manpower. There may also be better sources of manpower and methods of developing future managers more suitable to individual agency needs. For instance, the Department of Health, Education and Welfare relies heavily on utilization of present employees for internships and the Department of Housing and Urban Development recruits a wide range of people for the program rather than only MI eligibles.

Additional measures must be taken by policy-makers to communicate with management interns and to consider their views on matters directly affecting them. There are also several methods that could be used to increase an intern's identification with his agency. Measures as basic as involving interns in study groups, inviting them to attend and participate in staff meetings, and considering their observations and constructive recommendations for offices in which they have worked are not universally used. Some management intern programs have been altered without inviting or considering the views of the interns.

Additional consideration must be given to the value of the prolonged in-depth assignments versus a series of relatively short rotational assignments. Most agencies now use the rotation method and some of these assignments, in the eyes of interns, are not of sufficient duration for them to feel truly involved in the work of the office.

There are few reliable bench marks by which to judge management intern programs. Most completed research has concentrated primarily on agency retention rates of interns, but none of it suggests what is good or bad retention. It has even been said that agencies should lose more management interns than they do and that agencies lose the good interns, retaining the persons they should lose. These comments notwithstanding, it would seem clear that from agency standpoint keeping its interns for an average of three years would be a minimum requirement. If an agency keeps its interns for an average of less than three years, it is losing on its intern investment.

The question with which all users of the management intern program must be concerned is: How should a management intern program in the federal government be conducted to assure a good return on an investment? While they are backed by experimental data, people working most closely and most concerned with federal management intern programs generally agree that the following points should prove beneficial in constructing and conducting a management intern program:

1. A management intern program must be tailor-made for each agency. Techniques used successfully in one agency cannot automatically be applied to another. The finest intern programs are those which are tied very closely to agency needs.

2. Programs must be flexible. They must be designed to allow variations in typical patterns described in training agreements. Agencies often bind themselves to rigid programs when Civil Service Commission standards permit and encourage flexibility. The CSC needs to improve its efforts to assist agencies in developing flexible programs.

3. Interns themselves must be involved in the planning and coordination of management intern programs. This includes working cooperatively with them in identifying and selecting assignments and final positions.

4. Supervisory support must be obtained. Some agency coordinators have been handicapped in operating their programs by lack of supervisory support. Supervisory support is a commodity not automatically granted; coordinators have to earn it, and good coordinators know there are ways to get that support.

5. Programs must have a higher purpose than simply bringing in new talent. Ultimately, the highest purpose of the management intern program is to

get vitality into management, to introduce new ideas into the agencies, and to get new ways of working an old established operation. The program can be used to bring about change to a much greater extent than it is now used.

6. Continual and imaginative evaluation is necessary to assure that management intern programs are meeting the current needs of agencies. It would appear that inadequate attention is given to collecting data on certain aspects of this program, the first year cost of which approaches five million dollars even in lean hiring years.

These six points are not guaranteed to result in a perfect management intern program, but overlooking any of them is almost certain to result in a second rate product. The federal investment in intern programs is substantial and more systematic evaluation is necessary.

The Management Intern Program is probably one of the most successful of the programs to attract, develop, and retain quality employees for government service. The efforts of planners and program coordinators have made the program generally responsive to federal needs. The quality of those recruited for the program has caused it to be considered as an important source of federal recruiting. The Management Intern Program and its predecessors have been influenced by changes in society and especially by employment conditions and educational systems. There are indications that the program will continue to be revised as long as such a program is required, and there is reason to believe that it will be replaced when it is no longer needed. There is no question, however, that much more needs to be known about the effects and effectiveness of the Management Intern Program before intelligent decisions can be made on its new directions.

Notes

1. Unpublished data from Federal Executive Inventory and conversation with Mrs. Sally Greenberg, Executive Manpower Planning Specialist, Bureau of Executive Manpower, U.S. Civil Service Commission, June 4, 1971.

2. Jonathan A. Slesinger, *Personal Adaptation in the Federal Junior Management Assistant Program* (Ann Arbor, Michigan: The Institute of Public Administration at the University of Michigan, 1961), p.2.

3. Nathan Mandell, "The JMA Program," *Public Administration Review,* May 1953, pp. 106-107.

4. Ibid., p. 111.

5. Slesinger, *Personnel Adaptation,* p. 2.

6. Mandell, "JMA Program" p. 107.

7. Karl Stromsen, *The Work of the National Institute of Public Affairs, 1934-1939* (Washington, D.C.: NIPA, October 1949) pp. 1-4.

8. Mandell, "JMA Program", p. 104-108.

9. Philip Young, "The Federal Service Entrance Examination," *Public Administration Review,* December 1956, pp. 2-3.

10. Much of the information in the following sections of this chapter is derived from the 1971 Management Intern Fact Sheets.

11. U. S. Civil Service Commission, *Trend of Competition and Selections, 1956-1969,* Washington, D.C., (updated by interviews in May 1971).

12. Office of the Secretary, Department of Health, Education, and Welfare, "Proposal to Modify the Selection of Management Interns," letter transmitted by a selection of minority candidates and sent to the Management Intern Coordinators, February 1, 1971.

13. U. S. Civil Service Commission, *Letter to Management Intern Eligibles,* Form WA 38, September 1967.

14. Manpower Sources Division, Bureau of Recruiting and Examining United States Civil Service Commission, "Survey of Management Interns," informal paper, March 1970.

15. Greenberg, conversation.

16. Interview with Dr. Ronald C. Semone, Associate Director, General Management Training Center, Bureau of Training, U. S. Civil Service Commission, April 1971.

17. U. S. Civil Service Commission, "Survey of Management Interns," informal paper, 1966.

18. Executive Director, United States Civil Service Commission, "Summary Report . . . Survey of Management Interns appointed during 1965-66," transmitted by memo to agency and department directors of personnel, March 25, 1969.

19. Ibid., March 1970.

20. Executive Director, U. S. Civil Service Commission, letter to directors of personnel on management intern survey, October 23, 1969.

11

The Congressional Fellowship Program: Maximizing Participant Observation in Studying Politics

RONALD D. HEDLUND

A recent increase in the number of political intern programs again has raised questions regarding the epistemological merits of participant observation.[1] To the rigorous empiricist who recognizes the acquisition of knowledge only through one's senses, participant observation hardly qualifies as a systematic and valid research strategy. Its unsystematic, almost haphazard means for exposing the investigator to the research problem raises questions of validity and representativeness. Further, the sometimes subjective, almost intuitive nature of the processes used in observing phenomena raises questions of interpretation and reliability. At the other extreme, the pure rationalist doubts participant observation because it advocates extensive use of sensory experience. While the rationalist may appreciate the participant observer's use of intellect and logical deduction in arriving at conclusions, the use of one's senses as an input to these processes generates skepticism.

Advocates of participant observation do not deny that it is in many ways unsystematic and intuitive and that it relies upon total sensory experience; rather, they defend participant observation because of this very combination of traits. A recent anthology on participation observation takes note of its nonrigorous, experiential character and points out the logical research consequence.

Because of the rather omnibus quality of this blend we call participant observation it has not lent itself to the standardization of procedure that social scientists have come to expect of their methods, as in testing, survey, laboratory, and ecological work .... The techniques of participant observation

The author gratefully acknowledges the assistance of many persons in preparing this chapter: especially Leslie Jarvis, who assisted throughout the analysis; Evron M. Kirkpatrick, Walter E. Beach, Thomas Mann, and a number of former fellows, who spent considerable time discussing the Congressional Fellow Program; the 296 former fellows who completed and returned the complex mail questionnaire used to study the program; Thomas P. Murphy and the public management intern seminar at the University of Missouri – Kansas City who criticized an early draft of this chapter; and, the Congressional Fellowship Program Advisory Committee, especially its Chairman William J. Keefe, who provided a grant to the author and assumed all direct study costs. However, the author alone assumes responsibility for the analysis and interpretation in this chapter.

are regarded as difficult to communicate or teach. The nonquantitative nature of the results causes difficulties in presenting evidence and proof for propositions.[2]

These characteristics led George J. McCall and John Simmons to characterize participant observation as a "style" of research rather than a method. Such a distinction is made primarily for reasons of conceptual clarity. As commonly used in social science research, a method denotes a way of doing things such as collecting information through a survey. Participant observation, on the other hand, does not refer in the same manner to a way of doing something; rather participant observation is a social role assumed by someone so that he may gain insight about a complex organization. Even the nature of this role varies to such a degree that generalizing about it is not possible. Thus to characterize participant observation as a method is to ascribe to it characteristics that it does not in fact possess.

Closely related to the nature of participant observation is its purpose. In professional jargon, participant observation is universally cited for giving one a "feel" for a situation. It offers the observer an opportunity to get close — physically, intellectually, and emotionally — to the reality of a complex situation. James A. Robinson noted that

"Having a feel for a situation" may be likened to the state of being comfortable in it, of believing that one has the salient facts of the event, of knowing something of what to expect next, of taking many things for granted, of predicting without being surprised by the future. The basic intellectual operation involved in acquiring "feel" is that of drawing an analogy between one's experience and the new set of circumstances in which he finds himself. . . . "Feel" is an analogy from earlier experience, and the sensitivity of one's political "feel," the originality of his political "insight," depends in part on the quality of prior political experience.

The fully engaged political participant feels comfortable when he has learned most of the attributes of his new role, its jargon, skills, and expected activities. His present experience coincides with earlier experience. In other words, when one becomes "socialized" to a new role he acquires "feel." The observer who wants a "feel" for politics must undergo some of the same socialization as the politician.[3]

By providing one a firsthand view of a political situation, participant observation advances one's general understanding of that situation and indirectly aids scholarly research.

Participant observation also has a more direct role in assisting empirical research. Here experience has proved useful initially in the predata collection stages of empirical inquiry. Participant observers appear to have some advantage over others in identifying important factors and specifying, in hypothesis form, the probable relationships among factors. Later, participant observation also has been useful for imparting meaning and significance to empirical research findings. Vidich and Shapiro commented:

What the survey method gains in representative coverage of a population is probably of no greater methodological significance than the increased depth of understanding and interpretation possible with participant-observation techniques. This is evident when we contrast the position of a survey analyst and a participant observer when both face the problem of interpreting the *meaning* of a question. The desk chair analyst can give at best an intelligent guess based upon sketchy pretest and tabular data. The observer, in contrast, can call upon the wealth of experience with the lingquistic habits, the attitudes, values and beliefs of the group and provide a much richer, and probably sounder interpretation.[4]

Finally, many political scientists report access to previously closed research situations for a participant observer. The reluctance and timidity of organizational personnel in allowing an outsider to study congressional committees, governmental bureaus, and party caucuses sometimes dissipates when the investigator becomes a legitimate participant observer.

Given these twin goals of developing a feel for some political situation and assisting in the empirical research efforts of an investigator, many potential political scientist observers have asked how one makes maximum use of these opportunities. What situational conditions optimize participant observation? How can the potential observer best prepare for his new role? What organizational steps can be taken by the sponsoring agency to assist participant observers? And what types of persons are most successful in maximizing opportunities for observation?

In order to answer these questions in a systematic manner, the remainder of this chapter will consider three topics: (1) the most desirable setting for participant observation; (2) one well-known, politically oriented participant observer program and its attempt to create this setting; and, (3) the factors that seem to advance or retard the establishment of this setting. In exploring the first of these topics this chapter will rely upon a growing body of literature discussing participant observation and intern programs.[5] The other topics will make use of data collected in an evaluation of one of the best known of all political intern programs—the Congressional Fellowship Program (CFP).[6]

The Optimal Participant Observer Setting

The literature and lore of participant observation is replete with statements regarding what constitutes an optimal organizational setting for participant observation. With the twin goals of developing a feel for the situation and conducting empirical research in mind, four major features would seem to characterize the setting conducive to these goals.

The first feature relates to the nature of the relationship established by the observer with significant others in the organizational setting. Advocates use a number of adjectives to describe the nature of this relationship including warm, frank and personal; but all seem to agree that the creation of a cordial and trusting interpersonal relationship is essential for developing feel and conducting research. In discussing this aspect R.J. Snow concluded that "Ideally, those persons well established in the research and environment will perceive the newcomer [the participant observer] as affable, as a peer, as one willing to work hard, and as one who poses little threat to their roles."[7] Such a relationship would assist the establishment of credibility and of access to the inner workings and personal attitudes of other participants in the organizational setting.

The second aspect of a desirable setting is the role assumed by the participant observer. Obviously the role an observer plays will be partly dependent upon the kind of relationship he establishes with the significant others; however, the observer may be assigned a social position and a role to play in the organization that is at some variance with the personal relationships established. "What an observer will see will depend largely on his particular position in a network of relationships.[8] The role assigned to the participant observer will affect how he approaches the organizational setting. In political organizations, especially those headed by an elected public official, a role as a trusted staff member is thought to be especially appropriate. After extensive exposure to Capitol Hill, Alan Fiellin noted that "the staff role is particularly strategic for learning about legislative politics. . . .[9]

In order to develop feel, it is also important that the observer assume work duties representative of the organization's mission. If the organization is involved in public policy formation, a participant observer whose work duties are routine and secretarial would encounter difficulty obtaining an accurate perception of that organization. While exposure to a variety of organizational activities may be preferable to some observers, others may seek opportunities to concentrate in more limited activities. The liabilities of this latter course, while obvious, need not impair the maximum usefulness of participant observation unless this strategy removes the observer from the organization's major activity patterns.

Finally, having opportunities to observe significant and representative organizational activity is deemed critical for optimizing participant observation. Reflecting on the availability of observational opportunities, Snow commented upon the observers physical location in the organization's environment.

The participant observer may discover that the strategic physical location of his desk or working space in the research environment will have direct implications for the quality of data he is able to collect. . . . A researcher should locate himself strategically to maximize observation opportunities if he can do so without offense to others.[10]

If close physical proximity to significant others affords more opportunities to observe important behavior, then being located in major office traffic patterns should assist in optimizing participant observation. Thus a participant observer is more likely to develop feel and to conduct valid, systematic, and empirical research in an organizational setting where he is able to develop a warm and trusting set of personal relationships, to assume a role providing direct and immediate access to important organizational activity. to undertake important and representative work duties, and to be physically located where he is able to observe significant organizational activity.

The Congressional Fellowship Program

In order to evaluate the attainment of a conducive participant observer setting, data from a survey of past participants in one of the most widely known political intern programs, the Congressional Fellowship Program, were examined. This program has brought promising young scholars, journalists, and public officials to Washington, D.C. and provided them a firsthand view of Congress through an intensive six-week orientation and a nine-month working assignment on Capitol Hill.

A mail questionnaire soliciting opinions and evaluations of the CFP was distributed in mid-October 1970 to 420 past participants.[11] A total of 296, or 70 percent of the questionnaires sent out were returned. Analysis of these 296 questionnaires indicates an exceptionally representative response rate for various categories of participants — academics (mostly political scientists), journalists, and civil servants. Somewhat greater variation, sometimes exceeding 10 percent, was found for selected years of the program; but, these variations seemed to be random so that no period of years, e.g., the first eight years when only journalists and scholars were involved, is grossly under-or overrepresented.[12]

Certain aspects of this program differ dramatically from those of other intern programs. The CFP is organized to recruit older, more mature persons than is usually the case. The average age at time of appointment is 31.5 years and almost all have received at least a bachelor's degree with more than half having also received a master's. The stated program purposes minimize it as a means to secure permanent governmental employment, but only 17 percent reported no desire to remain in Washington after the program's conclusion. The desire to remain was highest for civil servants, many of whom had lived and worked in Washington prior to their selection, and lowest among academics, fewer of whom reported a desire to change positions or use the program as a means for securing a position. An actual opportunity to remain in Washington after the program was reported by more than four out of five respondents. Again significantly more civil servants and journalists reported having such an opportunity than did academics. This finding probably indicates that fewer academically oriented participants had the skills and/or temperament to remain as staff persons. More civil servants (92 percent) and journalists (60 percent) did in fact remain than did academics (40 percent); and many of these academics left Washington after just a few years. The type of position in which the person remained also differed. Journalists tended to work either as journalists or on the Hill while academics tended to work on the Hill or seek some other type of position; civil servants tended to return to executive agencies. These preliminary remarks about the CFP and its participants lead to the obvious question: how well does the CFP succeed in creating an optimal participant observation setting?

Relationship to Significant Others

The nature of CFP participants' relationships to significant others in the congressional setting was measured using four eight-item semantic differential scales. Through this technique the respondent's linguistic representation of a concept is used as a measure of the meaning he attaches to that concept.[13] Thus the fellows' perceived relationships to significant others can be specified by examining their judgments on pairs of descriptive polar terms. In order to provide these judgments, every CFP respondent was presented eight pairs of polar terms, each pair hypothesized to measure some aspect of the type of relationship established with a significant other (see table 11.1). The respondents reported along a seven-step continuum their perceptions regarding the nature of

Table 11.1. Semantic Differential Scale Items As They Appeared in Questionnaire

DIRECTIONS: THE PURPOSE OF THIS SECTION IS TO EVALUATE THE NATURE OF THE RELATIONSHIP YOU WERE ABLE TO ESTABLISH DURING YOUR OFFICE ASSIGNMENT BY JUDGING IT AGAINST A SERIES OF DESCRIPTIVE SCALES. IN ANSWERING THESE QUESTIONS PLEASE MAKE YOUR JUDGMENTS ON THE BASIS OF THE INTERPERSONAL RELATIONSHIPS *YOU* ACTUALLY ESTABLISHED. FOR EACH QUESTION YOU WILL FIND A DIFFERENT ASPECT OF THIS RELATIONSHIP BEING TAPPED. INDICATE THE EXTENT OF YOUR RELATIONSHIP BY CHECKING THE APPROPRIATE SPACE. FOR EXAMPLE, IF YOUR RELATIONSHIP WAS VERY CLOSE TO THAT DESCRIBED BY THE FORMER EXTREME, CHECK THE SPACE NEAREST THAT CONCEPT. IF SOME OTHER SPACE IS MORE APPROPRIATE, PLEASE CHECK THAT ONE.
 MAKE ONLY ONE CHECK FOR EACH QUESTION.

Very (1)	Fairly (2)	Slightly (3)	Neither (4)	Slightly (5)	Fairly (6)	Very (7)	
Accepting							Rejecting
Frank							Evasive
Repetitive							Varied
Definite							Uncertain
Deep							Shallow
Insider							Outsider
Personal							Impersonal
Labored							Easy

these relationships. This judgmental process was repeated for the four major types of significant others encountered during the CFP—the member of Congress assigned to during the first half, the congressional staff worked with during the first half, the member of Congress assigned to during the second half, and the congressional staff worked with during the second half. The semantic differential thus required a total of thirty two questions, each eliciting one judgment.[14]

The distribution of responses for seven of these eight items and for all four sets of significant others, for twenty-eight of the thirty-two judgments, is clearly unimodal and monotonic, indicating a comparatively high degree of consistency among respondents regarding the character of the relationships. The lone exception, the repetitive-varied item, consistently differs from the other seven. In terms of central tendency for these seven items and for the four sets of significant others, in every case the modal response category is strongly in the direction of an optimal relationship as described in the previous section – falling either in the "very" or "fairly" category and in the optimal direction, i.e., accepting, frank, definite, deep, insider, personal, and easy rather than rejecting, evasive, uncertain, shallow, outsider, impersonal, and labored. In none of these twenty-eight cases does the number of responses in the nonoptimal direction total more that 20 percent and in the majority of these instances it is less than 10 percent.

When each set of eight items is subjected to a factor analysis in order to determine the dimensionality of responses, two major factors can be discerned – one factor, composed of the seven items discussed above, seems to indicate the level of personal confidence perceived by the respondent in his relationship with the significant other; and a second factor, made up of the single remaining item, repetitive-varied, seems to be based upon the nature of the work assignment (see table 11.2). Additional credibility for this structuring is apparent in the consistent placing of items on the same factor for all four sets of significant others.

Regarding the nature of personal relationships established by post CFP participants with the objects of their attention – members of Congress and their staffs – a Kaiser Varimax rotated factor analytic solution shows that (1) two separate dimensions relating to the nature of this relationship can be identified in their responses; (2) one of these relates to the type of personal confidence the fellow perceived as existing with the significant other and the second to the pace of the work assignment; (3) this structuring of relationships is consistent during both halves of the Fellowship and does not vary depending upon the identity of the significant other; and, (4) congressional fellows seem generally to have been successful in creating a relationship they feel is conducive for acquiring feel and doing observational research in the organizational setting.

Role Orientation

Whenever one enters a new organizational setting, he assumes a social position

Table 11.2. Rotated Factor Analysis Solutions to Determine the Dimensions of the Relationships Established by Congressional Fellows with Members of Congress and Their Staff

Rotated Solutions

Descriptive Polar Terms	Member of Congress – First Half		Staff – First Half		Member of Congress – Second Half		Staff – Second Half	
	Personal Confidence Factor I	Work Assignment Factor II	Personal Confidence Factor I	Work Assignment Factor II	Personal Confidence Factor I	Work Assignment Factor II	Personal Confidence Factor I	Work Assignment Factor II
Insider	.866	-.065	.896	-.085	.895	-.081	.856	-.190
Deep	.855	.006	.827	-.038	.877	-.040	.861	-.111
Personal	.854	.031	.836	-.046	.863	-.031	.814	-.116
Accepting	.835	-.091	.862	.011	.813	-.086	.824	-.044
Frank	.760	-.193	.871	-.039	.851	-.023	.855	-.060
Definite	.741	-.069	.761	.024	.800	-.007	.814	.096
Easy	.587	-.279	.678	-.241	.704	-.163	.692	-.273
Repetitive	-.023	.968	-.041	.986	-.067	.993	-.081	.978
Percentage of Total Variance (cumulative)	55.3	68.1	59.5	72.1	61.1	73.4	60.0	72.5
Percentage of Explained Variance (cumulative)	81.1	100.0	82.5	100.0	83.2	100.0	82.8	100.0

and a role in the network of interpersonal relationships. He soon discovers that expectations regarding values, attitudes, and behaviors exist for any role and that ignoring these expectations can produce extreme tension. The interpersonal role judged most valuable for maximizing participant observation in a congressional office is that of staff. Since few other viable role alternatives exist, the success one has in adopting the role of staff becomes critical for developing feel and conducting research. In fact, 70 percent of past fellows indicated it is very important for a fellow to learn how to think like a staff member and another 25 percent indicated it is of some importance. Regarding their success in assuming the staff role, 55 percent indicated they were very successful and 35 percent felt fairly successful in learning to think like staff personnel. No one indicated a complete lack of success in assuming this role.

Office Duties

In order to obtain an accurate picture of the overall operation of an organization it is essential for the observer to become familiar with various office operations. Experience in a variety of office duties will provide such exposures and will concurrently provide information about the perspectives and behaviors developed by other members of the organization. Because of the highly individualized working style of congressional offices,[15] however, it is difficult to generalize about the most advantageous arrangement of work duties which might aid in developing feel and conducting research. Such uniqueness poses a difficulty in determining whether the duties assigned an observer expose him to the operations of that congressional office.

Congressional fellows were asked to indicate the proportion of time spent by the 296 respondents. Table 11.3 indicates that the greatest amount of a fellow's time was spent in duties generally considered an integral part of the congressional process – legislative assistance, policy research, and constituent relations. In most cases, however, the observers did spend some portion of their time in the more routine clerical types of duties. Although congressional fellows seem to spend large amounts of time on integral activities, which provide insight into important office operations, they also appear to be exposed to other duties thus giving them an overall perspective.

Opportunities for Participant Observation

Even if the observer has assumed an appropriate staff role, established appropriate relationships with significant others, and performed important duties, he may not be able to observe significant organizational activity. For example, he may be placed in a physical location so remote from the center of organizational activity that meaningful observation is impossible. Comparatively

Table 11.3. Average Amount of Time Spent in Various Organizational Duties During Congressional Fellowship

Type of Duties	Average Proportion of Time[a]	
	First-Half Assignment	Second-Half Assignment
Clerical	4.9	4.1
Policy research	25.0	26.1
Constituent problems	16.9	14.2
Press relations	11.9	11.4
Legislative assistance	26.7	28.4
Other	11.6	12.6

[a] These are average percentages for all 296 respondents and do not total 100% due to a small number of no responses.

few congressional fellows reported being physically located in the same office as a member of Congress, but generally speaking they were located in an adjacent office shared with staff members (table 11.4). While being located in the same

Table 11.4. Physical Location of Fellow in Relation to Significant Other (Percentage by Column)

Nature of Location	In Relation to Member of Congress		In Relation to Staff	
	First Half	Second Half	First Half	Second Half
In same office	11.8	7.8	73.0	62.5
In adjacent office in major traffic pattern	61.5	47.0	16.9	18.2
In adjacent office not in major traffic pattern	13.2	22.0	5.7	9.8
Physically separated	11.5	22.0	2.4	8.1
No response	2.0	1.3	2.0	1.4
Total %	100.0	100.1	100.0	100.0
N	296	296	296	296

office as a member of Congress would have certain observational advantages, many legislators spend considerable time elsewhere; thus, being located with staff members in a major traffic pattern probably probably provides an adequate opportunity for participant observation.

In spite of the idiosyncratic features of a work assignment in a congressional office, the congressional fellows studied appear to have been successful in creating an atmosphere conducive to participant observation. The personal relationships established with members of Congress and their staffs seem to be consistently warm, personal, and trusting as perceived by fellows. No apparent difficulties appear to have been created for the fellows in assuming a position and role advantageous for developing feel and conducting research. Exposure to a wide range of office activities with concentration in significant areas seems to characterize the experience of most fellows. And numerous opportunities for face-to-face involvement and observation apparently were afforded large numbers of fellows. With this encouraging report about the CFP's perceived success in creating an optimal participant observation setting, one is led to the third topic of this chapter: What factors seem to affect maximizing an organizational setting for participant observation?

Creating the Optimal Setting

A number of factors have been assumed to affect the quality of an intern program, especially success in creating a setting conducive to developing feel and conducting observational research. In a recent monograph that evaluates several politically oriented intern programs, Bernard C. Hennessy concluded that three types of factors affect program quality; (1) the attributes of the interns; (2) the nature of the offices in which the interns serve; and (3) the pedagogical nature of the program. Based on his extensive experience with intern programs, Hennessy then formulated thirteen generalizations regarding how each of these factors affects intern programs. These generalizations relate to the training, skill and experience of the intern; the size, complexity, and type of office; and, the planning, preparation and involvement of the program director.[16]

Although a direct test of Hennessy's generalizations was not always possible using the CFP data, information on specific variables related to the personal, situational and programmatic factors was collected. This section of the chapter will consider the effects of these variables on the relationships, roles, duties, and observational opportunities of CFP participants. Due to the multiple measures used for both independent and dependent variables and the consequently large number of associations to be considered, only selected associations of statistical *and* theoretical importance can be considered here.

Personal Qualities of the Intern

One of the major behavioralist assumptions regarding the study of politics is that the attributes and experiences of the actor have some effect on his behavior. According to this perspective, persons are not ciphers who have no effect on their own behaviors; rather, their characteristics and experiences have a profound influence on their beliefs and actions. If this stance is accepted regarding political actors, the same should follow for political interns. For instance, the CFP requires that applicants be interviewed by a three-man panel which determines, among other things, if the candidate has the necessary personality, temperament, and background. In spite of this effort to secure participants who are compatible with the requirements of working in a congressional office, certain types of fellows have experienced greater success than others.

Fellows with prior experience in politics and the legislative setting are thought to be better prepared for work assignments and observation in congressional offices. These previous experiences seem to sensitize one to practical politics and legislative mores so that when one begins an office assignment he is immediately able to assume important tasks and intelligently to observe and interpret behavior. Although all three political-legislative exposure variables investigated — prior political involvement, prior exposure to Capitol Hill, and specialization in Congress or legislative behavior — are significantly related to at least one feature of the optimal setting, the overall effect appears to be minimal. Three of these four significant associations are with the proportion of time spent in various work duties, suggesting that prior political-legislative interest and involvement has some affect on the kinds of work a fellow assumes. For example, table 11.5 shows that a high level of previous political involvement is significantly associated with the proportion of time spent during the first half assignment in policy research; however, the failure of the other two significant

Table 11.5. Proportion of Time Spent in Policy Research During the First Half Assignment by Prior Political Experience (Percentage by Column)

Proportion of Time	Level of Previous Involvement				
	Very Much	Somewhat	Little	None	Total
None	10.0	11.4	16.4	25.8	16.9
Up to 10%	18.0	12.5	27.9	23.7	20.3
10-20%	22.0	19.3	16.4	16.5	18.2
20-50%	34.0	46.6	34.4	29.9	36.5
50-100%	16.0	10.2	4.9	4.1	8.1
Total %	100.0	100.0	100.0	100.0	100.0
N	50	88	61	97	296

Chi-square = 24.1 $p < .02$

relationships regarding work duties to occur during the first assignment raises questions about any wide-spread initial advantage because of prior involvement. The fact that these significant relationships are observed later during the second assignment period perhaps indicates that in some instances a reinforcement of prior exposure through additional work experience is necessary before its impact will be discernable.

Another set of factors hypothesized to be important are the reasons a person has in applying for the CFP. Three differing types of motivations were investigated — the opportunity for practical political involvement, the chance to conduct research, and the desire to enhance or advance one's occupational status. Such differing motivations are expected to reflect a differing orientation and approach to work and observation in the office setting. Regarding the types of work undertaken, fellows placing a high or low level of importance on the practical involvement aspects of the program are significantly different from those indicating a middle or no level of importance. For example, the former types are significantly more likely to do clerical work during both assignment periods than the latter group – chi-square $p < < .05$. Further, those with a high or low level of practical motivation consistently reported greater success in achieving an optimal setting. They indicated significantly more success in learning to think like staff (see table 11.6) and in developing high levels of personal confidence – chi-square $p < 0.025$ – in their congressional relationships during the first assignment. These findings may indicate that fellows with a high motivation for practical involvement are so committed that they

Table 11.6. Success in Learning to Think Like Staff by Importance of Practical Involvement (Percentage by Column)

| Success in Learning to think like staff | Level of Importance | | | | |
	High	Medium	Low	None	Total
Very	59.5	47.2	52.9	50.0	56.4
Fairly	34.0	47.2	41.2	25.0	36.5
Some or little	6.5	5.7	5.9	25.0	7.1
Total %	100.0	99.9	100.0	100.0	100.0
N	200	53	17	12	282[a]

Chi-square = 28.2 $p < .001$

[a] Fourteen respondents did not provide the necessary information.

willingly assume all duties, even those considered routine and clerical. A similar behavioral pattern may be demonstrated by participants with a low practical motivation because they feel compelled to be accommodating in the office setting. On the other hand, fellows with some practical orientations may feel sufficiently secure so that they can avoid clerical duties, and persons with no practical orientation may be indifferent to creating favorable opinions among office personnel and thus may not assist with routine work. Additional evidence supporting this interpretation is found in the greater success reported by those with high or low practical motivations in learning to think like staff members (chi-square $p < 0.001$).

The analysis of research and career advancement motivations suggests that their effect on developing feel and conducting observational research is less important and pervasive than was discovered regarding practical orientation. For example, the significant relationship between the importance of research and the amount of time spent in press relations seems spurious because of the effects of a third variable, type of background. The relationship between a career advancement orientation and physical isolation from the member of Congress also appears spurious in that program year is related to both. A high motivation for research is, however, associated with the relationship established with staff and the ability to assume a staff role. In these instances a high motivation for research seems to impair creating a warm personal relationship with staff and learning to think like a staff member.

Perhaps the most striking differences regarding the effects of background factors can be seen for educational-occupational experiences and orientations. As previously indicated, the CFP specifically recruits participants from three discrete backgrounds — academic, journalistic, and bureaucratic. Educational experiences, relating to level and type, and occupational duties vary systematically according to the type of participant. The effects of these variables on the work duties assumed are impressive. For example, academic participants with Ph.D. degrees consistently spent more time in policy research and general legislative assistance work than did other participants. Journalists, not surprisingly, reported more time in press relations (table 11.7), and the bureaucrats more time in constituent relations and policy research. No differences regarding

Table 11.7. Proportion of Time Spent in Press Relations during Second Assignment by Type of Participant (Percentage by Column)

Proportion of Time	Type of Participant			Total
	Journalist	Civil Servant	Academic	
None	29.7	48.6	70.1	52.4
Up to 10%	10.8	31.4	22.2	22.6
10-20%	8.1	13.3	1.7	7.4
20-50%	36.5	5.7	4.3	12.8
50-100%	14.9	1.0	1.7	4.7
Total %	100.0	100.0	100.0	99.9
N	74	105	117	296

Chi-square = 97.4 p<.001

the amount of clerical work for types of fellows are observed. During the first half assignment academic fellows reported being physically located most closely to the member of Congress and bureaucrats most distant; however, for the second assignment, no differences regarding physical location were reported. Thus, if some advantage is available to academic fellows for direct observations, it would seem to be an initial advantage only.

Certain isolated relationships are observed between other features of a fellow's background and success in achieving an optimal participant-observer setting. Prior involvement in other intern programs seems to affect fellows only in their perceptions of work assignments. Fellows with previous intern experiences reported their work assignments to be more varied than did those without such experience. Since no evidence is found that they did in fact do different kinds of work than those participating for the first time, this difference seems to be perceptual. One can hypothesize that previous involvement in intern programs does prepare one mentally and emotionally to cope better with the strains and mundane features of a work assignment, but has little affect on the fellow's success in creating an optimal setting. Perhaps this finding is idiosyncratic to the CFP because the extensive orientation period is sufficient to prepare those fellows without prior involvement for the work assignment and for systematic observation.

A few personal background variables are found to have no independent relationship with any of the variables studied. These included participant's age, level of education, and degree of self-recruitment. Further, many of the variables discussed above seem to have a limited and highly selective effect on creating an optimal setting. Personal background factors appear to have greatest impact in the types of work duties assigned.

Situational Factors in the Assignment

A second set of factors with obvious influence on the setting, but largely beyond the control of the intern, relates to the actors and organizational features of the office assignment. An unwilling member of Congress can effectively deny access to the intern by assigning him routine business and isolating him from office activity. Also the type of office, its organization, and personnel can clearly prevent a fellow from doing research and learning about the member of Congress and his office. Only by seeking an accommodating office, negotiating with office personnel, and leaving an undesirable setting can the fellow deal with these influencing factors. Since evaluations of each office assignment are required from every fellow and are made available to subsequent fellows, some information is provided regarding the nature of the office and that member of Congress; however, if that office has never had a fellow, the only alternative is to seek other sources of information. While some adjustment and negotiation regarding a fellow's duties and access sometimes takes place, any change toward a more open atmosphere depends entirely on the member of Congress and his staff. Yet, in the seventeen-year history of the CFP, very few have left an office during the assignment.

The program is organized so that fellows can seek assignments in three different types of offices — with senators, House members, and congressional leaders or committees. Fellows normally are required to change office assignments after the first half so that exposure is possible to two offices, one in the House and one in the Senate. Although variation across individual offices is likely to be considerable, similarities in office organization are likely to be substantial among senators, or among representatives, or among leaders. Consistently significant differences in the types of duties fellows perform are

194

found based on the type of office. Assignment in a leader's or committee office generally resulted in significantly more time being spent in policy research (chi-square $p < 0.002$) and less time in constituent problems (see table 11.8) and legislative assistance (chi-square $p < 0.001$). Differences in the types of work for House and Senate are also important. A Senate assignment compared with one in the House seems to result in more time on policy research and legislative assistance and less time on constituent problems.

Table 11.8. **Proportion of Time Spent in Constituent Problems during First Assignment by Chamber (Percentage by Column)**

Proportion of Time	Chamber			Total
	Senate	House	Leadership	
None	18.1	25.3	55.2	26.4
Up to 10%	33.3	22.2	27.6	25.4
10-20%	20.8	16.5	6.9	16.6
20-50%	27.8	32.0	6.9	28.5
50-100%	0.0	4.1	3.4	3.1
Total %	100.0	100.1	100.0	100.0
N	72	194	29	295[a]

Chi-square = 24.7 $p < .01$

[a] One person had no assignment during the first half.

The type of assignment also affects the physical isolation of the fellow from the member of Congress. This relationship is perhaps in part a result of the varying amount of office space made available to these three types of members. Fellows assigned to leaders, who generally have dual office space, are most likely to report being physically separated from the member (see table 11.9); those serving with House members, who usually have less generous office space than senators, are most likely to report being in the same or an adjacent office in the major traffic pattern. In terms of observational opportunities, then, a House assignment would appear to maximize and a leadership assignment to minimize such chances.

Finally, relationships perceived to be high on personal confidence were most frequently reported for assignments in the House (chi-square $p < 0.001$). This finding probably reflects the close physical proximity to the member of Congress during the House assignment and the reported greater access to members of the House.

In an effort to measure an office's receptivity to fellows and the degree to which office personnel accommodated participants, fellows were asked to indicate their satisfaction with the office assignment and the division of time among various duties. These two measures are, at best, indirect indicators of the degree to which fellows were integrated into the organization and accepted by

Table 11.9. Physical Isolation From Member of Congress during First Assignment by Chamber (Percentage by Column)

Nature of Location	Chamber			
	House	Senate	Leadership	Total
In same office	16.2	5.6	0.0	12.1
In adjacent office in major traffic pattern	70.2	56.9	25.9	62.8
In adjacent office not in major traffic pattern	9.4	25.0	11.1	13.4
Physically separated	4.2	12.5	63.0	11.7
Total %	100.0	100.0	100.0	100.0
N	191	72	27	290[a]

Chi-square = 95.7 $p < .001$

[a] Six respondents did not provide the necessary information.

staff members. Admittedly, satisfaction indicates other things as well, but one would expect an accommodating and friendly staff to strongly affect one's satisfaction with an office assignment. A high level of satisfaction with an office assignment and with the division of duties is consistently related to the amount of time spent in activities other than policy research and press relations.[17] A satisfactory assignment and division of duties is also significantly related both to the fellow's physical location and his perceived success at learning to think like staff; those with higher levels of satisfaction tend to be located more closely to the member of Congress and his staff and also tend to report greatest success in adopting a staff role. As tables 11.10 and 11.11 show, both measures of satisfaction are strongly related to the perceived level of personal confidence. The troubling aspect in discussing level of satisfaction as an independent variable measuring the nature of the assignment is the probable contamination. These measures partly reflect other factors including the types of duties undertaken and the types of personal relationships established.

Another indication of the importance of the situation is the significant continuity from the first to the second assignment. The type of work undertaken during one assignment period is strongly related to that undertaken during the second. A similar pattern is also observed for the type of relationship established. Some evidence even suggests that the first half office experience may neutralize the effects of other independent variables.

The Nature and Organization of the Program

Probably the most difficult task in evaluating an optimal participant-observation setting is to assess the role of the program itself. If sufficient time and effort are given in preparing interns for their office assignments, much more success is likely to be noticed in their utilizations of opportunities for developing feel and

Table 11.10. Personal Confidence Relationship with Member of Congress, First Assignment by Satisfaction with Division of Duties (Percentage by Column)

Nature of Relationship[a]	Level of Satisfaction				
	Very Satisfied	Somewhat Satisfied	Adequate	Somewhat/Very Dissatisfied	Total
High level of personal confidence	56.5	24.5	0.0	0.0	40.4
Medium level of personal confidence	28.6	46.8	43.8	18.2	35.1
Low level of personal confidence	14.9	28.7	56.3	81.8	24.5
Total %	100.0	100.0	100.1	100.0	100.0
N	161	94	16	11	282[b]

Chi-square = 62.8 p<.001

[a] Standardized factor scores from the rotated solution were trichotomized to determine levels.

[b] Fourteen respondents did not provide the necessary information.

Table 11.11. Personal Confidence Relationship with Member of Congress, Second Assignment by Satisfaction with Office Assignment (Percentage by Column)

Nature of Relationship[a]	Level of Satisfaction				
	Very Satisfied	Somewhat Satisfied	Adequate	Somewhat/Very Dissatisfied	Total
High level of personal confidence	58.9	26.0	14.6	0.0	41.1
Medium level of personal confidence	29.1	43.8	17.1	7.1	30.0
Low level of personal confidence	11.9	30.1	68.3	92.9	28.9
Total %	99.9	99.9	100.0	100.0	100.0
N	151	73	41	14	280[b]

Chi-square = 96.4 p<.001

[a] Standardized factor scores from the rotated solution were trichotomized to determine levels.

[b] Sixteen respondents did not provide the necessary information.

conducting research. For example, the program can orient participants to the general and particular features of the institution and setting; it can provide them with the information necessary to serve as contributing participants; and, it can familiarize interns with the techniques of systematic observation. Furthermore, the program can provide the ongoing intellectual content that Hennessy argues is necessary for a successful internship, and it can protect the participant observer from an unnecessarily hostile office setting.[18]

Unfortunately, the best means for evaluating the programmatic effects on the intern experience is through an analysis of comparable programs or through a systematic variation in the essential features of a program. The first alternative is not plausible because the CFP differs in many critical respects from other participant observer programs.[19] While the second alternative in its pure experimental format is also not plausible, an approximation is possible if one considers the program as organized by differing directors. This strategy assumes that interdirector variation is a valid indicator of programmatic effects. Intradirector differences were not examined since four persons served in this capacity only one year each.

In the seventeen-year period for which data were collected, eight persons served as directors. Statistically significant differences are observed only for the proportion of time spent in clerical work during the first assignment. This finding does not indicate major programmatic effects as measured by the differing directors.

Programmatic effects were also examined by comparing periods when the CFP differed regarding size and level of bureaucratic participation. Three periods were considered: 1953-61 when the program was small and only academics and journalists participated; 1961-65 when it was slightly larger and bureaucrats participated but in small numbers; and 1965-70 when the program was considerably larger and about half were bureaucrats. Significant increases in the proportion of time spent in policy research and press relations are noticeable in the recent periods, but these changes may reflect as much the increase in certain skills available with more bureaucrats as any programmatic effect. Thus consistent and far-reaching programmatic effects on developing feel and conducting research are *not* discernable in the CFP data.

Summary and Conclusions

This chapter set out to consider three topics: (1) what is the most desirable setting for participant observation; (2) how well did one politically oriented program create this setting; and (3) what factors affect the establishment of this setting?

After a review of relevant literature and recent discussions of intern programs, four attributes were described as characterizing an optimal participant-observation setting: (1) a warm and trusting set of personal relationships;

(2) assumption of an organizational role that provides access to the observer; (3) experience in important and representative work duties; and (4) the availability of opportunities for intern observation and involvement.

Data from participants in the 1970 CFP study seem to indicate that fellows were fairly successful in optimizing each of these four characteristics. Using a semantic differential scale, fellows reported perceiving a high level of personal confidence in their relationships with significant others, these relationships being distinguished by the participants from the nature of their work assignments; no participant reported a complete lack of success in assuming the role judged most appropriate — that of staff; fellows generally seemed to be performing office duties likely to be representative of overall office activity; and although comparatively few fellows were physically located in the same office as the member of Congress, most were not completely isolated from face-to-face contact.

Certain personal attributes were significantly related to some of these four features. Prior political and legislative experience seemed to have some bearing on the types of work duties assumed but was negligible on the other features of an optimal setting. Fellows' motivations in applying for the program were related to the types of work performed, to the types of relationships established, and to success in playing the role assumed. Of greater importance seemed to be the motivation toward pratical involvement. Regarding the three major types of educational-occupational backgrounds found among fellows, their greatest effect was on the types of work duties. No significant differences among academics, journalists, and bureaucrats were found regarding the type of relationships they developed with members of Congress and staff or with their perceived success in assuming a staff role. While prior involvement in participant-observer programs did appear to prepare fellows better initially for the types of situations likely to arise, no other effects on the optimal setting were discovered. No discernable independent effects were detected for age, level of education or recruitment patterns.

The most important and pervasive factors affecting the setting were those associated with the office situation. The type of office assignment and fellow satisfaction with that assignment were both significantly related to virtually all features of the optimal setting. Assignment to someone in a leadership position seemed to place the fellow in a setting significantly less conducive in developing feel or conducting observational research. Careful attention to these situational factors seems to offer the greatest potential for maximizing participant observations.

Finally, no important differences were found for the various programmatic aspects studied. Perhaps systematic variation in these factors was not sufficient over the years to affect the quality of the observational setting. Thus, in further optimizing the CFP for developing feel and conducting research, the greatest short-term effect would probably occur through alterations in the situational features, especially in the reception given to fellows by significant others.

Changes in the types of people recruited might affect the types of work performed, but few effects are likely to be observed elsewhere. Unfortunately, situational features are more difficult to change than are the qualities represented by interns or the program's organization and content.

Notes

1. A major expansion in participant observer intern programs took place in the late 1950s and early 1960s primarily under the sponsorship of the Citizenship Clearing House and its successor, the National Center for Education in Politics (NCEP). Bernard Hennessy indicates that between June 1958 and September 1966, the NCEP and its state affiliates sponsored 2,153 under- graduate student and 107 graduate student interns. See Bernard C. Hennessy, *Political Internships: Theory, Practice, Evaluation* (University Park, Penn- sylvania: Pennsylvania State University Press, 1970), pp. 13-15. With the shifing of foundation money from such projects in the mid-1960s, many programs and the NCEP itself suffered and some even disappeared. The recent return of some foundation support to intern programs, e.g. the Ford Foundation support of the American Political Science Association State and Local Intern Program, and the increased interest by students in practical experience has resulted in a moderate revival of political intern programs.

2. George J. McCall and J.L. Simmons, *Participant Observation: A Text and Reader* (Reading, Mass.: Addison-Wesley, 1969), p. 2.

3. James A. Robinson, "Participant Observation, Political Internships, and Research" in James A. Robinson (ed.), *Political Science Annual: An Interna- tional Review, Volume Two — 1969* (New York: Bobbs-Merrill, 1970), p. 77-78.

4. Arthur Vidich and Gilbert Shapiro, "A Comparison of Participant Observation and Survey Data," *American Sociological Review* 20 (1955): 33.

5. The term intern is generally used as a synonym for participant-observer. Both denote a period of particial involvement by someone in the ongoing work situation of some organization. The intention is to provide involvement for persons normally outside the organization under actual conditions so that opportunities are available to observe how practice differs from theory.

6. Ronald D. Hedlund, "The Congressional Fellowship Program: 1971 — Revitalization or Retirement," Washington, D.C.: The American Political Science Association, Spring 1971.

7. R.J. Snow, "Participant Observer Analysis," in Donald J. Freeman (ed.), *An Introduction to the Science of Politics* (New York: The Free Press, forthcoming).

8. Arthur J. Vidich, "Participant Observation and the Collection and Interpretation of Data," *American Journal of Sociology* 60 (1955) reprinted in McCall and Simmons, *Participant Observation*, p. 78.

9. Alan Fiellin, "The Study of Legislative Behavior through Participant Observation," paper prepared for the 58th Annual Meeting of the American Political Science Association, St. Louis, Missouri, September 1958, p. 1.

10. Snow, "Participant Observer Analysis," p. 31.

11. The total number of participants in the CFP between 1953 and 1970 is 435; however, due to deaths and unknown addresses, questionnaires could be sent to 420.

12. For a more detailed examination of the sample, see Hedlund, "Congressional Fellow Program".

13. See Charles E. Osgood, George J. Suci, and Percy H. Tennenbaum, *The Measurement of Meaning*, Urbana, Ill: University of Illinois Press, 1957, especially chapters 1-3 and James G. Snider and Charles E. Osgood (eds.), *Semantic Differential Technique*, Chicago, Ill.: Aldine Publishing Company, 1969.

14. The CFP splits the participants' office assignments so that almost everyone works in two congressional offices. Thus it was necessary to ask about the relationships for both first and second half assignments.

15. See for example Donald G. Tacheron and Morris K. Udall, *The Job of the Congressman*, 2nd ed. (New York: The Bobbs-Merrill Company 1970), pp. 43-52, and 303-11.

16. Bernard C. Hennessy, *Political Internships*, pp. 110-17.

17. Appropriate chi-square measures were:

Proportion of Time	Satisfaction with Office		Satisfaction with Duties	
	First Half	Second Half	First Half	Second Half
Clerical	$p < .001$	$p < .001$	$p < .001$	$p < .001$
Policy research	$p > .05$	$p > .05$	$p > .05$	$p > .05$
Constituent problems	$p < .01$	$p < .05$	$p < .01$	$p < .02$
Press work	$p > .05$	$p > .05$	$p > .05$	$p > .05$
Legislative assistance	$p > .05$	$p < .01$	$p < .02$	$p < .001$

18. Hennessy, p. 114-17.

19. Some of the essential differences include (1) an intensive six-week orientation, (2) recruitment of more mature and sophisticated participants, (3) a mix of academic, journalistic, and bureaucratic participants, and (4) minimal assistance in securing office assignments.

12   The White House Fellows

BERNARD ASBELL

David Lelewer, 29, boyish-faced and earnest, a member of a new breed near the top level of government, was sitting in an undistinguished cubbyhole painted in bureaucratic cream-and-greeen at the Department of Health, Education and Welfare. In that 107,000-employee behemoth, he could easily have passed as a deputy assistant payroll supervisor. "Secretary Finch," he said, "gave me this desk right between his and the Under Secretary's office so I could pop in all the time. But I prefer getting away from Washington, going out to the *other* end of government programs. In my short time here, I want to make a *difference*."

In the Cabinet Room of the White House, President Nixon was chairing a meeting of the Urban Affairs Council. The subject was hunger among Americans. The president began putting some tough questions on nutrition and food supply. Answers flowed, specific and precise, mostly from a young lady seated behind Secretary of Agriculture Clifford M. Hardin. After the meeting, the president learned that the young lady, Caro Luhrs, was a medical doctor, and not a government employee in the usual sense. She had been specially selected for a one-year stay to work and learn at the secretary's side. Like Lelewer at HEW, she was a White House Fellow. Each year, eighteen or so outstanding young Americans are selected for that enviable status. Until five years ago there was never anyone quite like them in American government.

As any student of modern bureaucracy knows, a new government program, no matter how gorgeously designed, has a way of going wrong, turning up results that nobody intended. Here goes the story of a program that has gone wrong. Well, sort of wrong, in that it's producing results that nobody intended — and everybody concerned is just delighted. The White House Fellows program bears a lesson for every kind of large organization of human beings — whether a corporation or university or local government — that is trying to refresh itself by spreading leadership among ambitious, able young men and women.

Back in 1964, President Lyndon B. Johnson expressed concern over the widening chasm between government and young leaders. He asked some of the best minds around what to do about it, and one of the ideas — it came from John W. Gardner, then president of the Carnegie Corporation — really grabbed LBJ's imagination. The idea was to search about for young people who showed outstanding career promise in business, the professions, scholarship, journalism,

This chapter was originally published as follows: Bernard Asbell, "Each Year, A Brand New Bunch of Fellows," *Think*, March-April 1970, pp 2-7. It is reprinted by permission of the publisher and the author.

local civic leadership, and bring them to Washington to learn about government's problems by working as personal staff assistants to cabinet officers and White House advisers. The idea was not to keep them in Washington, but to send them home after a year and replace them with a new crop; not a talent raid of local communities by big government, but enrichment of individuals by giving them an extraordinary opportunity to broaden their experience.

Now, as never before, the landscape is dotted with young leaders in local government and private industry who know how to engage federal government as a partner – how to *use* central government for local progress – because they have worked both sides of the street.

For example, John W. McCarter, Jr., young staff member of a Chicago management consulting firm, was named a White House Fellow three years ago and was assigned to the director of the Bureau of the Budget. Returning home a year later, he was appointed director of finance for the state of Illinois. A "classmate" in Washington, Harold A. Richman, a fellow assigned to Secretary of Labor Willard Wirtz, has just been appointed – at 32 – Dean of the School of Social Service Administration of the University of Chicago. His successor at Labor, Doris Kearns, is now teaching a course at Harvard on the American presidency.

Fellow Kimon S. Zachos (Justice Department) returned home to be elected to the New Hampshire State Assembly. John A. DeLuca (White House) has become executuve assistant to Mayor Joseph Alioto of San Francisco. Jane Cahill (Housing and Urban Development) is executive assistant to the chairman of the board of IBM. William R. Cotter (Commerce) is in charge of Ford Foundation grants in Colombia and Venezuela.

Free to be Original

All to the good. That's just what Johnson and Gardner invented the White House Fellowships for, and why President Nixon is enthusiastic about continuing them. Where the program has gone "wrong" – producing results that were not at all intended – is that it has enriched, on a more permanent basis as well, the supply of young blood to the government itself. Three fellows under President Johnson have been appointed by President Nixon as Deputy Assistant Secretaries of HEW. One of thse, Bob Patricelli, a fellow at State under Dean Rusk, must have learned something about diplomacy. In his job at HEW, he mediated among contending cabinet members and White House advisers in helping compose one of the most complex bills of the current administration, the proposal pending in Congress to overhaul the welfare establishment. The highest ranking ex-fellow is Ronald B. Lee, Assistant Postmaster General for Planning. One of three blacks who presently hold the rank of assistant secretary, Lee helped develop the proposal to convert the Post Office Department to a quasi-private corporation.

Because the tenure of fellows is fixed and short-lived and their status special, they are seldom assigned continuing duties in the daily grind of the departmental machine. Therein lies perhaps their greatest value to the improved running of government. Fellows are free to look at problems with fresh, unbureaucratic eyes – free to be original.

Take, for example, an adventure cooked up by Lelewer at HEW and his counterpart at the Department of Justice, David Miller, whose fellowship year of 1968-69 straddled the Johnson and Nixon Administrations.

Two "Alienists"

"We decided," recalls Lelewer, "that one contribution we might make to the incoming administration was to try to provide some new insights into the problems of school desegregation, which we knew each of our new secretaries would have to face." They arranged to visit school districts threatened with cut-off of federal education funds – one in the North, a suburb of Detroit, and several in the South – to see "what was happening at the other end." The fellows talked with teachers and parents, black and white, and with elected officials, some of whom had lost reelection as reprisal for appearing to cooperate with federal officials.

"What we saw was alarming," recalls Lelewer. "First of all, when the federal government cuts off funds, what it's cutting off is compensatory education money meant to help the most disadvantaged, who are mostly black. They were becoming the real victims of federal action.

"Secondly, the officials we met, for the most part, were people who believed in working with 'the system,' who accepted the idea that schools had to be turned around on this issue, but who realized it was tough politically. When our talks got really frank, we found that what they wanted was a court order, getting a federal judge to say, 'You *can't* do this, you've *got* to do that.' Then they felt they could achieve school desegregation as required by law – and still get reelected."

Returning to Washington, the pair of fellows briefed Secretary Robert Finch and Attorney General John Mitchell, orally and in writing. In a short time, the administration launched a new policy of emphasizing court orders in desegregation cases rather than abruptly cutting off subsidies to districts. "I'm not going to say," Lelewer points out, "that our findings were the only input that led to the new policy. But I know we were listened to seriously, not because we were experts, but because we had done some hard digging and were viewed as very objective."

Secretary Finch corroborates Lelewer's assessment: "Anything that a fellow comes up with, when it hits the secretary's desk, may very well get a higher degree of attention than something from an assistant secretary, because these fellows have a unique status. Unlike regular officials, they have no gain to seek. They're not fighting for position or to defend a posture. They're here to do their thing and go back to wherever they came from, probably in an enhanced position no matter what. In law, we call such people alienists, people who are free to testify in a very objective and disinterested way. For that reason we — at least, I — give the fellows a very high degree of credibility."

The opportunity to make important contributions does not by any means come automatically with the glamorous title of White House Fellow. A busy, hard-to-reach cabinet officer can easily ignore the young intern — and some have chosen to do so. Each fellow has to fight his way in — in the words of Jane Cahill, "by building equity through just plain hard work." Miss Cahill, who knows whereof she speaks, had the special problem of being assigned to Housing and Urban Development only a short time after it had been created as a cabinet department. "Nobody," she says, "not even Secretary (Robert) Weaver was sure how all the parts of the department were to fit together. The last problem he needed was finding work for a fellow he didn't know, didn't choose, didn't know he could rely upon."

Miss Cahill searched for and found her own work, especially by urging Under Secretary Robert Wood to give her assignments. One particularly laborious — but successful — chore was preparing detailed testimony for a Senate hearing to be given by Secretary Weaver. Her "equity" mounted. Before long, when Weaver lost his top administrative assistant, he appointed Miss Cahill to fill the critically important post for the remainder of her fellowship year.

An extraordinary example of "building equity" is the case of John S. Pustay, an Air Force lieutenant colonel who won a fellowship in 1966. Pustay, holder of a Ph.D. in international affairs and author of a book, *Counterinsurgency Warfare*, was assigned to the State Department.

"The first four weeks were very disappointing," he says. "I couldn't break through the people around the Secretary. The men at about the fourth level down, it seemed, were making busy work for me, giving me cables to read, setting up briefings at one area desk after another, making me be some sort of dilettante. Then came my first break, during the preparations for President Johnson's Asian trip that was to culminate in the Manila Conference. I was to go on the trip, but in a sort of noncapacity. I went to Ben Read, Secretary Rusk's special assistant, and told him I didn't want to be a 'traveling guest,' but a regular *working* member of the team. He was skeptical about 'downgrading' a fellow, but he put me to work compiling briefing books on each country for the President and Secretary, proofreading official statements, digging up facts, legwork, whatever had to be done."

Soon after the tour, Pustay traveled with Rusk to Vietnam as a personal assistant. He had broken through to where the action was.

Alone in Vietnam

"One of the things that came up at our briefings in Saigon," Pustay says, "was a growing concern about anti-American feelings among the South Vietnamese.

Later, in Washington, I asked the secretary for permission to go back to Vietnam for a personal fact-finding study of those feelings. I traveled South Vietnam alone, lived for four weeks with district chiefs in the Delta area, unarmed, sleeping in huts, eating fishheads and barley for breakfast. When I got back I briefed the secretary and he had me brief the president. What I reported was that the feelings were what I call 'anti-situational,' not anti-American. If the presence of Americans was creating a housing shortage for example, the proper remedy wasn't dropping leaflets about the democratic way of life, as we'd often been doing, but building places for people to live in."

Pustay wound up a member of the secretary's top-level five-man "working group" on Vietnam, which daily monitored the military, diplomatic, and intelligence reports and formulated suggestions for changes in plans and policy.

Hudson Drake, administration manager at North American Rockwell, was assigned as a fellow to Vice President Hubert Humphrey during the closing months of the last administration. Between whirlwind trips with his fast-stepping boss, Drake assembled a history of the expanding vice-presidential duties since the tenure of John N. Garner in the 1930s. Then he devised a plan to improve the organization of the vice-presidential staff and presented it to his incoming boss, Sprio T. Agnew, who readily adopted it.

A pair of fellows, Harold Richman at Labor and William R. Cotter at Commerce, came close to reducing the size of the cabinet. Exchanging information about their departments, they perceived much overlap, some functions they felt were obsolete, others that might be assigned to other departments. The two men began spending luncheons, evenings and weekends designing a merged department to be headed by a secretary of Business and Labor. The following January, President Johnson proposed the departmental merger in his State of the Union address.

The kinship among fellows leads to an unusual network of communication among governmental departments. "It's often easier for one of us to get information from another department by calling *our* guy," says one fellow, "than for a cabinet officer calling *his* guy — the other cabinet officer. We see ourselves as a group as well as members of departments. I think cabinet members realize we can be very useful to them in this way."

When Fellows Leave

If the network of fellows is effective inside the government, it is no less so after they leave. Says one former fellow, "Nobody hesitates to ask the help of anyone else. If one of these guys calls, whatever he asks, I'll do it." When Kim Zachos of New Hampshire became vice-chairman of Manchester's Model Cities Committee, he solicited the knowledgeable suggestions of fellows and ex-fellows everywhere, enriching his local plan. He surveyed them again to help find a first-rate man to direct the local project. At the Urban Coalition, Chairman John Gardner has recruited ex-fellows to his staff and called upon others for volunteer tasks; they, in turn, call upon still others. Ex-fellows who teach at universities regularly enlist others as guest lecturers and consultants in course development. One fellow went on to become a congressional candidate in a Massachusetts primary. His classmates contributed funds and several took time off to help in person.

"That's all part of what John Gardner had in mind," says Stephen Strickland, former acting director of the fellows program. "He was harking back to the days of Jefferson when the talented men in the country knew each other. When a job needed to be done, they knew who could help them get it done."

About a thousand young Americans, age 23 to 35, apply for Fellowships each year, or are nominated by their employers or friends. From these, a group of about 100 is selected for interviews by one of eleven regional panels of business and civic leaders; each panel forwards perhaps a half-dozen nominations to the Commission on White House Fellows in Washington. Chairman of the commission is Arthur S. Flemming, president of Macalester College and former secretary of HEW; his predecessors were Judge William Hastie and David Rockefeller.

Hopeful as the applicants are, those who survive the early screening are almost always startled to find themselves among the 30-or-so finalists invited to a final-selection weekend with the Commission at Airlie House, a retreat near Washington. Harold Richman recalls his feelings:

"I'll never forget that bus ride to Airlie. I knew not a soul. I sat next to this good-looking guy from Georgia, 23 years old. We both looked at each other as though to say, 'I don't know how I got here.' His name was Tommy Johnson and he had just come out of Harvard Business School and had written a big paper on automating the printing industry. This guy knew nothing but Harvard — and Georgia, where he planned to go back and help an old family friend run a string of newspapers. Tommy wound up assigned to Bill Moyers, stayed on as deputy press secretary at the White House, and for two years was the guy who turned off the President's bedlamp at night and was the first to see him in the morning, went to all the summit conferences and circled the world twice." Johnson is now in Texas as LBJ's executive assistant.

During the selection weekend, the sixteen-man commission divides into five or six interviewing teams, each meeting with every finalist at formal interviews, coffee hours, cocktail parties, by rotating partners at meals — any excuse for scrutinizing candidates formally and informally. At the final get-together, each receives a sealed envelope informing him that he has been chosen — or is given the devastating news that he has not. Then all, winners and losers alike, attend a White House ceremony and reception with the president.

The Tension Builds

Before assignment to departments, the fellows meet with cabinet members or agency heads, these meetings based on mutual expressions of interest (fellows' resumés are circulated among cabinet officers. Meanwhile a new tension builds. Where will each be assigned? Each fellow is asked to state four or five preferences. Almost all ask for the White House. Of eighteen fellows in the current class, twelve also listed HEW. The man who got it was Wilson K. Talley, not a social activist but a nuclear physicist from the University of California. The idea, which has evolved over the five years, is not to cast a man according to his previous specialty but to broaden his experience — and to enrich his department with new viewpoints.

Each secretary sees the biographical sketches of all the fellows. One current fellow, Judge Allen Dickson (he's a lawyer, but Judge is his name, not a title), was told: "You didn't list it as a choice, but Secretary of Defense Laird is interested in you." "Why me?" Dickson asked. "He'd like to talk to you and tell you." Dickson spent a couple of days at the Pentagon, including an hour with Laird, who convinced Dickson that his business experience at General Mills in Minneapolis would be a valuable asset to the Defense Department. Dickson accepted.

Added to direct involvement in government is a formal year-round education program — at dinners, lunches, around conference tables and through travel, financed by participating agencies. Carnegie Corporation picks up the tab for the lunches and receptions with notables. In Washington the fellows meet with senators and ambassadors, under-secretaries and congressional aides, private citizens ranging from journalists I.F. Stone and David Broder to economist Milton Friedman and warfare analyst Herman Kahn, from a group of former convicts and drug addicts to welfare recipients and black militants.

Nineteen sixty-nine fellows flew to Cape Kennedy to view the first launching of men to the moon and to New York for three days at the United Nations. On a trip to San Francisco, the fellows met with street workers of Chinatown and Hunters Point, lunched with Berkeley students of the Third World Liberation Front as well as Chancellor Roger Heyns, toured in police squad cars and dined with the police chief, pumped Mayor Joseph Alioto on the problems of running a city, heard a dozen members of the state legislature argue whether federal tax sharing should flow through states or go directly to cities, and conferred with Governor Ronald Reagan — all in a one-week visit. For the first time this year, fellows have also been traveling abroad, meeting with high American and native officials.

For all this, what do the fellows come out with?

David Lelewer: "We all started eager to meet people, learn our way around, see how it all works. I think we were surprised that in a short time we were able to *give* something. I came away with much more faith in the ability of an individual to make a difference. Not only the top individual, but a deputy assistant secretary or a program chief or a Grade 7 or 8 administrative assistant who works hard and earnestly."

New Lenses

Others speak of seeing government actions through new lenses, of gaining new insights which they have brought to their corporate or local civic jobs. Colonel Pustay brought his new insights back with him to the Air Force: "I've been able to explain to peers and seniors how a proposed Air Force policy might be viewed, say, at State or at the White House. I'm able to say, 'This is the way it looks to us in our blue suits over here, but let's look at the things *they're* concerned about.' " Pustay's experience is expected to serve him especially well on a tour of duty to which he has just been assigned — at Brussels, on an international staff for strategic planning at NATO.

The fellows program totally changed my life," concludes Walter J. Humann who, along with his predecessor at the Post Office Department, Ronald Lee, was a member of a five-man committee that developed the plan for a postal corporation. In terms of personal advancement, last year Humann became the youngest (32) board-elected officer of LTV Aerospace Corporation, where he is corporate secretary. He doubts the appointment would have come to him without the extraordinary experience of his fellowship year. But more emphatically, Humann adds: "I came back here with a deep feeling that there's more to the way you ought to spend your life than just trying to increase earnings per share. There are problems in the community, in the state and nation that demand attention."

Not one to settle for mere sentiment, Humann, after leaving Washington, started a nationwide organization called The Citizens Committee for Postal Reform. It has raised $200,000 and maintains a staff in Washington. "I never was aware before that year in Washington," he says, "of what one man's potential really is."

Ask almost any fellow to summarize the meaning of his year in Washingon, and almost always he starts out the same way: "It totally changed my life." It's hardly surprising that such extraordinary exposure to the practice of public responsibility — to the inside workings of big government — would alter the course of a rising young American enroute to his own practice of responsibility. What is more surprising — at least what no one expected — is how the presence of these young Americans has in so many ways, small and not so small, influenced the workings of government.

13

The Washington Semester Internship Program: The Case of the State University of New York

MICHAEL WEAVER

Choosing An Academic Program

In planning a program for social science majors in Washington, D.C., two approaches immediately become apparent. One is an internship experience in which the student is placed in a governmental agency, interest group organization, or a congressional office. There he works and observes government in action. Usually, a paper or a series of papers on some problem or aspect of the political process is the basic determinant for the grade. The educational experience largely becomes a function of the individual's capacity to observe intelligently coupled with the willingness of the field supervisor to allow the student to do meaningful work and be privy to the politically interesting things that occur during the internship.

A second approach is to develop a course of study for students in which Washington resources — both research facilities and government officials themselves — are utilized to the fullest possible extent. The student is directed by one or more faculty members within a structured curriculum and the grading is based on class participation, examinations, and term papers.

The two approaches have several things in common. In both cases, the student is given the opportunity to study in Washington and observe the political system in operation. In both cases the underlying pedagogical assumption is that a unique and different kind of learning experience occurs in this setting as compared to the traditional on-campus classroom situation. In both cases, the study of politics presumably becomes more relevant to the student. The real strength of the internship can become its Achilles' heel. The assumption implicit in this approach is that a student will obtain unique insights into the political process as a result of the constant day-by-day exposure to the activities taking place in the office to which he is assigned. There are at least four risks that must be considered in this approach. Not all of them can be controlled by the program director. They are:

1. Will the agency or office give the student meaningful work to do? Performing clerical duties such as typing, stuffing envelopes, and running errands is hardly the ideal situation for the intern.

209

2. Will the agency or office confide in the student about his problems? Essentially, what is involved here is a trust factor which must be established between the student and the sponsoring office. If the field supervisor is reluctant to confide in the student or if he is usually excluded from meetings where policy and decisions about policy are being made, his internship is not likely to be very meaningful as an educational experience.

3. Will those who supervise his work be capable of giving their time (and willing to give it) to cast the problems or processes in a larger conceptual or theoretical framework? The supervisor with the time may not have the skills required to guide the student just as the supervisor with the skills may not have time.

4. Will it be too late in the term to move the student elsewhere if it becomes apparent that the risks cited above become real? Time passes quickly in this kind of program and a substantial portion of the semester can go by before the student realizes that the experience is not contributing toward improving his understanding of the political process.

To reiterate, then, the very strength of the internship program — an in-depth study through constant exposure to the continuing processes and problems of governing — contains within it risks which can invalidate the student's educational experience.

A Washington-based course of study is designed to offset these possible deficiencies. Like the internship program, it assumes the student comes to Washington having been equipped by the political science department of his home campus with the theoretical tools necessary to discover meaningful relationships between classroom political science and practical politics. Unlike the internship program, it offers the student an opportunity to test his theories through an enriched curriculum which emphasizes diversity in its offerings. Through these courses, he investigates the reality of politics as perceived by the bureaucracy, the executive, the Congress, the courts, the political parties, and such paragovernmental areas as the Washington press. The stress is on interrelationships within the political system. The student begins to tie together the several theories presented to him in on-campus courses into a larger, better integrated, and more comprehensive theory of the dynamics of the political system. It can be said that in the internship program — if ideal conditions exist — the student learns a great deal about a tiny operation. From that experience, he is able to generalize about the larger system, thus profiting from his experience. It is similar to the problem associated with the case study approach in a regular classroom situation. If the case study is well chosen and executed, the political process is revealed and the subject matter of the case serves merely as an illuminator. If it is poorly done, the subject matter of the case becomes paramount in the student's mind and the dynamics of the political process he is supposed to be seeing becomes obscured.

The diversity contained within a course program for the Washington student hedges against this problem. A semester is not sacrificed if a particular part of a course turns out to be trivial, irrelevant, or lacking the necessary elements needed to uncover the larger system. If course A (or more likely, some part of course A) turns out to be inadequate to achieve the goal of greater understanding, courses B, C, and D are there to offset this shortcoming.

Diversity is not the only advantage of the Washington study program. Another strength is the more structured situation in which the student finds himself. At least for the undergraduate, the structured experience, containing some of the elements to which he has become accustomed on campus, provides reinforcement, tends to allay his anxieties, and makes it less likely that he will panic as he embarks upon a course of study dramatically different from his earlier academic experiences. In addition, the structured situation provides a full-time teaching faculty member or members in Washington whose professional responsibility is to assist the student in clarifying, theorizing, and integrating what he is learning about the governmental process. Thus, the very important process of conceptualization and generalization is not entirely dependent upon the ability and generosity of a harried supervisor, as is the case with the internship program.

Those who planned the State University of New York Washington Semester Program carefully considered the strengths and weaknesses of the two approaches and concluded that the study program with its diversified curriculum and structured situation had greater potential for achieving the desired education goals. It was felt that after the Washington-based faculty member had obtained some experience in conducting an academic program in the nation's capitol, a recommendation could be made on the feasibility of adding an intern program.

Proposing an Internship Program

Since Washington programs are expensive, there are several alternatives to consider before placing the faculty member in Washington. Three approaches have been used successfully. First, a single institution may undertake its own small program.[1] Second, the school may subcontract certain courses to schools in the Washington area.[2] Third, several schools may form a consortium to jointly finance the program.

The State University of New York chose this last approach. In February 1967, a thirty-page prospectus, "Semester in Washington" was adopted by four western New York institutions — Brockport, Cortland, Geneseo, and Oswego. The initial plan was modified during 1967-68. By 1969, a twelve-hour course of study was offered. Each week the students read both professional and popular literature on the assigned topic, discussed the material thoroughly, and formulated questions to be presented to expert speakers invited to discuss the matter.

By 1970 three more colleges — St. John Fisher, SUNY at Buffalo and the

State University Center at Buffalo — joined the consortium. Courses included a series of abbreviated case studies, the politics of congressional reorganization, a special lecture series, and independent study.

In the spring of 1970, representatives of the participating colleges in the State University Washington Semester Program met to consider the future of the program. The Department of Political Science at Brockport — acting on recommendations the director of the Washington Program proposed — and the cooperating colleges agreed to establish the program on a year-round basis and to initiate a fifteen-hour intern program beginning in the fall of 1971. The director had reported that the intern program appeared to be worthy of experimentation for four reasons:

1. Considerable interest was expressed by officials in Washington to see the consortium move in this direction.

   The Washington professional (whether he is on Capitol Hill, in the federal bureaucracy, or associated with an interest group) is greatly concerned about today's university student and the manner in which he relates to the political system. Alienation and disaffection with the system expressed as it has been through campus turmoil is as disturbing to them as it is to most academicians and college administrators. Receptivity to an intern program and a willingness to sponsor student-interns was clearly revealed in a series of discussions with Washington officials in the spring of 1970.

2. The Study Program, having operated for two years in Washington, had brought to the attention of the staff, a substantial number of potential intern-sponsors.

   An intern program, to be successful as an educational endeavor, requires a talented and well-trained field supervisor. Many individuals possessing the traits necessary for supervising interns were identified as a result of their participation in the regular program.

3. A rich and generally untapped source for interns was discovered. Student interns tend to concentrate either on Capitol Hill in a congressional office or committee, or in the federal bureaucracy. Interest groups (except for the more obvious, e.g., Common Cause) tend to be overlooked. The legislative office of associations such as the National Farmers Union, the National Chamber of Commerce, or the AFL-CIO with their extensive interest in virtually all of the issues in the political arena appeared to contain the necessary elements for an exciting and educationally enriching student internship.

4. The Study Program could be utilized to supplement the intern's academic program.

   It was expected, when the intern's schedule permitted, that he would participate in the activities scheduled in the regular program.

It was further agreed by the cooperating colleges that the program be expanded to provide for a maximum of forty students per term of eighty over the year with the students having the option to choose between the two programs. However, the intern program was designed to be the smaller of the two, and only upper-division, well-qualified students were to be selected.

Developing the Intern Program

The original prospectus for the intern program proposed a double internship over the semester. In the first half of the term, the intern would work in the legislative office of an interest group. In the second half, the intern would move to Capitol Hill, locating himself with a congressional office, standing committee or subcommittee which in some manner felt the impact of that interest he had interned with originally. For example, a student could work with the National Council on Hunger and Malnutrition and then move to Capitol Hill to intern with the Select Committee on Nutrition and Human Needs or with the House or Senate Agriculture Committee. In addition to his internship, he would participate in some of the activities in the regular program as well as in the weekly seminar for interns. The seminar would draw heavily upon the individual experiences of the interns. Each intern would be responsible for conducting one or more of the weekly seminars on such subjects as interest group formation, interest group coalitions, interest group-agency relations, interest group-executive relations, interest group-congressional relations, and so forth.[3]

Clearly, the underlying assumption of the intern program is that cognitive development occurs to a large extent in ways which make it nonmeasurable with the ordinary tools of evaluation (examinations, oral reports, term papers, and the like). So far as this aspect of learning is concerned, the intellectual growth and educational development of the student is unique and known only to him, at least in its totality.

On the other hand, certain parts of the program can be expressed by the student in both oral and written form. His ability to undertake and execute these responsibilities forms the basis for his grades. Three grades were to be awarded; they were derived from the following documents:

1. Major Research (two course credits)

   Depending upon the particular internship, each student would complete a major research paper or a series of smaller research papers to be submitted for evaluation by the faculty supervisor.

2. Work Experience (two course credits)

   a. Field Supervisor's Evaluation

   Each field supervisor would present a written evaluation of the intern's work-study experience. He would be asked to comment on the intern's work performance, judgment, written and oral expression, adaptability, and originality. In addition, the faculty supervisor would meet periodically with the field supervisor to discuss the intern's work.

b. Intern Evaluation

Each intern would prepare a paper describing his experience. The paper should include but would not necessarily be limited to: (1) a detailed description of the work experience, (2) an evaluation of the intensity and extent of commitment to the program by the sponsoring agency and supervisor, (3) an analysis of the internship program as to its effectiveness as an educationally sound program, and (4) an accounting of the ways in which the intern experience did or did not illuminate the larger political process.

3. Seminar (one course credit)

Each intern would prepare and present orally for seminar discussion an analysis of some part of his internship which he deemed to be of interest and worthy of consideration by his colleagues. He would be expected to contribute to the discussion in seminar. In addition, he would be expected to present his research to the regular study students where the subject matter relates to one or more of their courses. Finally, he is expected to take advantage of learning opportunities offered by the regular program.

1970-71 Academic Programs

Twenty-two interns and forty-four regular study students participated in the State University of New York Washington Semester Program during the academic year 1970-71.

During the fall, a course on the American presidency was added to the curriculum of the regular program. In the spring, Dr. Edward Janosik, chairman of the Department of Political Science, State University College at Geneseo, New York joined the staff to offer a course on the legislative process. Dr. Oleszek developed a course on the "Congress, the Courts, and the Executive — Cases of Conflict," and the six-hour public policy course was continued. More than seventy-five Washington officials participated including such well-known politicians and scholars as Ambassador Averill Harriman, Senators Javits and Bayh, former White House Press Secretary George Reedy, House of Representatives Minority Leader Gerald Ford, and political analysts Richard Scammon and David Broder.

The newly-initiated intern program started cautiously with the selection of six students. Early in the term, it became evident that the proposed double internship required modification if not total abandonment. The interns reported shortly before the middle of the term that they had just begun to get involved deeply in a project with their sponsoring agency. Moving to Capitol Hill at this juncture would involve another time-consuming orientation and was not likely to be productive. A semester passes too quickly to support two enriched internships. In this semester the matter was made more complicated by the uncertainty associated with the Congress's adjournment for the November 1970 elections. As it turned out, only one intern moved to Capitol Hill. The program was then modified to provide the option for a double internship if arrangements satisfactory to the student, faculty, supervisor, and field supervisor could be made.

A second problem arose in the placement of the interns. It had originally been intended to place the interns with interest groups. However, most of the fall interns came to Washington with fairly well developed ideas of what they wanted to do in their research as well as the agency to which they wanted to be attached. Consequently, greater emphasis and effort was made to match student interest with the appropriate sponsoring agency, whether it was an interest group or not. Fall placements were made at the National Association of Counties with this student later moving to the House Banking and Currency Committee, doing research on public housing for the rural area; the National Farmers Union, researching and preparing testimony on the Foreign Trade Act; two students at the Office of Economic Opportunity, one developing an OEO policy for the aged poor, the other investigating internal organization problems; and two students at the U.S. Civil Rights Commission, one compiling and analyzing data on desegregation practices in Southern parochial schools, and the other examining interventionist approaches toward the elimination of discrimination.

In the spring, sixteen interns were selected for the intern program. Placement opportunities were expanded to include Capitol Hill under the direction of Professor Janosik, who had joined the teaching staff for the semester. Interns were placed on Capitol Hill with the Senate Judiciary Subcommittee on Constitutional Rights, the Senate Labor and Public Welfare Subcommittee on Migratory Labor, the Senate Committee on Housing and Urban Affairs, the Republican Conference Committee, and with the congressional offices of Senator Birch Bayh and Representatives Nick Begich, Andrew Jacobs, David Obey, and Peter Peyser.

Interest groups sponsoring interns in the spring included: The National Farmers Union, The National Council on Hunger and Malnutrition, and the American Bankers Association. In the federal bureaucracy, students were placed with the Treasury Department, the Equal Employment Opportunity Commission, the Department of Housing and Urban Development, and the U.S. Civil Rights Commission.

In evaluating the twenty-two interns, the staff of the Washington Semester concluded that in nineteen cases, the experience had greatly benefited the student. Three were adjudged as having been marginal, if not failures. Inadequate field supervision by the sponsoring agencies and/or weak students appeared to account for these outcomes. A highly successful internship was regarded as one where the student was presented with an opportunity to generate input, if not impact, into the political system. The work of three interns clearly reveals this opportunity.

A student from Geneseo interned with the Senate Subcommittee on Migratory Labor. He came to Washington with a deep interest in the problem, having worked on the problems of migrant workers in upstate New York. In addition to his major research on housing for migrant farm workers, he developed a Migrant Farmworkers Bill of Rights. The bill contains fourteen titles including collective bargaining rights, child labor, minimum wage, social security, voting rights, housing, health, and the establishment of a national advisory council on migratory labor. It is expected to be introduced into the United States Senate in the 93rd Congress which begins in 1973.

A Brockport student had served as a summer intern with the Rochester, New York city government, where he developed a deep interest in the revenue-sharing proposal. With the assistance of Representative Barber Conable of New York, he was able to obtain a position with the office of the Assistant Secretary of the Treasury for Economic Policy. He was assigned the task of preparing data comparing the administration's revenue-sharing proposal with other alternatives, notably tax credits and welfare federalization. His study formed the content of a speech given by Assistant Secretary Murray L. Weidenbaum before the Forum on Federalism, St. Louis University, and it later appeared in *U. S. News and World Report*. He was also responsible for handling requests for information by members of the Congress on the effect the proposal would have on their districts.

A third student, also from Geneseo, was assigned to the Office of Economic Opportunity where she was responsible for developing an OEO policy of the aged poor. The completed project reached the desk of the then director of the agency, Donald Rumsfeld, for consideration and disposition.

Earlier in this chapter, four questions — identifying risks inherent in intern programs — were discussed. How real are those risks and how can they be avoided? On the basis of one year's experience in processing interns, it can be concluded that the elimination of those risks lies in identifying field supervisors who are talented, knowledgeable, and genuinely interested in working with students. The benefits to be derived from the intern experience do not arise in a vacuum. Inadequate supervision or lack of commitment by the field supervisor will cause the internship to fail no matter how glamorous the surroundings might be. Thus placement in a particular agency is far less important than placement with a good supervisor, no matter what the agency is.

Conclusion

"This has been the greatest educational experience of my life" is the most common opening line in student evaluations of their Washington experience. While that remark is deeply satisfying, the staff of the program recognizes that the real value of this program to the student lies in the unselfish contributions hundreds of Washington officials have made to the program over the years. It is to them that the students should direct their gratitude.

As far as the future is concerned, the State University of New York will continue its Washington program. An exciting opportunity awaits next year's students with the addition to the staff of Mr. George Reedy, press secretary to Lyndon B. Johnson and author of *The Twilight of the Presidency*. Mr. Reedy will offer a course on the American presidency. Other plans include the development of a study program in international relations and American foreign policy and the establishment of a summer intern program.

The mission is to provide students with educational opportunities they find deeply satisfying and rewarding and to continue to work toward the goal of academic excellence in all of the programs. The challenge is great. The competition is rigorous and likely to increase as students continue to seek more relevance in their education.

Notes

1. An example of this is the Colgate University program, now in its thirty-seventh year of operating a spring semester program. Ten to fifteen students are placed in internships and are closely supervised by a faculty member who accompanies them to Washington.

2. American University has three such programs. The Washington Semester focuses on the whole political system; the Washington Urban Semester concentrates on urban politics; and, the Washington International Semester investigates international relations and American foreign policy.

3. For example, an intern assigned to the Emergency Committee for Full Funding of Higher Education could lead a discussion on the formation of new interest groups, and as a case study, the strategy and tactics employed by that group during the HEW appropriations controversy. He could have the other students read material such as: Anthony Lewis Dexter, *How Interest Groups are Represented in Washington*.

Part 4
Executive and Organization Development

14

Executive Development:
Executive Seminar
Center Style

Ever since Socrates spoke to Nocomachides about the art of management, the subject of executive leadership has been a matter of both public and private concern.[1] The recommendations of the Second Hoover Commission and the question of an elite senior civil service are but the latest manifestations of this continuing dialogue, which has been severely limited by the lack of specific American experience. Recently, however, there has been some action worthy of note.

The Civil Service Commission created Executive Seminar Centers in Kings Point, New York in 1963, and in Berkeley, California in 1966, and a Federal Executive Institute in Charlottesville, Virginia in 1968. These first two aim at middle managers, while the institute is designed for the top cadre of civil servants (GS 16-18, the "supergrades"). This chapter concerns the seminar centers, for they will, I suspect, serve as a model for future middle-management training both in and outside the federal government. They are the showcase for federal management training, and I think it is fair to say that some of the commission's prestige and leadership in the training field rides on their success.

The Intergovernmental Personnel Act should bring state and local governments more heavily into the training field, initially in cooperation with the federal government, and with some attendance at these centers. From this contact, the concept or center style may spread to state and local applications. Finally, it is quite likely that this center concept will be expanded to at least a third location, and it will be appropriate to consider alternative strategies before the pattern is hardened. The sum of these events alone makes some review of the center philosophy, *modus operandi*, and future worthwhile.

But there are some other reasons for discussing the centers. One is the need to underline the emphasis on the outside lecture method as a development and teaching process, noting its strengths and weaknesses in the center context, and thus suggesting that alternate strategies in future seminars might also prove fruitful. A more serious consideration is the difficulty in broadening specialists into generalists.[2] This is the basic function of the centers, but it is more easily stated than accomplished, and the difficulties should be known to those considering these types of seminars. Obviously, both these issues have

This chapter originally appeared under the same title in *Public Administration Review*, September-October 1970, pp 553-561. It is reprinted with the permission of the publisher and the author.

221

implications far beyond the centers themselves.

This article proceeds as follows: the first part will outline briefly just what the centers aim to do and how they go about it, while the second part will evaluate the matters of the lecture method and the broadening of specialists. The first part will be factual, the second more impressionistic. Both facts and impressions, I think are necessary to put the centers into perspective.

General Information on Centers

The centers are aimed directly at the supply of future top-career civil servants, that is, at those who are the middle managers now. These men and women are at the GS 14-15 level ($20-$24,000). To the extent that any one pattern exists, they supervise at or above the second level or provide staff aid to top personnel. They are not yet heads of operating divisions or agencies. They can aspire to these levels, for those who attend the center programs average about forty-five years in age and twenty years of federal service, and are thus both relatively young and well experienced. They are, according to the center brochure, "at the point in [their] career when attained or potential position and responsibility dictates that [they] expand [their] views, attitudes, and understandings beyond agency and functional boundaries."

Establishment of the centers grew from the increasing awareness of the need for broadening technicians, specialists, and other professionals so they could accomplish a management job marked by concerns and constraints which are government-wide, rather than limited to a single agency. The centers developed as one of the components of this development process. These needs explain why the centers are interagency, with fifty-five participating agencies; why they concentrate on the governmental process and with broad policy issues; and why they cover government-wide management issues such as unionization and PPBS rather than being concerned with techniques and skills.

Curriculum

The curriculum consists of eleven two-week courses, given from one to six times a year, with seventeen courses per year at each center. There are two types of seminars: core and program. The four basic core seminars cover: (1) the management of organizations, (2) the administration of public policy, (3) the environment of federal operations, and (4) federal program management. A fifth, management of public policy and programs, covers the latter three in four weeks, as an option to agencies desiring a more concentrated course. The program seminars cover: (1) the national economy, (2) the effects of techno-logical development (3) intergovernmental relations, (4) social programs and economic opportunities, (5) international affairs, (6) national security policy, and (7) resource management.

Over 1,200 managers attend these seminars each year, evenly divided between Berkeley and Kings Point, averaging some thirty-eight for each individual two-week course. As of July 1969, some 5,500 managers have taken one or more courses. Somewhere between five and ten percent of the participants are repeaters, indicating an overall tendency to spread out attendance rather than concentrating it on a few highly select managers. The stated commission policy calls for the middle manager to take all four of the core curriculum courses before a "comprehensive view of the federal environment can be obtained," but this is hard to accomplish for many reasons. Sheer numbers alone, with 58,000 GS 14s and 15s in the civilian service, plus the much larger pool of GS 13s who are often sent by their agencies, accounts for much of this spreading out. Agency preference for a thin rather than concentrated dosage probably explains the rest.

Course Content

Both centers rely primarily on outside lecturers, with a range of group discussions, readings, and cases to round out the program. Typically, there will be a morning and an afternoon speaker, preceded by group discussion or workshops in the early morning and followed by assigned readings or group projects in the evening. Lecture periods normally are for two or three hours, with prepared statements no longer than an hour or so, followed by a break and a question-and-answer period in which the speaker is "fair game." These discussion periods are off the record, to reduce participant and speaker defensiveness, and are characterized by rather active exchanges. The function of these lectures varies, but includes not only information on the insight into a variety of topics, but sometimes downright provocation as a spur to learning. The interagency mix of participants contributes considerably to the breadth and depth of discussion. The topics, taken from a recent Berkeley course, included the following range: local government policy-making, income maintenance systems, Congress and the party system, the role of the career official in the administrative process, and science, technology, and public policy. In addition, there were a number of required readings such as Richard Neustadt, *Presidential Power;*[3] John Gardner, *Self-Renewal,*[4] and C.P. Snow, *Science and Government.*[5]

Most courses range widely in this fashion, extending all the way from broad public issues to federal administrative processes and back again.

During 1968-69, almost 40 percent of the Kings Point lecturers and 55 percent of the Berkeley lecturers were from academia, with the balance from federal agencies and private sources. Many of the nonfederal speakers have had government experience, imparting a stronger federal flavor to the courses than is apparent from the programs. The centers have somewhat different styles, moreover, since Berkeley has more academic input and tends to draw from field officials, while Kings Point has a much heavier weighting of Washington participants and speakers.

Financial and Administrative Support

Centers are financed by sales of spaces to agencies. A 1969-70 space cost $500. This money, placed in a working fund early in the fiscal year, pays for the center staff, room and lodging at the Kings Point Merchant Marine Academy or a Berkeley hotel, building and classroom maintenance, and the costs of visiting lecturers, readings, etc. This financial arrangement is no small aid in planning, since an assured total of funds is avaible in July, rather than waiting for individual course sales later in the year, as other commission training programs must do. A few of the fifty-five participating agencies take up most spaces. In the Berkeley center in 1969, the nine Departments of Health, Education, and Welfare, Interior, Treasury, Air Force, Navy, Army, National Aeronautics and Space Administration, Commerce and Atomic Energy Commission, in that order, took seventy-five percent of the slots. Certain agencies that have strong management development programs, such as Internal Revenue (Treasury) and Social Security Administration (HEW), seem to subscribe much more strongly than most others.

The centers are arms of the commission's Bureau of Training, operating out of Washington with small staffs of a director, four associate directors, and clerical help. The staffs arrange courses, the commission sets operating policy, and overall policy is decided by an advisory group of training or personnel officers from major departments in Washington. This group meets rarely, and most decisions are thus made by the commission. In effect, the centers are nonprofit, consumer-owner organizations operated by the central control agency for training.

How Are the Centers Doing?

Acceptance of the center programs by their agency clientele has been gratifying to the commission. Demand for spaces continually exceeds supply, and a third center would have been filled in 1969-70. Participants consistently rate courses "excellent" or "very good" on the evaluation sheets and many later write favorable letters to the center or program director. A Berkeley center survey of 423 of the 1966-67 participants indicated that the vast majority were enthusiastic about the seminar they completed. Most noted that they did more reading, particularly in new areas; that they have a different attitude toward government and the political process; and that the center helped them to be more effective administrators. They felt that the primary benefit came from the opportunities to consider broader aspects of their job, to exchange views with other federal executives, and from general intellectual stimulation.

There have been favorable comments and articles in such diverse publications as the *Los Angeles Times West*,[6] and the *Civil Service Journal*,[7] both carrying the article "Life with the Power Children," by John Weaver, and *The Federal*

Times,[8] as well as passing comments in many professional journals commenting on personnel and manpower trends in the federal government.[9] One public administration textbook devoted a portion of the chapter on training to the centers.[10]

There is a lack of empirical evidence regarding positive, center-induced behavior changes in participants, as is the case with most training programs. Adequate tools for obtaining such evaluation are not presently available, and until they are it will be necessary to rely on judgmental values such as mentioned above. It is clear that these noted judgments and the agency demand for courses indicates general satisfaction with the centers.[11]

Lectures and the Center Concept

Perhaps the heart of the center concept is the reliance on outside lecturers. This particular approach, or training technique, deserves further comment.

Almost universally, lecturers are outside persons, either from the government, academia, or private life. They serve two main purposes, first as the substance for the course itself, and secondly as the technique or device for stimulation of participants to learn, discuss, and debate. While other devices such as debates, reading assignments, buzz groups, movies, and deliberately provoked discussions are also used, lectures provide the core of the intellectual stimulation that happens at the center. The core of the center concept is the stimulus of new ideas and the dialogue between speakers and participants arising out of the lectures. Experience indicates that the lecture emphasis is the best way to make maximum impact on participants in a short period. Alternate forms of course structure such as small group projects, heavy doses of reading, group workshops, and discussions have proven effective as supplements to the lecture method, but not as replacements for it.

It is not surprising that lectures have such a dominant position. Most training and executive development courses make heavy use of them, and people have come to expect that they will be associated with training courses. The academic model has had an effect also, since most college teaching is done this way. Participants have become used to lecturers as a learning device in their careers, since our administrative culture seems to put a heavy weight on having an expert or scholar or specialist inform learners or trainees, the communication pattern generally flowing primarily one way. These reasons are supplemented by the nature of the federal managers' working environment. At the middle-management level there is constant pressure to produce, implement, change, and react, not contemplate or conceptualize. The manager is generally quite specialized and highly motivated, which means that he works very hard, under pressures noted above, in relatively narrow areas of conern. The predominate ethic is often to get the job done in a hurry with limited funds and relatively little concern, at his level, with long-range program impact. The behaviour patterns developed by these administrative constraints work against a course designed to emphasize reading, reviewing, researching, conceptualizing, and applying to concrete situations. Hence, in a two-week course, managers desire to work hard, but in programmed ways. Most desire to be told what to do. Most cannot be turned loose in the library for browsing and musing over their role in government, but it has proven relatively effective to assign short, provocative articles or essays for morning discussion periods. This is why the lecture approach, with its greater ability to focus directly on an issue, works more effectively.

This discussion of the lecture method at the centers is meant neither to idealize it nor to imply that all learning and development takes place with a speaker. Quite the contrary. While lecturers provide the core of the course, they are by no means the only learning experience. The personal interaction of class members with each other is a most significant course effect, and participants probably learn as much from each other as they do from any structured part of the course. Most of this learning from each other takes part during small group discussions, while going over the assigned readings, and during meal and break exchanges. Highly meaningful to the participants, this experience tends to be retained long after the lectures have been forgotten. For example, there is at least one or more member of each class who has not heard of the planning, programming and budgeting system or who has never dealt with employee unionization. The experience of their peers with these matters is an eye-opening experience to them, and one that cannot be dismissed as a lecturer's ivory tower.

The importance of these experiential types of learning is at least as important as the informational/stimulation type largely making up the lecturers. That is why primary speaker emphasis is a mixed blessing. It prevents deep involvement in group discussion over time, and largely rules out other training or development techniques such as major group projects and reports. When these latter techniques are used, they are necessarily subsidiary, and so regarded by the participants.

Another drawback is that lectures are easy for the participant to disengage (turn off) from without being noticeable to their peers. Group pressure tends to flag. Lectures require a passive reaction by participants, who sometimes become "sponges" soaking up new ideas and information but with limited involvement with peers or the speaker. Their potential involvement, the essence of growth, has been scratched rather than plumbed. The lecture method is a safe, sure, and noncontroversial way for the centers to operate, but it may fall short of tapping the full potential of participants for teaching and learning from themselves.

Alternate Strategies

So far all that has been said is that while the lecture method is highly successful and well suited to a short course, it does have certain drawbacks and reduces the time available for other training methods which rely more on the individual participant's input and involvement. This is, of course, a matter of judgment, although no more unrealistic than the assumption that a successful technique (i.e., lectures) should never be changed. There are other ways to structure management training courses than primary reliance on outside lecturers, and since other agencies may develop their own centers and the commission may extend the numbers of centers to three or four, alternate strategies might well be considered. The first two assume continuance of the present structure, with slight changes, while the second two suggest more drastic changes.

Alternative One. This might be called the "modified lecture" course. It provides for continuance of two-week courses, divided into possibly four modules, or topic areas. Each module would call for extensive reading, discussion, group exercises, and role playing around the topic theme. One major speaker for each theme, to open, close, or accelerate the class discussion, would be used. This speaker would be a top government official or someone of major stature in a related field. This should maintain the high level of interest in a short course that a very prominent speaker can provide, while throwing participants on their own resources for a larger share of the time. A structured part of this option could be participant presentations if their expertise fell into the proper topic.

Alternative Two. This "solid-core" alternative would reduce course offerings to three core sessions, increasing each one to three weeks. Each session would have a different focus. One might be a research/analysis course, where participants are required to develop a major policy or research paper on a topic related to their job or agency. The result, hopefully, would be to develop a participant's ability to function at a high-level staff capacity. Normally, the class would discuss the papers.

The second course would be an information/policy course, with major federal issues described, analyzed, and placed in perspective. It would emphasize familiarity with a broad range of federal issues and programs, and extensive readings. This is quite similar to the present administration of public policy course.

The third course would be management development, in which participants perform simulated management tasks and receive peergroup feedback. The overall goal would be to help the participant experience his education in situations where he is expected to behave as an executive. In-basket exercises, simulation, gaming, and role playing all are techniques which might be used in this course. So could organizational development training devices such as T groups and sensitivity training, which are somewhat controversial but still used by a number of federal agencies.[12]

Each participant would be expected to attend all three courses.

Alternative Three. This option stresses the development of agency in-house training capacity, involving a deliberate commission effort to export training expertise. Centers would be rented out to agencies, probably on a scheduled basis, and the center staff could help the agency develop middle- and top-level management training programs. While some agencies do not need this aid, many do, and the commission could render a major service here. The final decisions on content would be made by agencies, but the center would be a major asset in developing these courses and coaching with the best training practices. Strictly speaking, this is not necessarily an alternative to the overemphasis of lectures, but it is likely that the mix of course techniques coming out of this use of the centers would stimulate use of many optional techniques.

Alternative Four. This alternative, the "management exchange and feedback" option, conceives of the centers as essentially a management development way station, processing the exchange of middle-management executives or staff specialists between agencies. After the exchange had been arranged between agencies, the centers would serve as intellectual and information centers where the potential exchangee could undergo briefings, participate in training courses of his new agency, take special courses if he is to do special types of work such as policy analysis, and mentally prepare himself for a new assignment. After the exchange, the centers could serve as a debriefing stop, where the returning exchangee could outline his work and prepare any evaluations necessary, act as a management resource person to regular center classes, or lecture other specialists in interdepartmental management and policy issues. While this sort of function could be carried on without the centers, if federal agencies ever make heavy use of the Commissions' Management Inventory for permanent or short-term assignments, this center function would institutionalize the exchange process. It would be a forum for broadening management capabilities in federal agencies and possibly coordinating these exchanges. This idea is clearly avant garde, but it would not require heavy resource commitment, and possibly one specific center could be the focus for this or a similar function.

There are endless permutations and combinations of these suggestions and no doubt much better ones can be developed by training specialists. At any rate, the possible openings of new centers inside and outside the federal government provides the commission and other personnel agencies a real chance to experiment with a successful pilot program, and to try other approaches.

Specialists, Generalists, and the Center's Role

This topic has perhaps the widest implications for managers and trainers. As mentioned earlier, the official center function is to help middle managers expand their views, attitudes, and understanding beyond agency and functional boundaries. I hope that the experience of the centers can shed some light on the practical difficulties of broadening specialists for higher responsibilities.

Participant Expectation

One problem which should be noted is the value bias which makes specialists less worthy than generalists, at least in the management training field. In designing training, often we assume that all middle managers are "upward mobiles" who crave higher office and larger responsibilities. This view does not reflect reality, at least as far as center participants go. Perhaps it is not true of any large group of middle managers. Most, I suspect, are well adjusted and happy in their present positions, either having decided they do not desire the headaches of management or having calculated that they are unlikely to reach top positions and adjusted their expectations accordingly. Most of the persons attending the centers do not anticipate promotions to supergrades. They come, I think, for many reasons, but generally not with the expectation that the center will be an integral part of their preparation for top-level positions. They expect to learn new ideas, meet new people, "recharge their administrative batteries," and gain intellectual stimulation, but do not envision applying the experience in a top policy position. This clearly deflects part of the center training, which is based on the expectation of larger responsibility. It certainly can miss the committed program type of executive, such as some park rangers, who want no part of pure administrative tasks. There is very likely no way to completely bridge this gap, partly because middle management is such a broad category and partly because of the variability in human nature. The center experience merely underlines the problem, cautioning developers of similar programs of what they may expect.

Timing

Another pragmatic issue involving the center is the difficulty in specifying when in a participant's career broadening will have effect. This brings up the whole question of evaluating behavior changes due to training. Nobody knows if interagency, broad-gauge seminars are effective in widening perspectives and developing insight. Most persons accept them as an act of faith, a sort of training theology.[13] There is usually a general bland acceptance of the value of broadening and of those management training or development courses which have this in mind, resulting in tremendous difficulty in evaluating the impact of this training-induced behavior changes. As far as I can tell, little is being done to investigate it. Hence, we don't know how and when to make available broadened perspectives to a career executive (if one training device can do such a complex thing), and this makes it virtually impossible for agencies and the centers to pick the best people at near optimum time.

The Selection Process

Probably the major trouble area is the agency selection process. A very high percentage of center participants simply are not ready for the course they attend. Some are at the wrong time in their career, which cannot be easily remedied. But others are near or eligible for retirement. Many have not had the preliminary training in management that the centers assume. Many do not have jobs requiring a broad perspective of the federal government, even though they meet the grade requirements. Some are notified so late that they cannot mentally prepare for the two weeks, or even complete a review of the advance materials. But these complaints always will occur, to a greater or lesser degree, in any training course. The real criticism of agency selection is, I think, the total lack of any concept of career planning in most agencies. Most participants at the center, for example, are not really at that point in their career when interagency concerns and government-wide policy matters are crucial to their development. They are there because they wanted to come; because they could be spared for that course; because their immediate supervisor thought they should go; or many other reasons similar to these.[14] These reasons may be appropriate in individual cases, and may serve some needs of the agencies involved very well. But they indicate the overall lack of agency career planning and of the difficulty in assembling forty managers who are relatively similar in career outlooks and prospects for a two-week broadening course.[15]

The difficulties mentioned in this section are to a certain degree symptomatic of all middle-management training. The consequences should therefore be evaluated, if only to learn the true cost of the present seminar center system. It falls short of agency demand, and would be hopelessly short if all managers were to attend the five courses (four core plus one specialty) prescribed by the commission as the optimum. In addition, as was noted above, the agency selection process is quite random and much training is going to participants who do not expect to move up to higher policy levels.

I think a case can be made that the present process tends to suboptimize, and that this will become more and more apparent as time goes on. Sooner or later, the commission may have to choose between a thin system providing almost all middle managers with one or a few courses, or a heavy system that devotes most middle-management training resources to a small, fairly select group. Either choice can be justified. A thin approach would stress the potential in every manager, and the need to upgrade management capability at all levels. However, it would involve an enormous training commitment over the present level of expenditure of time and money, and poses equally major logistical difficulties. A heavy system reverses the arguments. It can be assimilated relatively easily into the system, and with some work by the commission and the agencies, identification of the most promising executives could be made. The drawback is that it is a form of elitism, much as the senior civil service was, and is objectionable to many persons, both inside and outside the government. This type of forced choice is not popular and is generally ignored. I think ignoring it will move toward a form of unintentional heavy system, due to the lack of funds to expand centers as rapidly as demand increases. Those who are able to attend more than one course will be so rare that they make up an unintentional select group. This, if and when it occurs, is of course a choice. These two alternatives call for a choice that all sizable jurisdictions must make in contemplating center-type middle-management training.

Summary

This chapter has sought to outline the operation of the centers; to comment on two major operational matters, the use of the lecture method and the selection process, which involves the issue of training generalists. Four options for curriculum diversification were suggested, and two alternatives regarding participant selection were noted.

The centers seem to have proved themselves, and are highly regarded by their client agencies. Possibly now is the time for the commission to consider some of the questions raised here, since it is dealing from strength and because new centers may be proposed shortly. Beyond this, any actions taken by public agencies on center-type middle-management training should also be aware of these issues.

Notes

1. Xenophon, *Memorabilia and Oeconomicus* (Cambridge: Loeb Classics, Harvard University Press).

2. When linked with the emergence of a professional public service, this issue is a major concern today. See for example, Frederick Mosher, *Democracy in the Public Service* (New York: Oxford University Press, 1968), chapter 4; and Corinne Gilb, *Hidden Hierarchies: The Professions and Government* (New York: Harper and Row, 1966).

3. Richard Newstadt, *Presidential Power* (New York: John Wiley and Sons, 1960).

4. John Gardner, *Self-Renewal* (New York: Harper and Row, 1963).

5. C.P. Snow, *Science and Government* (New York: Mentor Books, 1962).

6. *Los Angeles Times West,* October 8, 1967.

7. *Civil Service Journal* 8, no. 3 (March 1968).

8. "Resident Centers Give Best Training," *The Federal Times,* April 23, 1969. This was part eight of a focus on training series.

9. See Roger Jones, "Developments in Government Manpower: A Federal Viewpoint," *Public Administration Review* 27, no. 2 (June 1967), pp. 134-41.

10. Marshall and Gladys Dimock, *Public Administration* (New York: Holt, Rinehart, Winston, 1969), pp. 240-43.

11. For studies into evaluation of management development, see Wilbur Ferguson, "Qualitative Evaluation of Training Using Student Reaction,"

Training and Development Journal 22, no. 11 (November 1968), pp. 34-42; Ralph Catalenello and David Kilpatrick, "Evaluating Training Programs – The State of the Art," *Training and Development Journal* 22, no. 5 (May 1968), pp. 2-9; and Vera Kohn and Treadway Parker, "Some Guidelines for Evaluating Management Development Seminars," *Training and Development Journal* 23, no. 7 (July 1968), pp. 18-22.

12. Many may not be familiar with the practices of, and controversy over, sensitivity training. It is essentially an unstructured situation in which the group determines what it will do and how it will operate. By attempting to elicit openness on the part of participants, it focuses on the development of a high level of interpersonal relationships and communication skills. This emphasis on openness may build conflict and threaten many persons, and some practices allegedly do permanent damage to persons. The concept and problems of implementing this type of training in the federal government are well covered by Robert Golembiewski in "Organization Development in Public Agencies: Perspectives on Theory and Practice," PUBLIC ADMINISTRATION REVIEW 29, no. 4 (July/August 1969), pp. 367-77. A good discussion of sensitivity training can be found in *Industrial Relations,* 8 (October 1968), with articles by Marvin Dunne and John Campbell, "Laboratory Education: Impact on People and Organizations," pp. 1-27; and Chris Argyris, "Issues in Evaluating Laboratory Education," pp. 28-40.

13. See, for example, "Management Training: An Act of Faith," *Dun's Review* (December 1968), pp. 46-49.

14. These observations are well supported by a questionnaire survey of 67 participants in two spring 1969 seminars at Berkeley. Based on this survey, the selection process appears to be somewhat random, and many participants had no idea why they were attending the seminar. A 1965 Kings Point survey of 307 supervisors revealed slightly different results. Here most responses indicated that participants were selected because of their current position and responsibility by higher authority upon supervisory recommendation. These differences may reflect either a higher selection standard at Kings Point, or merely different views of the selection process between supervisors and subordinates. In the Berkeley case, even if supervisory and higher levels had excellent criteria for their selection choices, I would still criticize the process, because the individual managers do not comprehend it.

15. For a view that career development should be subordinate to individual development, see Ralph Salvagno, "The Myths of Career Development" in *Training and Development Journal* 23, no. 3 (March 1969), pp. 46-48.

15

The Federal Executive Institute — Academy for the Bureaucracy

FRANK P. SHERWOOD

To understand the Federal Executive Institute, it is helpful to know that at least part of the reason for its creation was a growing awareness of the insularity of the federal system and the parochialism of the average executive. Illustrating this is the fact that 80 percent of the people promoted to supergrade positions are promoted within the same department they have been serving. This insularity is, I might add, characteristic of all our government organizations, from city governments to state governments and on up to the federal system.

This awareness, that men at high levels of responsibility need to look upward and outward, as well as in and down, was important in 1958 when the Federal Employees Training Act — the basic authority for such enterprises as the Institute — was passed. That act, by the way, because it establishes training as an integral part of management activity and allows the manager to use funds for training as he does for any program activity, is perhaps the most important piece of personnel legislation in the country's history.

At the institute, we operate on the assumption that everything in the system is temporary. We try to make the things we do relevant in a shifting, turbulent situation. We appoint from the staff a project manager — we call him dean — for each eight-week session. Can you imagine a university with a different education program manager each semester? We've had about eight deans now; no one has repeated. We consciously take a faculty member who hasn't been in the system very long and build him into the role. Each of them comes with a quite different set of assumptions. An economist — a system analyst — is running the next session, and we've been going through a lot of questioning of assumptions with him. Because each dean, with his team, is responding to what he sees happening in the environment, each session is fairly different from every other.

We provide the dean with a budget of $9,200.00, which is what we regard as our variable cost for a session. He uses those funds, within some modest constraints, very much as he wants. A recent dean loved to have all kinds of speakers and to buy books, so we had a cost overrun, and a lot of thrashing about that. It was good for the system. One thing it does is cause the fellows to put the heat on me. For example, we're trying a visiting scholar and practitioner program now, and it is expensive. So the dean is saying that this is experimental and the institute ought to pick it up. We are taking a look at the $9,200.00 figure and considering raising the pot. This requires us to look at the bigger

233

financial picture. The procedure has caused cost-consciousness and consideration of alternatives, but in a noncontrollist way.

I might mention a couple of other things about the institute and its effort to free up the system. The way in which we're financed gives us freedom to make choices and puts a burden of responsibility on everyone. It also makes rewards possible and is self-generating.

We consider our staff to be on temporary assignments up to three years. However, some are career civil servants and as a result a desire is sometimes expressed for more stability in the system. Also, we spend a lot of time in team meetings going over ground that some of us have gone over before. But the self-generation happens when guys will not accept our experience. They insist we go back over the ground and test the premises and the evaluation. They force us to look again at things.

The staff consists of twenty people, fourteen of whom are professionals. There is no hierarachy to speak of. We've built in a tremendous amount of feedback activity, and we've worked at the team-building OD thing, but with dubious success. What strikes me is that no matter how much communication we have, it's not enough. We had an issue recently involving OD. Some of our faculty members are themselves specialists in team-building, and sometimes I am irritated with myself when I bring in OD people, as though we did not have our own resources for this. Not long ago, the OD people suggested I have an advisor to myself for a couple of months and indicated a particular person. I said no. I like the man, and I'm sure he could provide some valuable insights. However, I made the point that we have faculty members with competence. If they can't feed me what the outside man would, there is something wrong with our system.

Twenty percent of the men at the institute have Ph.D.s and over 50 percent have master's degrees. By any measure, they are society's elite in capability. Despite this education, they need help in the kind of conscious worrying that says, "Who am I? What am I up to? What is my responsibility for helping create values and norms for the system of which I'm a part?" They don't deal comfortably with these questions.

Because we are an interagency program, we have guys with the dandiest expertise you've heard of. One man almost cancelled because a French submarine sank and he's the key man in finding submarines. Institute executives specialize in exotic things that I didn't even know existed, and there is no single body of knowledge that all of them need.

So we create a range of alternatives as rich as possible and expect them to sort out what's meaningful for them. We have a team-building exercise that provides the individual an opportunity to look at his goal structure — what does he want for himself and how does he want to contribute? We feel that that is his task as a mature, successful person.

All too frequently, the statement is made, "Gosh! I feel uncomfortable because I'm not sure I'm doing an organization thing." Or, "I've always been told what I'm supposed to do and what is important. The only test I know is whether or not something will contribute directly to the organization."

I say that this is a pretty short-run view of life. If you seek to become a better person, you look at what you want to have happen, you look at yourself, determine how you will contribute. But these men are uncomfortable with that.

Why are they like this? Is it something about the educational system, the entire process they go through? Is it the climate of the federal establishment? Is there something in the federal executive selection process? It could be all of these things.

I think you must start with a question about the personality of the federal executive. The research on this subject is not very good, but one study was done in the late fifties by Norman Martin. Some reanalysis of the data shows that federal executives tend to be basically dependent and nonachievement-oriented. Devastating charges! Many of them came into government at a fairly early age, twenty-four years on the average, and they do talk a lot about security. In that sense they are dependent, and people who are dependent are often hostile toward the authority that, at the same time they want, in a love-hate relationship. Our experience at the institute seems to validate the research.

Another thing to look at is the educational system, a system that I believe emphasizes conformity. It says, "Don't think for yourself! Get in step!" Most of the men in high levels of government have had highly technical education – very few have had a classical liberal arts education – and I think the problem is particularly great in technical education.

I met a fellow recently, deputy director of a major bureau and a good illustration of this problem, who doesn't even seem to have a concept of our modern culture. He is willing to learn and he's certainly not dumb – these guys aren't dumb – but he has not seen the big picture and he also, along with many others, feels threatened by the question of personal goals.

This reminds me also of a friend whose college-age son asked him about his philosophy of life. The boy, a college student, had come home in a state of emotional disarray and the question came up during the course of an all-night rap session between father and son. My friend realized with a jolt that he hadn't thought much about his philosophy since he was in college.

One thing we look for in a leader is that he be a learner. If you take seriously the idea that the executive today is responsible for *what* happens more than *how* it happens, then you know that he must be tuned in to a vast array of things happening around him. Furthermore, those things are continuously changing.

It follows, then, that the learning process becomes very important in the executive function. While he has increasing demands on his time in all aspects of his work, the executive also has a rapidly growing amount of data, from a broader and broader spectrum, that he must process before he can make a sound decision.

And frankly, we are discouraged at where we have to start. The average executive is no further along in learning skills and attitudes than he was when he left college. For instance, he has a terrible problem with roles at the institute. He figures that the professors ought to be the givers of knowledge and he the receiver. We at the institute are specialists, too, and we have things we can give. But the man who can bestow all knowledge and wisdom just isn't there. The executive must learn to deal with this and take responsibility for his own learning.

It is just as it often is in school. Kids put the responsibility on the teacher, saying "Okay, run something by me. Maybe I'll accept it; maybe I won't. But if I don't, it's your problem."

When we look at the institute's experience, it is obvious that all people don't learn in the same way. We put about twenty-five books, all kinds of books from *Growing Up Absurd* to *Managerial Psychology,* in the room of each man at the institute. Some of the men are compulsive about those books, and I'm sure that some of the same ones haven't learned a thing from reading them. And I feel that part of each person's skill development task is to determine how he learns best.

A third factor to consider in exploring what it is that makes the average executive as he is, is, of course, the system itself. It does things to the people in it. Let me describe a problem we've had. The institute was charged with three goals for its educational program. One is to develop managerial capability, another is to enable executives to work collaboratively in the system, and the third is to help the government to be more responsive. All of this is directed, of course, to the education and development of the individual executive – his personal growth.

Yet the notion that executive development is for people causes big problems. Some say it is inappropriate for the government to spend money on personal development. It is considered unclean for a man to leave the institute saying, "I've personally grown out of this!" Concern about personal values and where an individual is going get little approval in the system.

These difficult questions of philosophy, of goals, of personal contribution to society, not only *must* be addressed, but I also feel that people really *want* to address them. It goes with a healthy personality.

I mentioned that one of our institute goals is to help the men develop skills for working collaboratively. We feel that a leader must recognize the interdependence of everyone in the organization and in the system. The leader, instead of being dependent or dominant, must be able to live in a milieu where it isn't clear who is boss. Taking his own share of responsibility for what happens, he recognizes that others are involved and seeks collegial ways of working things out. This requires an ability to work in groups, particularly in problem-solving groups where the hierarchy factor is not very significant. It also demands a climate of trust and open communication.

Most of the men at the institute are not used to this kind of situation, and they become very frustrated in it. I remember, though, one institute graduate who told us of a meeting he led after his institute experience. It could have been a committee meeting just like dozens of others he had gone through. However, he suggested those present spend an hour getting to know each other. It turned out to be, he reported, a much more productive session.

Another institute goal is to help the men become more attuned to the contemporary environment. We do several things to provide this kind of enclosure. A speaking program brings in, for informal dialogue, a number of major government figures. With our complex government, we have a tremendous range of individuals, and their influence has been valuable. In addition, the executives have their own speaking program in which they talk about their specialties. This provides a wide variety of topics, from drugs and narcotics to what's ahead for NASA. In a workshop program the men go to Washington for three days and − dividing into broad special areas such as domestic policy, foreign policy, or science policy − visit congressmen and others involved in that realm.

Also, in their policy management studies, many of the men work on areas of social significance. For example, an Air Force computer specialist who had never seen a ghetto lived in a Philadelphia ghetto for three days and was, I believe, very much changed by the experience.

In addition to experiential things of this sort, we simulate the university by having two series of seminars of about five meetings each. The amount of reading is relatively light, but there is opportunity for a lot of open discussion. Seminar topics vary but are of critical importance such as black history, the city, and moral values in the society.

An important factor working at the institute has to do with how men are selected to come, what they are told about it and what their expectations are. It is significant that this varies greatly from one federal agency to the next. Typically in those agencies that have highly articulated executive manpower programs, selection for the institute is regarded as a real honor.

On the other hand, many a man comes very reluctantly. In his agency, being sent to the institute may be like being grabbed up and kicked out the door. Perhaps within his agency, understanding of, or communication about, the program is poor and the man is sure he is being sent because something is wrong with him.

The fact that the institute program provides a very personal and individual experience probably means that this will continue to be a problem. However, more significant is the fact of great differences among agencies in attitudes toward executive change and development. Four organizations, the CIA, the Navy, NASA, and IRS, come to my mind as agencies in which individual competence − and I'm talking about leadership competence rather than technical competence − is highly prized. Within them there seems to be recognition of the fact that things aren't going to go if there aren't good leaders around. There is, therefore, a commitment to the executive as a person.

Of the agencies mentioned, all, except perhaps IRS, are and have been well financed; they haven't been scratching for money. They are staffed sufficiently to make a training investment that supports that commitment to the individual. In some cases this condition is coupled with a systematic way of approaching the executive process, a process that includes specific growth expectations, ongoing planning, and planned job rotation. A man coming to the institute from this organization has good data on where he has been and where he is going. He does not feel lost.

Out of every sixty men there are, roughly, five who wish they hadn't come and spend much of their time proving they were right. Nearly everyone who wants to be there comes out feeling good about it.

This is due to the fact that in my teaching, I've found that fellows who have had related work experience can get a lot more out of a classroom situation. They have more motivation to understand and greater recognition of the dimensions of the problem. This is also true, of course, at the Federal Executive Institute. We don't use case studies because the men have their own experience to draw upon.

This does not imply that the work experience should necessarily precede the academic experience. I don't believe it should be entirely one way or the other, and that complicates the scheduling. I feel that working part time and going to school part time is dysfunctional. When you're doing something you want to do, you should be able to stay with it all day, rather than be boxed in by a rigid two or three hours work period followed by three hours school, then work again. This would have all kinds of problems. In the federal system, internships occur after the educational experience and are often seen as a first career step. This, I believe, intensifies the socializing problem that's bugging many young people.

In our educational system with its heavy reliance upon grades and tendency toward teacher-student relationships in which students are passive receivers, how do you encourage risk-taking? How do you teach tolerance to ambiguity? Is the intern experience meaningful in this regard? It can be, and I think sometimes it is, but I'm skeptical about internships. For one thing, practitioners in the system are often trying to socialize young people into their systems. With a heavy emphasis on that, there is little encouragement of risk-taking. My own internship experience, many years ago, was frustrating. I was angry throughout the experience, and it was perhaps because of those feelings that I didn't go into the federal government. We were shoved around and given unimportant things to do. There was a systematic putdown that is, from what I can tell, still going on.

For one thing, I honestly think that teaching the generalist concept is not real. At USC in the city manager program, we honored the generalist myth, and though a number of our people did go into city management, many more did not. We didn't give them what they needed to get started in city management. Many others who went into very specialized roles found much of their education not very helpful.

Not only graduate education but also the entire educational system ought to be more concerned with process and less concerned with content. By the time you get to graduate school, some fairly specific targets are necessary. Then both school and work experiences can be more meaningful. Let me give you an illustration. Let's say a person wants to become a manager and a leader. He really believes he can do the things that are required, but he has no real way of knowing without some appropriate experiences. Suppose this man, then, becomes a trainer. In doing this he must develop skills for identifying people's needs and for utilizing resources. He must learn how to develop people's capabilities and bring them together in meaningful ways. These are also the skills he must have as a leader in any kind of organization. Also, he would be in on relevant things. There's no way of making training totally irrelevant. I also see system analysis, the kinds of things that are going on in Michigan, as leading in the same direction.

It is an overstatement, however, to say that starting a person in training inevitably involves the organization only in training and nothing else. There are lots of examples of people who started in training and have gone far beyond it. Increasingly, many leaders are saying that they make few decisions any more. Rather, they help to see that decisions are made.

At the institute, I have noticed different degrees of expertise between executives from technical agencies such as the AEC and NASA contrasted with executives from social agencies such as the OEO and HEW.

The more sophisticated managers are in the hardware and defense areas. A tragedy of our society is that there is more sloshing around, more uncertainty, in our human resources agencies. There is also a lack of willingness to spend money on training, in a situation where, because of the numbers of variables and the complexity of constituencies, training needs far exceed those in agencies where targets are clear.

In general, the head man at a "technical" federal agency should have an expertise in the specialty of that agency. That points up another problem with the generalist concept. There's no place to go. There are jobs in the system that don't require the engineering or whatever degree, but they are in the minority by far. I might put in here that the person with a training background, coming up his own specialist route, probably has a better chance at getting one of the top jobs than the one with a more ambiguous background.

The question of the generalists and specialists in federal agencies is a mixed thing, and it varies from agency to agency. For example, whether or not I call the Park Service director a generalist, he's never been out of the Park Service. However, he is one of the more sophisticated managers in the country, partly because of the kind of managerial training system the Park Service has. Every park superintendent, though parochial in the sense that he has always been in the Park Service, is managerially sophisticated. A man might start as a ranger, be tapped for leadership, and begin a process that will build his leadership capabilities. On the other hand, IRS executives can more accurately be called generalists. They often come to those positions out of other agencies; some of them have degrees in administration. But opportunities are limited. Something like 2 percent of these federal executives have been educated in the schools of public administration. I don't want to put it down, however. Interesting possibilities do appear. Also, I think there is more opportunity for generalists in state and local government.

And there are people like Burt Harding. A graduate of Syracuse University in public administration, he distinguished himself as a deputy commissioner in IRS and acquitted himself well as number two man in OEO under Sargent Shriver. He got out of government for a year, but came back because he likes government and loves what he's doing.

Another one is Elmer Staats, comptroller general, who has a Ph.D. in public administration from Minnesota. I also know that the General Accounting Office is looking for PA people, because they are being called upon to do some of the most important work in government, and they must get out of their accounting rut. By the way, in a few years I think the GAO, of all places, will be the most exciting place in government for a generalist.

Another change in the years ahead will be the Organization Development movement. I believe many of you in public administration have to see yourselves as developing skills in the change process. You have to think of the PA person, if you want to talk about a generalist, as an applied social scientist, and the area for that is the change process: How do you help people deal with new dimensions of the system? How do you provide bridges for them? The Organization Development movement is currently the hot one, but I think it's going to be supplanted by more concern with management by objectives theory. PPBS is dead and OD isn't going to quite catch on. One reason is that it is linked too much with sensitivity training and hasn't enough specific operational legitimacy. And, in fact, the things that are done in OD can be done within the rubric of management by objectives. It's important to recognize that there are two schools of management by objectives theory. One is a hierarchical school in which the manager says, "I'll set the objectives and I won't bother you with a lot of detailed supervision, but boy are you accountable!" The other school sees it as a more collegial process in which the parties to the behavior collaborate. Instead of accountability, the question is "How can I help you get where you and I agree we wnat to go?"

OD is being harmed, in my opinion, by the emphasis on group dynamics. True, there is a tremendous need for improvement in group skills, but that's not the whole thing. I'm interested in how people receive behavioral cues in organizations, and one thing I've been looking at for some time is our financial processes. There's nothing more debilitating to motivation and acceptance of responsibility.

Let's say you, a manager, want to buy a typewriter. First, you make a claim in your budget proposals. Even if the budget is approved, you probably have to repeat the process, saying, "Hey! How about that typewriter?" Then someone tells you when you can spend the money and you finally have approval. Now someone comes along and says, "We've decided to buy all L.C. Smiths this year," so you have to buy an L.C. Smith, regardless of how your secretary feels about it. You are given no freedom. You are told whether, when, how, and what to do, and in a sense that you are not mature enough to make a judgment. If I want to buy an IBM typewriter, I buy an IBM typewriter, but that's not true in a lot of federal agencies.

I did a study of financial controls in the California state colleges, and I have a feeling that many of their problems can be attributed to the issue of financial control. A top official at one of the colleges, in a responsible position, couldn't make the decision to split a job and hire two half-time people. He had to get approval from Sacramento.

Regarding the problems of group size and group decisions, it has been argued that large groups need someone to direct them. There are two problems with this. One is a question of how many people you want involved in a decision and this requires a consideration of the quality of the individual versus the group decision. There is, by the way, some data that suggest that many kinds of decisions are better when group-made. This also involves the question of how much participation and involvement you want for other reasons, and the consideration becomes a matter of basic values.

The other element has to do with group size. If you're going to have a problem-solving session, you must have a small group and provide air time for everyone. One way to make sure the committee process won't work is to get the group too large. There are ways of handling that, though, the obvious one being to break up into smaller groups, then come back together and determine the agenda for a larger group. Even when you want 100 people involved in a decision, there are ways of building in participation and involvement.

The question of defining leadership in a group can be thorny. Sometimes there is abdication, with people saying, "To hell with it. You do it and don't bother me." Or there is conflict. People see it as a means of securing image and reward. They all want it, and they don't care about the group.

There is, in essence, a judgement whether that kind of function – the feedback function – should be performed by someone within or external to the system. The organization has to build the capabilities and arrangements that will cause it to happen in the organization, one way or the other. Given the people we have, I think we ought to be able to do it for ourselves.

In my own organization I see myself as in a critical boundary position between the outside world, which is real, and the world inside the institute – also real. To us, the world outside is in some ways a hostile one. I remember an incident having to do with sensitivity training. The situation was touchy. Among other things, there was a fear that our persistence in offering such training would result in a prohibition on all long-term training. Because I felt the rest of the staff had not had the same opportunity I had to experience that environment, I decided the staff could not accurately understand the motives of the outside forces. I cancelled the labs without prior staff discussion. I don't see how you can avoid this occasionally.

The leader has to believe in the reality he perceives, and sometimes others within the organization seem to be completely out of touch with that reality. I see a city manager, particularly, as sharing the kind of boundary position in which I find myself. When he sees another person in his organization as living in a cocoon, he cannot have complete confidence in that man's judgment on a particular issue, and their relationship, at that point, is not pure.

In order to build confidence so that this reality can be shared, we try to work with it, and the only thing I know to do is to run as open a system as possible. But I think of another incident that came up around something called the Feds' Manifesto. Eleven young people in the federal government issued a "Federal Employees for a Democratic Society Manifesto." I don't remember all of what it contains, but generally, it was that there should be more T-groups; there should be more discussion in agencies about things that young people want to discuss, and probably most consequential, that a person shouldn't have to administer a program he doesn't believe in. In other words, he shouldn't be called upon to do anything that doesn't go along with his value system. Of course, this an outright attack on hierarchy. It says that authority is no longer the ultimate value. We suggested that executives read the manifesto in our newsletter, not endorsing it, but saying that it's the kind of thing that ought to be read by people who want to understand the generation gap. I got considerable static on this and was told by important people in my world that I shouldn't have included it. Next thing I knew our problem was known to just about everybody in our world, it seemed.

If a place is not made available for young guys to come into government service and not only hold to their values but even be part of implementing or making policy, I suspect that many people will be turned off and leave government; others will come in; there will be more activism, and there will be some bending on the part of the government. If older people can stop being bugged by the fact that kids don't like the institutions, we'd have some basis for negotiation. Let me add that there are a number of executives who see the problem. Everybody in the system isn't in the same place. However, an interesting thing about the eleven who signed the manifesto is that they developed their militancy in the government, not having been involved in college activist movements. That's a sad commentary.

As one just over thirty, I feel like the last defender of the court who is very glad reinforcements finally arrived. We're talking about a different set of assumptions that cut to the core of traditional beliefs.

I think many of them are saying that the system is far different from the theory. They're not throwing over the theory itself, but the institutions which have grown up around it and which supposedly represent them. It's a shock, though, to hear that the federal bureaucracy is not even willing to listen to the manifesto.

I think there is a basic disagreement on the issue of authority. To the kids, authority is not the ultimate value, whereas older people think the system is falling apart if the hierarchy principle doesn't persist. I'm also thinking back to something Merton talked about — the question of terminal versus instrumental values. There's a frightful tendency for us to displace the terminal values with instrumental ones. By *terminal* I mean life and liberty questions — the end states we desire. What happens is that we can never operationalize the end states so we create a set of procedural values that will presumably take us there. They become the things we honor. If I live by instrumental values, those are the ones I'm going to be up tight about.

Yet, my early decision not to enter the federal government had nothing to do with my undergraduate training. Rather I had a vague impression that the bureaucracy seemed so big that I could see few rewards for myself. I found it stifling. However, my experience was limited, and I think I probably made a mistake in judgment. There are some exciting agencies and opportunities to do creative things.

Many people allege that to be a leader in government today, an individual must have charisma. This gets to a fundamental question of what's going to happen to the leadership process. As organizations become more unglued, as there is less coordination by means of establishing jurisdiction, there will be more question of who does what. Leadership roles will become less a matter of clear-cut distinction between so-called program and nonprogram decisions and the idea of the administrator working on only the big things will be left behind. He will have to make himself felt in ways that are less clear, and that's a harder thing. It seems to me that this will call for men with more personal magnetism. Charisma will be an important dimension of leadership. I don't foresee any diminution in the leadership role; I do see more opportunity for more different kinds of people doing things in different ways.

In summary, the bureaucracy will provide more and more opportunities for this leadership. In an increasingly pluralistic society, I see the bureaucracy becoming more political and bureaucrats becoming more confident and more politically potent. This increasingly pluralistic, highly specialized society inevitably points up cleavages and requires conflict resolution. This makes the job in the bureaucracy in many ways more attractive because the administrator is hearing many messages, and in order to deal with them he must insert his own values and needs. Our system is so diverse that I'm increasingly more uncomfortable about a monolithic view of it. You can find within it every kind of human under the sun.

16

The Intergovernmental Personnel Act: Manpower, the Quiet Crisis in Federalism

DAVID B. WALKER

For lack of statesmanship, a
nation sinks:
the saving of it is a wealth of
counsellors. . . .
When no one is consulted, plans
are foiled:
when many are consulted,
they succeed. . . .
A man who listens to healthy
reproof
will rank among wise men.

PROVERBS

Manpower has been one of the most critical dimensions of the crisis in contemporary federal-state-local relations. But only recently, with the enactment of the Intergovernmental Personnel Act of 1970, did it become a focal point of national concern and action.

Federalism's Unsettling Scene

But this should come as no surprise. American federalism today is a far different governmental system than what it was a decade or two ago. Moreover, the expectations of the American people as they look to this system have shifted dramatically. Certain facts concerning recent intergovernmental relations underscore these broad generalizations and highlight the crisis in public management and personnel at all levels.

First, since 1950 the nation's gross national product has more than tripled, and our people have come to enjoy higher standards of living and the benefits of modern science and technology. With this advancing affluence, however, along with our soaring population and galloping urbanization have come persistent demands for more and more public services, and a resulting burgeoning of governmental budgets. Witness the fact that during the past decade per capita public spending for domestic purposes rose by more than 97 percent, far

245

surpassing the 63 percent hike in per capita expenditures for defense purposes and 76 percent rise in per capita personal income.

Second, this demand has hit most severely those levels of government whose fiscal and administrative systems are most shackled by statutory and customary limitations, whose revenues are most dependent on slow-growth tax sources, whose elected officials are most subject to hostile voter reaction to new tax levies: the states, counties, cities, and towns. Yet, over the past decade, state and local government expenditures rose at an annual average rate of 9.4 percent compared to 7.3 percent for direct nondefense spending by federal government, and those expenditures now account for over two-thirds of all such civil governmental outlays (i.e., all outlays save those for national defense and international relations).

Third, since the end of World War II, nearly three-quarters of the nation's population has concentrated in urban areas and over half of these citizens now reside in suburbs. Moreover, while nearly 80 percent of our taxable wealth and business activities are now produced in these same urban areas, the dynamics of recent urbanization have produced central cities with an increasing proportion of low-income, underprivileged, and undereducated citizens; with deteriorating community facilities and industrial plants; with a host of physical environmental problems; with a largely "mined out" property tax; along with a gradual flight of much of the community's leadership base to the suburbs.

Fourth, this same urbanization process has produced some suburbs with many of the problems of their core city neighbors as well as a meandering maze of newer jurisdictions exercising local autonomy and separate spending, taxing, and planning authority. It has produced then metropolitan areas as a whole where a few have area-wide decision-making procedures and programs that affect the region as a whole, and where none can effect a fair distribution of the cost of public services among constituent localities.

Fifth, our rural population is about what it was in 1960, but the farming population declined by 35 percent between 1960 and 1969. In terms of income levels, population growth, education, health facilities and housing, rural America is on the deficit side of any urban-rural comparison. This crisis in our countryside is juxtaposed against the flight of much of its leadership and skilled working force to the cities, the erosion of its revenue base, and the desperate need to revitalize rural county government.

Sixth, in the states there are major legal, program, administrative, and fiscal powers to alleviate central city agonies, to reduce core city-suburban disparities, to strengthen rural governments, to redraw the meandering local government map; in short, to cope effectively with one of the most critical, yet least publicized weaknesses in contemporary intergovernmental relations: i.e., the debilitating conflict between states and their own localities. Yet, in all too many instances state legislation works directly against central cities, encourages the jurisdictional jungle at the local level, impedes the development of fair and effective local revenue systems, and makes it difficult to attack area-wide problems on an area-wide basis. State tax collections did increase by more than 165 percent between 1959 and 1969, and state aid to localities nearly tripled during the same period, but central cities generally received a disproportionately smaller share of this aid than did suburbs and rural areas. Twenty-seven states by January 1970 had established departments of urban or local affairs, and this is quite encouraging. Most of these units, however, merely have technical assistance and advisory functions. Moreover, a majority of states have not involved themselves administratively or financially in federal-local development programs — urban renewal, mass transportation, water and sewage facilities, hospital construction, model cities, and the like.

Seventh, the federal response to these public service and finance pressures at the state and local levels has triggered an extraordinary, almost explosive, expansion of the grant-in-aid system. Federal aid to state and local governments experienced over a four-fold increase between 1960 and 1970. These grants now amount to more than 500 separate authorizations, an estimated $30.3 billion for fiscal year 1970, and approximately 20 percent of state and local revenue. More than 340 of these programs were enacted since 1963.

Finally, while this expansion in federal aid has provided much needed fiscal assistance to state and local governments and while the 258 percent hike in urban program funds between 1961-69 constitutes a noteworthy national response for the metropolitan crisis, other trends accompanying this rapid growth have had an adverse effect on the overall system. The extraordinary number and variety of these programs have created problems of overlapping, duplication, and fragmentation at all levels.

The increase in the number of eligible recipients, while frequently necessary to meet pressing problems at hand, has generated battle after battle over "bypassing" and program coordination problems among the affected jurisdictions. The highly technical nature of many of the newer programs — especially those relating to education, economic development, physical and mental health, poverty, and urban rehabilitation — have highlighted the need for additional and highly specialized manpower both at disbursing and receiving levels. Furthermore, the new style focus on the multiple manifold needs of specific regional groups, specific age groups, and specific economic categories have prompted cutting across categorical program lines, and this further complicates the management dilemma at all levels.

More active government at all levels; rapidly growing government at the state and local levels; a mushrooming of our metropolitan areas with their marvel of wealth and their myriad social, economic, and jurisdictional problems; a less publicized erosion of much of rural America; an evolving new role for the states which some are having difficulty in assuming; heightened tension between the states and their larger localities and among urban localities; and a rapid increase in the number, dollar amounts, and administrative problems of federal grants-in-aid — these are the basic features of contemporary federalism with which we contend.

The Personnel Angle of the Federalism Triangle

In broad outline, they dramatize many points of conflict in contemporary federalism. At the same time, they underscore the fact that the spirit of intergovernmental cooperation is not dead and that opportunities to revitalize it can be found at every level. Above all, these facts of federalism clearly indicate that improved management is about as critical as more money.

The personnel problem, for some, is but a by-product of the general management and money imbalances in the system today. And in a sense, this is true. A reduction of the fiscal imbalance by revenue sharing, tax credits, and welfare take-over at the national level, and by greater use of the personal income tax, assumption of the bulk of local educational load, and property tax reform at the state levels would go far toward providing the funds needed to attract and pay adequately the needed state and local personnel. Moreover, managerial innovations in the form of reorganized executive branches of state and local governments, curbing the proliferation of special districts, developing responsible regional mechanisms that can plan and implement programs of area-wide concern – to cite only the more obvious – would greatly facilitate meeting the heavy servicing demands placed on public personnel at the state and local levels. But the personnel challenge must be considered in its own context, while obviously relating it to those other facets of federalism's basic agenda for adaptation to the needs of the seventies. The gap in this area is just that great and its salient features that troublesome.

Some would have us believe that there is no manpower gap. Full-time state and local employment after all reached the 10.1 million mark in 1970, more than three times the federal figure and 80 percent greater than the counterpart 1960 total. The overall state monthly payroll soared to $1.6 billion by early 1970, or over three times the 1960 outlay, while the total local payroll passed the $4.2 billion mark, or two and one-half times the figure of a decade ago. In terms of jurisdictional categories, the states, school districts, and counties have had the highest employment rates over the past decade. In terms of functional categories, state and local employment in education and public welfare rose by 69 percent and 119 percent respectively between 1960 and 1970. Police rates increased by 48 percent and those in public health and hospitals by 45 percent during the same decade. All told, state and local governments now account for over 85 percent of all manpower engaged in civil governmental functions.

These figures underscore the fact that the states and localities have had to shoulder most of the manpower burden of meeting the growing popular demand for greater public services. They also tend to conceal many of the more subtle dimensions of what must be deemed a crisis situation.

1. They do not reveal, for example, that a shortage of qualified personnel, especially in the professional, administrative, and technical (PAT) sectors, has existed for at least a decade.[1]

2. They conceal the fact that about one-third of the top level municipal administrators retired during the sixties.

3. They do not indicate that at least twelve states still have no formal merit system except in those joint program areas covered by federal grant requirements; that the coverage in all but a handful of counties is very limited; and that about two-fifths of the full-time municipal employees are in occupational categories that are exempted under most merit systems, not to mention the 20 percent of the total municipal work force which is part-time.

4. These figures also fail to show the personnel difficulties experienced by chief executives in jurisdictions with old style, regulation-rooted civil service boards.

5. They conceal the fact that existing federal training aid under some seventeen programs has benefited largely program specialists, as has that under Office of Management and Budget Circular A-87, which permits training expenses to be included as "allowable costs" in individual categorical grant programs.

6. Above all, these impressive personnel figures in no way reveal the critical condition of central management people at both the state and local levels; as intergovernmental programs have expanded and become more intricate and interrelated, the line agency (program) specislists have increased their influence throughout the system; but the power, professional standing, and prestige of core management has not been strengthened commensurately in most jurisdictions, and this imbalance is a major factor affecting the position of chief executives, the status of comprehensive planning, the effectiveness of budgeting, the troubled condition of auditing and accounting, the broad problem of administrative responsiveness, and the public's cynicism regarding the capacity of government — all governments — to function.

A Response Emerges

The Intergovernmental Personnel Act of 1970 (IPA)[2] addresses itself to some, but not all, of the problems of recruiting and retaining qualified personnel, especially central management people, a problem which confronts state and local governments. Its initial predecessor, the proposed Intergovernmental Personnel Act of 1966 (S. 3408, 89th Congress) grew out of an awareness on the part of the Senate Subcommittee on Intergovernmental Relations, chaired by Senator Edmund S. Muskie, that more than good management practices, additional federal financial aid, greater flexibility and uniformity in grant administration, and greater decentralization of decision-making would be needed, if contemporary federalism were to be adapted to the pressing demands of the sixties and seventies. The Subcommittee's 1965 survey of "The Federal System as Seen by Federal Aid Officials" had found that manpower was considered to be one of the great gaps in intergovernmental relations.

The more-than-a-hundred middle management administrators of grant programs that responded to the survey revealed a profound awareness that the success or failure of their respective programs depended in large measure on the skills of their state and local administrative counterparts. While conceding that the implementation of intergovernmental programs even then had become a major state and local responsibility, they also evidenced considerable concern regarding the comparatively low salaries, meager in-service training opportunities, and limited merit scope of many state and local personnel systems. Over three-quarters of the respondents agreed that the inability to transfer retirement benefits and the loss of seniority were key factors blocking job mobility in these systems. A majority also concurred in the view that the operation of their respective programs would benefit by the establishment of more federally-supported training programs. Much of this, of course, merely corroborates Charles Adrian's assessment that one of the major points of conflict in the system arises "whenever the administrative personnel of a particular level for a particular function is not fully professionalized."

At the same time, the survey also documented a clear hostility between program specialists and political generalists; chief executives and top management generalists, in essence, were viewed by most of these program administrators as potential or actual opponents, subject to the whims of the electorate. Bypassing of general units of government, providing little or no grant information to elected chief executives and their budget officers, hostility to comprehensive area-wide planning, and opposition to any requirement that federal-local projects should conform to it underscore thier narrow program preoccupation.

In developing a legislative response to these and other intricate facets of the intergovernmental personnel challenge, the subcommittee drafted legislation that focused on some of the complaints of these federal administrators. But it also dealt with the needs of the core management sector of state and local government, a group that has been aided little by the rapid expansion of categorical grants, but whose function has become all the more significant as a result of this development. In short, the bill sought to strike a balance between the administrative generalists and the program specialists.

The intricate legislative history of this measure need not concern us here, save to note that the Johnson administration introduced its own intergovernmental manpower bill in the 90th Congress; portions of it subsequently were incorporated into the Muskie measure; the Senate passed a modified measure with floor amendments in 1968, but the House took no action; and considerable effort on the part of the public interest groups representing states and localities, the Advisory Commission on Intergovernmental Relations, the Office of Management and Budget, and the U.S. Civil Service Commission was required to secure agreement and favorable House action on a modified Senate-passed bill in 1970.[3]

The Intergovernmental Personnel Act

The basic thrust of the legislation is to help strengthen state and local governments through improved personnel administration and more effective recruiting and training. A modified block grant, discretionary grants, technical assistance, and other forms of nonfiscal federal support constitute the arsenal of approaches provided in the act.

Administratively, the measure puts, the U.S. Civil Service Commission into a lead role. The commission is the sole grant disbursing instrumentality under the act. It assumes the full responsibility for administering all merit system requirements in various existing federal grant programs, thanks to transfers stipulated in the legislation. It is authorized to join with state and local governments in cooperative recruitment and examinations and to provide technical assistance, on request, to jurisdictions seeking to improve their personnel management. The commission has already undertaken cooperative efforts in both of these areas under the Intergovernmental Cooperation Act of 1968 and plans to expand its technical aid under the IPA of 1970. Finally, the Civil Service Commission is charged with coordinating the training and personnel management technical assistance efforts of other federal agencies — all with a view toward reducing duplication and achieving greater effectiveness of the multiple federal activities in this troublesome intergovernmental area.[4]

Pursuant to these provisions, the Office of State Merit Systems of the Department of Health, Education and Welfare has been transferred to the commission. Within the commission a new unit, the Bureau of Inter-governmental Personnel Programs, has been established to help discharge its assigned duties under the act.

In terms of grant purposes, three basic uses are authorized by the IPA; personnel administration improvements, training, and government service fellowships. The development of a statewide personnel system, state efforts to strengthen local systems, manpower studies, improving one or more of the major personnel management functions, augmenting programs for the disadvantaged, and research and demonstration projects are some of the types of state-local personnel administration improvements that could be aided financially. The training title makes it clear that state and local employees in the PAT sector should receive primary consideration. Core management people no doubt will receive special attention. Both the act and its legislative history stress the IPA training grants are to help meet needs not adequately provided under regular grant-in-aid programs. The Government Service Fellowship grants will permit study at the graduate level for up to two years for PAT personnel. State and local governments will have wide discretion as to the candidates, the schools to be used, and the subjects to be studied. The IPA grant may cover travel, books, authorized related expenses, up to one-fourth of the selected employee's salary, and certain payments to the educational institution involved.

Regarding matching requirements, the Civil Service Commission may use grants to meet up to three-quarters of the costs of personnel administration and training grants until fiscal year 1976. Subsequently, even matching will apply.

In terms of allocation and grant type, the act earmarks 20 percent of the available funds for any one fiscal year to be distributed by the Civil Service Commission on a discretionary basis among state and local governments, relying on such factors as relative population, the number of employees affected, the pressing nature of the projects proposed, and the ability of governments to use the funds effectively. In essence these will be project grants and the commission will have considerable latitude in awarding them. The remaining 80 percent is to be allocated among the states on a weighted formula basis with the number of state and local employees and population serving as two factors that must be considered. A suballocation formula is also stipulated which requires the 80 percent to be further divided between the states and their localities using such factors as the number of their respective employees and the division of state-local expenditures. In no instance, however, will the minimum allocation for meeting local needs in any state be less than half the allotted state-area total.

The state-local relations provisions of the act provide a complicated but ingenious balancing of the personnel needs of both levels. These provisions, it might be added, were the most hard fought-out ones in the entire measure. In both the training and personnel administration titles, the states and their governors are given a good opportunity to develop broad state-local programs. The goal here is to encourage more effective, economical, and coordinated efforts in an area rampant with fragmentation. At the same time, general units of local government serving a population of 50,000 or more, either singly or in combination, also are directly eligible for grants. But there are some restrictions here. If a state government bases its application on a statewide plan developed pursuant to state law, and so notifies the commission, then local governments in their states in most cases are barred from receiving a grant. The state law involved, however, must establish a state agency with adequate authority, staff, and organization to develop and administer such a plan; it must provide technical and other support for carrying out its local components; and it must stipulate procedures that assure adequate local involvement in the plan's development.

In addition, a state may develop a plan that is the product of collaboration and specific agreement between the state and eligible general local governments. Where an eligible local government has agreed to be covered by such a state plan, it may be awarded another IPA grant only if its special needs are not met by the plan and if funds are available. Moreover, if these special needs fall in an area covered by the agreed state-local plan, then the local application can only be submitted with the approval of the state government. The same conditions would apply in the case of a state plan developed pursuant to law.

The intricacy of these various options should not conceal the fact that the act seeks genuine state-local collaboration in the training and personnel administration fields. The alternatives presented rest on the assumption that cooperation cannot be forced and cannot even be encouraged by a uniform, across-the-board approach, given the diversity of state-local personnel relationships in our fifty commonwealths.

On the nonfiscal front, the act authorizes all federal agencies to open up their training programs to state and local employees, especially those in the PAT category; it gives prior congressional consent to interstate compacts geared to improving personal administration and training; and it authorizes the temporary exchange of personnel between the federal government and the states and localities.

Finally and looking to the future, the act establishes an Advisory Council on Intergovernmental Personnel Policy which the president must appoint six months after the date of enactment. Composed of officials from all levels with at least half from state and local governments, the council is slated to study and make recommendations regarding personnel policies and programs, particularly as they affect these governments. It will report its findings and proposals to the president and Congress from time to time, but its first report must be rendered a year and a half following its establishment. Moreover, the act stipulates that this initial study should specifically consider the appropriate standards of a merit system and ways and means of promoting these standards. This report ought to provoke considerable controversy and hopefully engender a clearer understanding of how the needs of modern management can best be harmonized with those of merit.

Conclusion

The Intergovernmental Personnel Act symbolizes the fact that the nation is beginning to become aware of the manpower crisis facing state and local governments. Though its funding is modest ($15 million was expended in FY 1973) and its provisions do not deal with all aspects of the challenge, it can, if properly implemented, go far toward correcting a major problem in our federal system: the imbalance of bureaucratic authority and influence between and among the levels of government and between their core management sector and program specialists. Without this, the promises of any of the New Federalism's proposed fiscal, jurisdictional, and administrative reforms will fall far short of their mark. Devolution will be a detour. Decentralization will be the chaotic design of the program functionaries. And democracy with its promise of a responsible and responsive officialdom will become merely a distant dream.

Notes

1. See the study done in 1960 by the Municipal Manpower Commission. *Governmental Manpower for Tomorrow's Cities* (New York: McGraw-Hill, 1962).

2. *Intergovernmental Personnel Act of 1970*, 84 *Stat.* 1969. This was S. 11, 91st Congress, signed by the president on January 5, 1971.

3. See U.S. Senate, Committee on Government Operations, Subcommittee in Intergovernmental Relations, *Hearings, Intergovernmental Personnel Act of 1969*, March and April 1969, and Senate Report No. 91-489, October 21, 1969, and U.S. House of Representatives, Committee on Education and Labor, Special Subcommittee on Education, *Hearings, Intergovernmental Personnel Act*, November 1969, and House Report 91-1733, December 14, 1970.

4. See Robert E. Hampton, "Partners in Problem Solving! The Essence of the IPA," *Civil Service Journal*, April-June 1971, pp. 1-4.

17

The Application of Behavioral Science in Local Government Organizations: Some Political Implications

WILLIAM B. EDDY

Professional public administrators and their academic cohorts have traditionally gleaned through developments in the field of organization and management in search of approaches to greater effectiveness. This search has encompassed business as well as public management techniques and has reached into the disciplines of social science and various new technologies. Of course, several significant developments have occurred within public management itself. A relatively new approach labeled "organizational development" or "OD" is now available. There is evidence that the new approach holds promise for helping cope with some of the perennial problems of government institutions. However, OD is based on a somewhat different model of organization and a different value system than those under which many agencies presently operate. Thus it would seem to require rather careful examination.

Most of the earlier approaches to organizational effectiveness were related to the bureaucracy and administrative management models. They were based on a legal-rational philosophy and utilized "principles of management." These approaches have as their main focus the regularizing of organizational behaviors and procedures in order to achieve greater reliability. It is assumed that the organization will operate most effectively if all requisite performances are planned, organized, and programmed according to an established set of procedures and enforced by a hierarchy of authority.

This chapter will deal with the attempt to apply the new approaches to governmental organizations. The following propositions form the rationale for the positions taken:

1. Present organizational forms and administrative practices which exist in most local governments will not be adequate to solve our pressing urban problems effectively. Traditional bureaucratic organizations, which are characterized by a pyramidal authority or "command" system, clearly separated functional units, and systems of rules and procedures to direct work as their basic outcomes stress order, reliability and precision. In regard to the problems of the 1970s — these outcomes are not "where it is."[1]

Robert Saunders and Gerald Brown, University of Missouri – Kansas City, contributed importantly to this chapter.

2. In order to gain the necessary increased effectiveness, more is needed than simply beefing up the existing forms through more manpower, management information systems, and tighter controls. Basic changes in the way organizations are conceived and operated are necessary in order to bring about increased flexibility, better and more responsive problem-solving, more effective collaboration among operating units, and more widely shared participation in planning and decision-making.

3. The behavioral sciences have moved considerably past the "human relations" movement of the 1940s and 1950s in their ability to help provide avenues to organizational renewal. Approaches such as the family of methods often called organization development or OD — action research, survey-feedback, grid OD, organization revitalization, and others — have the capability of providing part of the answer to more effective performance.

4. In addition to the usual problems of overcoming internal resistance to change in implementing new programs, there is an additional dimension to the problem in local government. There may be important conflicts in traditions and values between applied behavioral science approaches and what are often termed "political realities." Change programs may be jeopardized, even though they are well-conceived and useful, if they run afoul of these "realities." The major purpose of this chapter is to explore some of these possible conflicts.

The Nature of Organization Development

The behavioral science theoretical underpinnings, methodologies, and goals of OD have been stated elsewhere and will not be repeated here.[2] However, it may be useful to summarize some of the organizational problem areas relevant to local government which may be amenable to behavioral science intervention.

1. The need for increased flexibility and adaptation to change. Continuing self-evaluation and renewal must become a way of life if organizations are to be able to adapt their structures and operations to forms appropriate for new problems in a changing world.

2. The need to shift from major emphasis on control, structure, and compliance to a focus on problem-solving, goal orientation, innovation, and risk-taking. Organizations conceived as mechanical systems are most effective in routine production and other repetitive tasks — not in solving a succession of idiosyncratic problems.

3. The need for more effective teamwork and collaboration within and across operating groups. Autonomous departmental units are no longer functional. Knowledge resources from a variety of spots in the organization need to be tightly integrated and brought to bear on complex problems

that do not confine themselves to variables within a single unit. Successful collaboration depends upon personal skills and approaches frequently lacking in traditional organizations.

4. Need for maximum utilization of human potential. Traditional organizational forms "put employees in boxes" in which only a fraction of their potential is developed and utilized. These tight boundaries rob the organization of much latent capability and contribute to personnel problems by making work less meaningful, less involving, and less intrinsically motivating.

5. Need for new conceptions of management, authority and leadership. The traditional assumption that all the authority in the organization is vested in the man at the top and that he brings about performance by "commanding" obedience is largely a myth in most public organizations (as well as private ones). There are many constraints on the command ability of the manager – including competition in the market, civil service regulations, and increasing professionalism. Further, and more importantly, the most valued behaviors simply cannot be brought about by demand. One cannot command people to be committed, to be innovative, to collaborate effectively, to be sensitive to the feelings and needs of others, to be more perceptive in their analysis of problems, to make better decisions, etc. Employees who do not want to do these kinds of things, who do not know how, or who feel threatened will not have their behavior changed much by command – except perhaps to become more defensive and constricted. Influence needs to be based more on problem-solving ability and relevance and less on status or tenure.

6. The need for more participative forms of organization. More of the decision-making and problem-solving activities of the organization need to be located closer to the points where the problems occur and the information about them is available.

7. The need to deal more directly and adequately with the identification and management of conflict and competition. Intergroup conflicts that are not resolved, but are either avoided or passed upstairs for arbitration, are likely to recur and to stymie collaborative efforts. Yet most organizations have very primitive mechanisms, if any, for dealing with conflicts and dysfunctional competition.

8. The need to conceive of the organization as a sociotechnical system, rather than as a rational-mechanical system. The various "people processes" of the organization must be better understood and facilitated. Communication, intergroup linkages, project coordination, and interpersonal competence must be built in "organically."

Perhaps even more important than the problem areas to which it addresses itself are the positions taken by many in the field of applied behavioral science regarding the appropriateness or inappropriateness of certain kinds of behavior.

These judgments are made on the basis of some combination of values, insights, and empirical evidence.

1. *Openness and authenticity.* Communication about facts, perceptions, ideas, and feelings should be free and open in all directions. People should be encouraged to "level" with each other – to be frank about their reactions. Feelings are viewed as important and appropriate aspects of interpersonal relations and should not be covered up.

2. *Trust.* A necessary component of effective collaborative relations is a level of mutual trust that will support openness, acceptance of others' positions, risk-taking, and mutual support.

3. *Theory Y.* McGregor's well-known alternative to Theory X (authoritarian management) asserts that most workers can be realistically viewed as potentially interested in work, responsible, capable of assuming responsibility. Better productivity ensues if people are managed less closely.

4. *Mutual Influence – Democracy.* Unilateral authority is not the best approach to management. Organizations work better if employees at all levels are allowed a sense of ownership in the process by having an opportunity to influence decisions and plans that affect them.

5. *Development of people.* The organization has a need and a responsibility to help its members continue to develop themselves as fuller, more competent and actualizing total persons.

6. *Confrontation.* Traditional avoidance of direct confrontation is dysfunctional. Norms that encourage avoidance of conflict, keeping feelings out of it, and compromising differences should be changed.

7. *Interpersonal competence.* Substantive technical knowledge is not enough. Organizational members need to learn operational skills in such areas as self-understanding, communication, confrontation, teamwork, and consultation.

Application of Behavioral Science in Political/Administrative Systems

Organization Development programs have been tried extensively in business firms.[3] There is less direct experience in public agencies. Robert Golembiewski and the author have discussed some of the problems of applying OD programs in government. Golembiewski's analysis emphasizes the federal government and focuses primarily on organizational characteristics that differentiate it from business. He lists the major differentiating characteristics of government as (1) multiple access (the system is more open to influence at many levels); (2) greater variety of interests, reward structures and values at subgroup levels;

(3) more competing command loci or influence centers rather than a clear-cut "management group"; (4) and weak linkages between political and career levels (which may mean between executives and operating managers).[4]

Golembiewski also discusses the unique "habit background" of public agencies. These are patterns within the institutional environment which may inhibit the process of change. Phenomena discussed include reluctance to delegate because of the need to maximize information and control at the top – where responsibility is affixed; legal specification of appropriate work behaviors; greater emphasis on security; stress on procedural regularity and caution; and a less strongly developed concept of professional management.

A previous article by the author identifies the following other possible reasons for minimal utilization of OD in government: (1) alternative change programs such as systems and procedures methods are more consonant with the legal-rational bureaucratic approach and are perceived as less threatening to the status quo; (2) some political scientists and public administrators are "natural enemies" of behavioral science – particularly in regard to its traditional "strong" leadership; (3) behavioral science is often seen as "tender-minded" with an undue focus on keeping employees happy; (4) participative approaches are susptected as cover-ups for management by committee or turning the organization over to the subordinates; (5) the values underlying applied behavioral science (discussed earlier in this chapter) may be in conflict with values inherent in some agencies.[5]

Other authors have, of course, discussed differences between public and private organizations that affect management behavior. Timothy Costello has described the unique characteristics of public agencies that may affect the ways in which change takes place.[6] His list – which refers to local government – includes:

1. Sudden and drastic changes in leadership
2. Goals and outcomes less amenable to measurement
3. More heterogeneous constituency – subgroups have conflicting interests
4. Decisions and policies are highly visible and more subject to critique
5. Local governments are subjected to more legal constraints and can make fewer of their own decisions than other institutions
6. It is much more difficult to "go out of business" – to shut down a facility or withdraw a service
7. Programs having immediate visibility and seeming to demonstrate progress may receive political priority over slower and less dramatic – though more meaningful – efforts

Political Issues Related to Behavioral Science in Local Government

The following points are hypotheses derived from the papers previously cited, experiences in OD programs in public agencies, and comments from colleagues. They are intended to stimulate further thinking about organizational change and renewal in local government, and about strategies of implementation.

1. There are, of course, the usual problems of interfacing any administrative system and political system. These include public mistrust of bureaucracy, politicians vs. administrators in policy formation, concerns about keeping the technocrats publicly accountable, generalized resistance to change, and political pressures in relation to programs. While these certainly are not unique to behavioral science applications, they may well be important factors.

2. There is a basic incompatibility between political systems and the "ideal" organization from a behavioral science point of view. Political systems are by nature *distributive*. They function to divide a finite amount of resources among various interest groups. This "cutting of the pie" is a win/lose game in which a variety of tactics are used to increase the reward to one group — which necessarily means they are decreased to others. The well-functioning administrative system aims at being *integrative*. Emphasis is placed on communality of purpose, collaboration, and win/win relationships. Ways need to be found to minimize win/lose competition among operating units, and to enhance shared problem-solving and planning. A highly integrative organization at the local government level may not serve the felt needs of politicians whose own goals require special out-put from a unit within the organization — to the possible detrement of other units.

3. Trust and openness may not be possible (or at least not perceived as possible) in situations with political implications. An official in NASA is quoted as saying: "we never punish error. We only punish *concealment* of error."[7] This policy is, of course, intended to reinforce openness. Many local government officials may feel they cannot afford this much risk, and may be much more concerned about concealing errors than whether or not errors were made in the first place.

4. Some of the techniques of the application of behavioral science involve dealing with the feelings, attitudes, and personal styles of participants. There is considerable misunderstanding, suspicion and prejudice against approaches such as sensitivity training and team building — and by association against their distant cousins such as group problem-solving meetings and planning retreats. They are seen as coercive and sometimes even subversive.

The author recently conducted a brief team-development program for members of a city council. The methodology involved confidential interviews with individual councilmen regarding intracouncil and council-management concerns followed by a retreat at which generalized interview data were fed back and discussed in some depth.

One council member refused to participate in the program and was quoted in the local newspaper as follows:

> I feel that the presence of a psychologist, regardless of what his title may be, is somewhat insulting to members of the council. I am quite sure than neither President Nixon nor Governor . . . would suggest such a thing to members of Congress or the Legislature.
>
> The role of the city councilman is to serve the people who elect him. I believe that rather than attending retreats we ought to be out in the districts conferring with the people, not psychoanalyzing one another.
>
> I personally do not believe in the techniques of group therapy, sensitivity training, or any other device which would reduce our individual thinking to the thinking of a group; that is, making the individual feel he is committing a mortal sin to have a thought of his own. . . .
>
> There is no substitute for training a councilman, and that is basically what these retreats purport to do, like conferring and meeting with the people in the districts and then reporting their views on the council. In other words, there is no substitute for "government of the people, by the people, and for the people." The administration needs to look no further for a philosophy nor do we need a psychoanalysis of the job we have been elected to do than to adopt the philosophy of government of, by, and for the people.[8]

5. Conventional wisdom, political thinking included, views "good" leadership, assertive-authoritarian leadership, and masculinity as essentially synonymous. Approaches to leadership which assert that subordinates should have upward influence, dissident points of view should be listened to, and solving problems is preferable to discipline are seen as weak and ineffectual. Two articles in the *Buffalo Evening News* illustrate what may happen. Warren Bennis, a leading behavioral scientist, resigned his position as executive vice-president of the State University of New York at Buffalo in protest against the way a student disturbance was handled. The newspaper reported the incident as follows:

> "I have throughout the sequence of disturbances, remained firmly convinced that police occupation could do nothing but exacerbate the troubles, that they were unnecessary," Dr. Bennis said in an interview.
>
> "I did not approve that decision then and do not approve of it now."
>
> Dr. Bennis, who retains his post as vice president for academic development, also criticized what he termed "a lack of candor" and unresponsiveness to student concern by the Regan administration since a clash between police and students Feb. 25 set off a student strike and a week-and-a-half of disorders on the Main St. campus.
>
> "I thought we hadn't done enough to demonstrate either sensitivity to the reactions on our campus, to the events on Feb. 25, particularly the police actions in Norton Union, nor did I feel that we had as an administration adequately communicated a responsiveness to the issues facing this campus," he said.

"If I felt we had done the best we could on these latter issues, and the violence had still continued, I might have then — but only as a last resort — called for the police occupation."[9]

In a subsequent meeting of the City Council, a councilwoman criticized the university administration. "The campus disorder," she said, "is separating the men from the boys. One of the boys has just resigned, thank goodness."

6. Organization development proposes that work time is legitimately spent working on relationship issues. Terms such as "team building," "working on the problem," and "processing" refer to the situations in which administrators do not do *work* in the traditional sense, but meet to talk about *how* they might work more effectively together. Politicians and the public may feel that this is wasted time and that people paid to manage local government ought to *know* how to work. The fact that human systems require *maintenance* in much the way that machines do is not widely understood.

7. Special problems may be caused by a press that maintains a traditional view of organizations and of local government. There is pressure for all "official" meetings to be open, and everything to be on the record. This condition reinforces closed, safe modes of behavior (you have to "watch what you say") and discourages sound problem-solving in groups. In order for groups to solve problems effectively, work out relationships, explore ideas, manage conflict, and make good decisions, an atmosphere of nondefensiveness, provisionalism, exploration, and trust must prevail. Very few, if any, members of the press presently hold concepts allowing them to differentiate between "dealing with policy" and "dealing with each other" meetings.

8. Laws and policies relating to accountability take a negative, defensive position. People are not to be trusted, they are not responsible, they must be watched. Applied behavioral science tends to pursue the opposite belief. Shared decision-making, looser controls, management by objectives, and decentralization and independence at lower levels may run counter to the needs of politicians. It may be perceived as better to run a highly controlled system which accomplishes less but runs less risk of scandal.

9. The hard sciences have managed to gain the trust of most people. The "soft" sciences of human behavior have not reached that point. They have no easily visible "better things for better living" or men on the moon to win friends. Further, the application of the medical model to the analysis of behavior has tended to associate psychology with the sick and the flawed — not a positive association in political terms.

10. In some (perhaps many) communities, training of any sort has not been legitimized — particularly when it costs money. "Professionals" are hired

into the public service at salaries that may be perceived as high, and they are supposed to bring all necessary knowledge with them. A yearly trek to the professional association convention can be justified as a way of keeping up with new development, but generally not an extended and relatively costly OD program.

11. The multiple access pointed out by Golembiewski allows for the resistors of change within the public organization (because of threat to status, for example) to gather support from outside groups who can influence the fate of change programs. Thus a counterattack against an OD effort may be launched via the press, political groups, or other interests with leverage.

12. Costello asserts that though the principal coin in the realm of politics is power, behavioral scientists have written more about the process of power equalization than about acquisition and effective use of power. The implications of this state of affairs may be that behavioral scientists are either uncomfortable or unknowledgeable in regard to one of the major dimensions of government, and that they may be ineffective in dealing with those who seek and use power.

There are doubtless other issues related to behavioral science in the political/administrative mix. And those listed probably apply differentially according to a variety of factors not presently understood. It is hoped that the listing will alert behavioral scientists and public administrators to avoid snags in the implementation of change programs.

Overcoming Resistance

Although it is risky to propose solutions before the problems are clearly defined, several possibilities for coming to grips with some of the difficulties listed above can be offered. First, the author has been personally involved in two major efforts to utilize OD ideas in the interface between administrators and politicians. The first was the council-manager retreat mentioned earlier. Although it was a very short-term program and was boycotted by one council member, it was deemed useful by most who attended. The other was a longer term effort to help elected and appointed officials in an urban county government develop better understanding and collaborative skills. The program is described in detail by Thomas Murphy.[10] Experience indicates that such efforts are feasible and worthwhile — but one must proceed carefully.

Second, Costello says that the behavioral scientist who would bring about change in municipal affairs must build a power backing. He may do this by (1) direct political activity in support of sympathetic candidates, (2) relating to strong community action organizations, or (3) personal cultivation or reaching out to men in power to gain understanding and personal acceptance. Although only the second approach has been clearly acceptable to the scientist, the third approach is most promising and is likely to be used more frequently in the future.[11]

Third, OD programs may need to be preceded by thorough informational and educational programs conducted both within and outside the organization. The need for change and development, the rationale, and case examples can be usefully pointed out.

Fourth, techniques worked out in other settings for overcoming resistance to change should be explored. For example, involving relevant political leaders in the planning and evaluation of OD programs, and encouraging them to feel a sense of ownership in the change process.

Fifth, behavioral scientists must be willing to devote time and professional thought to helping the public understand and accept the new operations and values that the OD approach proposes for organizations. Political and administrative leaders cannot be expected to opt for changes that are likely to undercut their support and endanger their positions.

Finally, in the long run behavioral scientists and public administrators may have to move from a defensive to an offensive stance. Too frequently the political system is accepted as the one that is fixed, and conventional wisdom is presumed to be indisputable. Those of us who think we know a better way to view the conduct of urban government and who think some of the politicians' views of what is management are wrong may have to say so in loud and certain terms.

Notes

1. Warren G. Bennis, "Beyond Bureaucracy," *Transaction,* July-Aug. 1965, pp 31-50 and John W. Gardner, *Self Renewal: The Individual and the Innovative Society* (New York: Harper and Row, Publishers, 1965).

2. Robert T. Golembiewski, "Organization Development in Public Agencies: Perspectives on Theory and Practice," *Public Administration Review,* July-August, 1969, pp. 367-78; William B. Eddy, "Beyond Behavioralism? Organization Development in Public Management," *Public Personnel Review,* July 1970, pp. 169-75; and Warren G. Bennis, *Organization Development: Its Nature, Origins and Prospects* (Reading, Mass.: Addison-Wesley, 1969).

3. Sheldon Davis, "An Organic Problem-Solving Method of Organizational Change," *Journal of Applied Behavioral Science,* January 1967, pp. 3-21; William B. Eddy, "Management Issues in Organization Development," in W.B. Eddy, et al. (eds.) *Behavioral Science and the Manager's Role* (Washington, D.C.: NTL Institute for Applied Behavioral Science, 1969); and Richard Beckhard, *Organization Development: Strategies and Models* (Reading, Mass.: Addison-Wesley, 1969).

4. Golembiewski, *"Organization Development."*

5. Eddy, "Beyond Behavioralism," pp. 169-75.

6. Timothy W. Costello, "The Change Process in Municipal Government," in F. Gerald Brown and Thomas P. Murphy *Emerging Patterns in Urban Administration* (Boston: D.C. Heath and Co., 1970), pp. 15-7.

7. Marvin R. Weisbord, "What, Not Again! Manage People Better?" *Think* 36 (January-February, 1970): 7.

8. *Kansas City Star,* February 7, 1969.

9. *Buffalo Evening News,* March 11, 1970.

10. Thomas P. Murphy, *Metropolitics and the Urban County* (Washington, D.C.: National Association of Counties, 1970).

11. Costello "Change Process," pp. 22-3.

Appendix
The National Center for Public Service Internship Programs

ROBERT F. SEXTON

The National Center for Public Service Internship Programs was established in November of 1972 in response to student demands for meaningful and career-oriented education; the increasing demand for trained and responsible public-service manpower; and academia's reevaluation of traditional higher education. It is located at 1140 Connecticut Avenue, NW, Washington, DC in the offices of the International City Management Association. It was established with the conviction that internships can be a vital ingredient in higher education. It is also based on the principle that government at all levels must be constantly renewed and improved by the infusion of new talent and new commitment in order to provide necessary services. Taken together, the needs of education and government will have to overlap and find common ground in order to meet the needs of each; internships can provide some of this common ground.

The National Center for Public Service Internship Programs grew out of a conference of intern directors, academics, and others held in Lexington, Kentucky, in October of 1971 under the auspices of the Kentucky Office of Academic Programs. More than anything, the conference pointed out a remarkable variety of internship programs, opportunities, and problems across the nation; twenty-two states and fifteen concerned institutions were represented.

It was obvious from the conference that (1) intern programs had grown to the point that further development without careful planning and research might be counterproductive, and (2) that virtually every program was carrying out functions individually which could be improved and simplified by cooperative efforts. Conferees were unanimous in demands for research (especially on topics such as the assessment of internship effectiveness), for information on funding sources, for exchange of internship placement information, and for evaluation of federal activities and legislation.

The basic need, then, was for communication among previously isolated operations. To facilitate this communication and to investigate possible institutional responses, a committee began work almost immediately after the conference (the National Planning Committee on Public Service Internship and Fellowship Programs).

Developments in education and government indicated that some concrete institutional device was desirable. The reform literature of higher education (for example, the Newman Report on Higher Education and the Carnegie Commission Reports) began to call for the increased use of experiential education, forecasting, hopefully, new academic respectability; institutional enthusiasm for experiential education came from the Union for Experimenting Colleges and Universities and many experimental and traditional colleges. Institutions of higher education devoted to public service education and interships, such as Sangamon State College in Illinois, appeared. Outside academia, institutions designed to assist students in their search for meaningful service-learning experiences become more visible (for example, Organization Response, the Commission on Voluntary Service in Action, the National Advisory Council on Education Experience Exchange Program, and CITY [Community Involvement Through Youth]).

For the public-service internship field itself most relevant were developments on the local, state, and federal levels. In response to increased demands for both manpower and participation by young people, numerous city governments and several states began or revitalized intern programs. In response to announcements of the work of the Planning Committee, hundreds of inquiries came from prospective intern supervisors asking for drafts of legislation, surveys of state programs, and statistical data.

Perhaps most telling, however, were developments on the federal level, where interest in intern programs was revived. The University Year for Action Program was already in operation, trying to accomplish, through grants to educational institutions, service-learning on a massive scale. The Intergovernmental Personnel Act, while not explicitly designed to foster intern programs, gave strong implicit support to the internship objectives of improving personnel in state and local government.

Three important internship bills in Congress also pointed out the need for a voice for those interested in internship programs. To date, there have been: one partial legislative success, one failure, and one case yet to be heard. All teach the same lesson: that research and model-building are desperately needed.

The partial success (partial because there is no appropriation yet) came in the Work Study for Community Service-Learning Program of the Higher Education Amendments of 1972 (PL 92-318). This legislation authorizes a $50-million annual appropriation through work-study "to pay the compensation of students employed. . . in jobs providing needed community services and which are of educational value." With passage it became apparent that suggestions and research by the internship community could be most important for effective implementation.

The failure of a second piece of legislation, Interns for Political Leadership, (S. 659, Higher Education Amendments), made the most telling case for the involvement of professional intern directors in the legislative process. This bill asked for the authorization of $10 million for internship stipends; interns were to serve in both state and federal government and were to receive college credit. Although Interns for Political Leadership had inherent weaknesses, the manner of its defeat in the House (after Senate passage) was important. To the surprise of observers, there was a large amount of House debate on this relatively insignificant piece of legislation (insignificant when compared to the total higher education package to which it was attached). Primarily, discussion centered on administrative weaknesses of the bill. These weaknesses might have been avoided by the advice of those familiar with intern programs; House supporters of the legislation were simply not armed with information necessary to defend it. The visible need, therefore, was for concentrated efforts by those expert in the intern field, first to see that good legislation was drafted and second to see that sympathetic legislators were armed with solidly researched information.

The third piece of legislation, introduced in the Senate in 1972 as Senate Bill 3141, proposes amendments to the Intergovernmental Personnel Act to create a state and local fellows program. This bill was not acted on in the 92nd Congress but will be reintroduced in the 93rd Congress. Although it is too early to judge results, it is obvious at this point that the legislation needs, in order to succeed, direct impact by internship experts.

Taken together, recent legislation has offered, and may provide, vast new sources of support for internships. In all cases, however, impact by those professionals most concerned with internships has been sporadic and haphazard. Individual project directors have devoted great amounts of time and have won important personal victories, but concerted effort has been completely absent.

The increasing number of internships, and increased interest, has also raised other questions. One involves the general educational quality of internships. It is probably beyond dispute that learning occurs when one does almost anything – the important question is: how is this learning to be maximized, equated to standard classroom learning and translated into credit, and directed toward specific types of professional development? The question arises because there are those who feel that a job, any job, is a learning experience and hence to be labeled "internship;" others feel that strict supervision, both at work and through special courses, is essential. Universities and colleges demand answers to these questions because they are important; their importance is multiplied by the expansion of new programs. The resulting need could be satisfied by a vehicle which would build the most desirable learning components.

The tendencies outlined above meant that some form of national coordination and communication was necessary. How are the individuals in broadly diverse fields to be pulled together for mutually beneficial efforts? The response was the National Center for Public Service Internship Programs. With a Board of Directors representing the broadest range of interested persons and a Washington-based professional staff, the Center's purposes are outlined in articles of association:

The Center shall serve the needs of public service internship and fellowship programs throughout the Nation, to encourage and facilitate the establishment and improvement of such programs, and to promote the acceptance of such programs as a significant and viable component of higher education. The Center shall cooperate with other interests, organizations, and individuals in education, government and the development of human resources.

While the process of defining a "public-service internship" may consume large amounts of time over the next few months, the main emphasis will be on true learning experiences in the broadest public sector. Public service might include government at all levels, nonprofit community-service agencies, community action groups, political organizations, professional associations, educational institutions, or organized interest groups of any kind.

What will the creation of the National Center mean for the future? In part, as an institutional response to present needs, it should help blend together heretofore divergent forces. By pulling together the resources of academia, government, the public service sector, and the interested public in general, new avenues and new quality should be available in the internship field. The Center will be an advocate for improvement and growth. The Center could produce a network for information exchange and hence vastly expanded service-learning opportunities for those who seek them. At the same time, research carried out with scholarly thoroughness should improve internships internally, and answer questions about long-range effectiveness, assessment, and funding. Research will also open new avenues of funding and ensure the continuance of existing sources. Program model building, for example, could greatly improve federal legislation and programs; model design will also be helpful to those drafting legislation on the state level. The use of existent resources will also be improved through discussion with funding sources and by the application of imagination to use of these sources.

To begin the flow of information, the Center will produce a Public Service Internship Newsletter, featuring reports from Washington, reports on new developments in local programs, and serious thought and research on important questions. The Center may also serve as a major resource and data bank, rich with information on programs around the nation. For program development, a series of topical or regional workshops might be held for persons interested in developing specific kinds of programs, or new relationships or interactions among sectors of the broad community.

In general, the Center looks forward to the day when internships are an integral part of American education, and when the full commitment of the human resources field is behind the use of internships. It is obvious that intern programs are not available to all those who might be able to take advantage of them, and that adequate financial resources are not yet available. As Don Eberly has said, ". . . no one should be excluded from this kind of experience simply for lack of funds, information, job openings, supervision, or counseling." I reemphasize this sentiment, and hope that, at least partially, the National Center, without seeking centralization, will help make quality internship experience available to any student who seeks it.

At the same time, to return to my original contention that internships have not yet taken their proper place as an ingredient of higher education, the Center should help facilitate communication between those experimenting with field placement in new forms and those who have been placing students in internships for some years. The Center should make it clear that innovation in education and innovation in internship are not necessarily two different things, that they are not mutually exclusive. At the same time, the public service community should be assisted and advised of the vast potential of this source of talent.

Index

About the Contributors

Bernard Asbell, author of the best-selling *When FDR Died* has served as a consultant to the Ford Foundation's Educational Facilities Laboratory, and has written another book, *The Improved American,* and articles on the American scene for The Reporter, Harper's, American Heritage, Horizon, The Saturday Evening Post, McCall's and other periodicals. He has taught non-fiction writing at the Bread Loaf Writer's Conference, Middlebury College, the University of Chicago, and the University of Bridgeport. He also has been President of the Society of Magazine Writers.

James M. Banovetz, editor and co-author of *Managing The Modern City* is Professor and Chairman, Department of Political Science, Northern Illinois University. Prior to his present assignment, he served as Director of the Center for Governmental Studies at NIU and as Director of the Center for Research in Urban Government and the Graduate Program in Urban Studies at Loyola University, Chicago. While earning his M.A.P.A. and Ph.D. degrees at the University of Minnesota, he also served on the staff of the League of Minnesota Municipalities. A frequent consultant for governmental agencies, he has served on the Urban Studies Fellowship Advisory Board of HUD since 1969 and has chaired the Board since 1970.

L.P. Cookingham, after seven years experience as an engineer in the Public Works Department in Flint, Michigan, was selected as Village Manager of Clawson, Michigan, a Detroit suburb. After four years there he was appointed City Manager of Plymouth, Michigan, also a Detroit suburb. Another four years found him as the first City Manager of Saginaw Michigan, inaugurating the Council-Manager government to replace the older Commission form. After four and one-half years in that position he was selected, in 1940, as the City Manager of Kansas City, Missouri following the ousting of the infamous Pendergast machine. What appeared to be a short-term assignment turned out to be a record-breaking tenure of 19 years. After resigning from the Kansas City position, he became Manager of Forth Worth, Texas where he served four years until reaching retirement age. He now resides in Kansas City and is still active as a municipal consultant.

William B. Eddy is Professor and Director of Public Administration, University of Missouri-Kansas City. He has formerly been Director of the University of Missouri's Center for Management Development and Associate Director of the Federal Executive Institute. Dr. Eddy is an organizational psychologist whose research and consulting interests involve the application of behavioral science to public organizations. He is a member of the American Psychological Association,

The National Training Laboratories, The International Association of Applied Social Scientists, and The American Society for Public Administration.

Frederick Fisher graduated from the University of Pennsylvania and has a masters degree in Governmental Administration. He was formerly the City Manager for State College, Pennsylvania. He was with ICMA as Director of Professional Development for three years. He is presently Vice President of the National Training & Development Service for State and Local Government.

Ronald D. Hedlund received an American Political Science Association grant to study the Congressional Fellow Program, data from which form the basis for the chapter included here. He is an Assistant Professor of Political Science at the University of Wisconsin – Milwaukee, specializing in legislative behavior and methods of research. Since receiving a B.A. degree from Augustana College (Illinois) and M.A. and Ph.D. degrees from the University of Iowa, Professor Hedlund has co-authored *The Job of the Wisconsin Legislator* with Wilder W. Crane, Jr., co-edited *The Conduct of Political Inquiry* with Louis D. Hayes, and contributed to the *Midwest Journal of Politics, Journal of Politics, American Journal of Sociology* and *New Republic.*

Richard D. Heimovics is a Ph.D. candidate at the University of Kansas in Human Relations. Concurrently he is also an Instructor in the School of Administration of the University of Missouri – Kansas City and a consultant to the Institute for Public Affairs, University of Kansas and the School of Medicine, University of Missouri – Kansas City. He was coordinator of programs for the Center for Management Development of the School of Administration, University of Missouri – Kansas City in 1970 and 1971 where he participated in management development programs in urban affairs, business management and public administration. Mr. Heimovics received a B.A. in Social Science from Dartmouth College in 1963. He received his MPA from the University of Missouri–Kansas City in 1969. Mr. Heimovics' other publications include two chapters in *Science, Geopolitics and Federal Spending,* D.C. Heath, 1971, titled "Geographic Distribution of Federal Research and Development Funds" and "Federal Support of University Research and Development"; "State Aid to Municipalities: A Comparative Study," for the City of Kansas City, which was presented to the 75th Session of the Missouri General Assembly in 1969; and, as co-author, "Results from an Ongoing Organization Development Program in a Public Agency", a presentation to the National Conference of the American Society for Public Administration in 1971.

Larry Hughes is a Senior Budget Examiner for Miami-Dade County, Florida. Hughes received his BA Degree from Graceland College in Iowa and then became a reporter for the *Kansas City Star.* He also served as a Peace Corps volunteer in India. Hughes received a MPA Degree from the University of Missouri–Kansas City in 1971 and served as assistant to the director of the MPA program.

James P. Jadlos is Director, Special Recruiting and Training Division, U.S.

General Services Administration, in Washington, D.C. In that capacity, he oversees or administers the agency's nationwide training and development, college recruiting, upward mobility and management intern activities. Prior to joining GSA, he was Associate Director of the U.S. Civil Service Commission's Personnel Management Training Center, where he designed and directed government-wide intern programs and conducted supervisory and management training. In his previous positions with the Civil Service Commission, he assisted in the conduct of personnel management evaluations in more than 25 Federal agencies. He was a U.S. Marine Corps officer for three years following his graduation from Syracuse University. His Masters Degree in Public Administration is from the American University.

Thomas P. Murphy is Executive Director of the Institute for Urban Studies, and Professor of Government and Politics at the University of Maryland, College Park, Maryland. From 1966 to 1971 he was Assistant to the Chancellor for Urban Affairs, Director of Graduate Public Administration Programs, and Professor of Public Administration, at the University of Missouri – Kansas City. He was also Executive Director of the Commission on Organization of Jackson County, Missouri, 1967-1969, and County Manager of Jackson County for six months in 1969.

From 1961 to 1966 he was at the National Aeronautics and Space Administration as Staff Assistant to NASA Administrator, James E. Webb, Assistant to the Associate Deputy Administrator, Dr. George L. Simpson, Jr., and Deputy Assistant Administrator for Legislative Affairs. His earlier government experience includes work with the Federal Aviation Agency, the U.S. General Accounting Office, U.S. Air Force and the Internal Revenue Service.

Dr. Murphy received his Ph.D. in Political Science from St. John's University, New York, in 1963; his M.A. from Georgetown University in 1960; and B.A. from Queens College in 1948. His articles on Congress, politics, urban affairs, budgeting and organizational structure have appeared in *Trans-action*, *The Economist*, *Western Political Quarterly*, *Ethics*, *Public Administration Review*, *Administrative Science Quarterly*, *Contemporary Review*, *Review of Politics*, *Union Theological Quarterly*, *Natural Resources Journal*, *New Leader*, and *Polity*. His prior books include *Metropolitics and the Urban County* (1970); *Emerging Patterns in Urban Administration* (Lexington Books, 1970); *Science, Geopolitics and Federal Spending* (Lexington Books, 1971) and *Pressures Upon Congress* (1972).

He has been active not only as a professor and an administrator, but also as a citizen participation, planning, management, organization, training, and budgetary consultant at the federal, state, and local levels. Primary involvements have been with the U.S. Department of Housing and Urban Development, the Office of Economic Opportunity and state, city, and county governments in Alabama, California, Iowa, Kansas, Maryland, and Missouri. Since 1969 he has been Director of Governmental and Educational Services for the Lawrence-Leiter Company of Kansas City.

Lewis J. Paper, formerly a Fellow at Georgetown Law School's Institute for Public Interest Representation, is a member of the District of Columbia Bar and currently a staff attorney with the Citizens Communication Center in Washington, D.C. He received the B.A. from the University of Michigan, the J.D. from Harvard University, and the LL.M. from Georgetown University.

John Rehfuss is Associate Professor of Political Science and Acting Director of the Center for Governmental Studies at Northern Illinois University in DeKalb. Born in 1934, he is married with three children. He received his Doctor in Public Administration from the University of Southern California in 1965. He has taught at San Jose State College, been assistant City Manager of Palm Springs, California, and worked as Associate Director of the U.S. Civil Service Management Seminar in Berkeley, California. He is the author of numerous articles in professional journals, and the textbook *Public Administration as Political Process.*

Robert F. Sexton is Coordinator of the Kentucky Office of Academic Programs and Chairman of the Board of Directors of the National Center for Public Service Internship Programs. He received his B.A. degree from Yale University and his Ph.D. from the University of Washington, and has been awarded Fulbright and Woodrow Wilson Fellowships. Prior to his present position as administrator of state legislative and administrative intern programs, Sexton served as an assistant professor of history at Murray State University; he has worked for the Peace Corps and Upward Bound, and held a Senatorial internship in Washington.

Frank P. Sherwood, who was born in Georgia in 1920, holds the doctorate in political science from the University of Southern California, awarded in 1952. In 1968 he became the first director of the Federal Executive Institute, which was established to provide for the development of top-level career officials. Before his appointment, he was director of the School of Public Administration, University of Southern California, where he served on the faculty from 1951 and from which he is on leave. He is President (1972-73) of the American Society for Public Administration, serves on the Board of Editors of the *Public Administration Review,* and is a member of the National Academy of Public Administration. In addition to several shorter foreign assignments, Sherwood was chief of a technical assistance mission to Brazil in 1962-63; its objective was to advise on the improvement of education for the public service in that country. He is author of *Institutionalizing the Grass Roots in Brazil* (1967) and co-author of *The California System of Governments* (1968) and *Administrative Organization* (1960). He has contributed to various professional journals and symposia.

Stephen Joel Trachtenberg is Dean of University Affairs and an associate professor of political science at Boston University. In addition, he is director of the Master of Urban Affairs program at the University's Metropolitan College. A graduate of Columbia University, Dean Trachtenberg received the J.D. from Yale

University and the M.P.A. from Harvard and is a member of the New York Bar. He has served as an attorney for the Atomic Energy Commission, an aide to a U.S. congressman, and as special assistant to the U.S. Commissioner of Education. An Executive High School Internship Board Member, he was named in 1968 a Winston Churchill Fellow of the English-Speaking Union and in 1970 one of Boston's ten outstanding young people by the Junior Chamber of Commerce.

David Walker received his B.A. and M.A. degrees from Boston University, and his Ph.D. from Brown University. He taught at Bowdoin College from 1956 to 1963, when he became Staff Director, United States Senate Subcommittee on Intergovernmental Relations. Presently, he is Assistant Director, Government Structure and Functions Division of the Advisory Commission on Intergovernmental Relations.

Michael R. Weaver is an Associate Professor of Political Science at the State University of New York (SUNY) at Brockport. For the past four years Professor Weaver has been located in Washington, D.C. serving as Director of the SUNY Washington Semester in Political Science, a year-round academic program offering a dual-track curriculum for upper-division undergraduates drawn from the SUNY system. Professor Weaver was born in Miller, South Dakota. He attended the University of South Dakota and the University of Rochester, and holds a Bachelor's and two Master's degrees in political science. In 1959 he joined the faculty at SUNY Brockport. He is married and has five children.